Standing Orders:
Rogers's Rangers, 1759

- Don't forget nothing.
- Have your musket clean as a whistle, hatchet scoured, sixty rounds of powder and ball, and be ready to march at a minute's warning.
- When you are on the march, act the way you would if you were sneaking up on a deer. See the enemy first.
- Tell the truth about what you see and what you do. There is an army depending on us for correct information. You can lie all you please when you tell other folk about the Rangers, but don't ever lie to a Ranger or officer.
- Don't ever take a chance you don't have to.
- When we're on the march we march single file, far enough apart so one shot can't go through two men.
- If we strike swamps, or soft ground, we spread out abreast, so it's hard to track us.
- If we take prisoners, we keep 'em separated till we have time to examine them, so they can't cook up a story between 'em.
- Don't ever march home the same way. Take a different route so you won't be ambushed.
- Every night you'll be told where to meet if surrounded by a superior force.
- Don't sit down to eat without posting sentries.
- Don't sleep beyond dawn. Dawn's when the French and Indians attack.

By Michael Lee Lanning

THE ONLY WAR WE HAD: *A Platoon Leader's Journal of Vietnam*
VIETNAM 1969–1970: *A Company Commander's Journal*
INSIDE THE LRRPS: *Rangers in Vietnam*
INSIDE FORCE RECON: *Recon Marines in Vietnam* (with Ray W. Stubbe)
THE BATTLES OF PEACE
INSIDE THE VC AND THE NVA: *The Real Story of North Vietnam's Armed Forces* (with Dan Cragg)
VIETNAM AT THE MOVIES
SENSELESS SECRETS: *The Failures of U.S. Military Intelligence*
THE MILITARY 100: *A Ranking of the Most Influential Military Leaders of All Time*
THE AFRICAN-AMERICAN SOLDIER: *From Crispus Attucks to Colin Powell*
INSIDE THE CROSSHAIRS: *Snipers in Vietnam*
DEFENDERS OF LIBERTY: *African Americans in the Revolutionary War*

BLOOD
WARRIORS
American Military Elites

Michael Lee Lanning

BALLANTINE BOOKS • NEW YORK

A Ballantine Book
Published by The Ballantine Publishing Group
Copyright © 2002 by Michael Lee Lanning

www.ballantinebooks.com

ISBN 0-345-44891-X

Manufactured in the United States of America

First Edition: November 2002

OPM   10   9   8   7   6   5   4   3   2   1

To
David Garland Neary

CONTENTS

✳✳✳✳✳✳✳

ACKNOWLEDGMENTS

✳✳✳✳✳✳✳✳✳✳✳✳✳

Research for this book was assisted by Anthony Horka, Office of the Assistant Secretary of Defense for Special Operations and Low Intensity Conflict; George Grimes, Public Affairs Office, U.S. Special Operations Command; Sergeant First Class Brian Sutton, Public Affairs Office, U.S. Army Special Operations Command; Joan Prichard, Public Affairs Office, U.S. Air Force Special Operations Command; Lieutenant Katie Licup, Public Affairs Office, Naval Special Warfare Command; Captain Mark S. Trott, commander, U.S. Army Sniper School; and Staff Sergeant Brian J. Reeves, USMC First Force Reconnaissance Company.

Special thanks go to Owen A. Lock for the idea for this book—and for his long-term editorial assistance and friendship.

As with all my writing, my most diligent editor and critic remains my wife, Linda.

INTRODUCTION

✳✳✳✳✳✳✳✳✳✳

*F*ROM the beginning of warfare, victory in combat has gone to the side whose infantrymen last occupied the territory in question. Regardless of technology, social sophistication, or political rhetoric, if the infantryman does not occupy the space, his side is not the ultimate victor. In that simple equation, nothing has changed.

Infantrymen, both soldiers and marines, do the majority of the fighting, experience the most hardships, and sustain the brunt of the wounds and deaths. They are the true heroes of the armed forces. American Civil War General William T. Sherman recognized the importance of the foot soldiers in his memoirs when he wrote in 1885, "All great wars will, as heretofore, depend on the infantry."

World War II journalist Ernie Pyle further explained in a 1943 dispatch, "I love the infantry because they are the underdogs. They are the mud-rain-and-wind boys. They have no comforts, and they learn to live without the necessities. And in the end they are the guys that war can't be won without."

It is the infantry that also pays the highest price to secure victory. When General Mark Clark was asked if he could see any similarities between foot soldiers of the First and Second World Wars, he replied, "They both did what a soldier has to know how to do very well—die."

Not only do the infantrymen suffer the most, but they also inflict the most carnage upon their opponents. They attack the enemy, destroy his assets, and mop up the battlefield. They figuratively bloody their hands by destroying their opposition

1

and then literally by going through the dead enemies' pockets in search of intelligence or souvenirs.

Even though infantrymen throughout history have decided the outcome of wars, commanders have recognized that small, specially trained units of carefully selected individuals can effectively perform dangerous, behind-the-lines missions to secure intelligence, capture prisoners, and free hostages. As combined units they can also affect outcomes of battles with their particular combat tactics.

In terms of a simple definition, then, *elites* has come to refer to carefully selected individuals, usually volunteers, who undergo grueling physical and mental rites of passage. After selection, these individuals receive training beyond the standard levels for traditional infantrymen, often being exempt from regimentation and bureaucracy. In addition to providing these special units advanced training and access to the most modern weapons and equipment, military officials set these units and individuals apart from the regular infantry by designating special uniforms, insignia, headgear, or footwear— which makes an elite troop instantly recognizable as such.

The elites gain more attention and accolades than other units. The American public prefers the different to the ordinary. Motion pictures, television, books, and other media tend to cast their military focus not on the everyday soldiers who do the majority of the dying but rather on individuals or units that are distinctive or extraordinary.

Members of many military organizations consider themselves elite even though they never experience the smell of gunpowder, the physical hardships of the battlefield, or the fear of death. Honor guards, musicians, pilots, doctors, and even pastry chefs certainly meet the requirements of the *elite* designation. Yet there are elites, and then there are elites. Regardless of the abilities and élan of the other specialists, their purpose and mission is to support the soldier who occupies space and ensures victory.

The real measure of true military elites is their proximity to the enemy. Killing from a distance—whether from the air, the deck of a ship, or an artillery base—results in an enemy who is just as dead. But it simply is not the same as looking into the eyes of the opponent, inflicting a fatal wound, and seeing a human take his last breath as his blood pours upon the ground.

Those who do the dirty work, and do it well, are the combat elites. These blood warriors are the best at what they do, and what they do is complex, dangerous, and more than a bit frightening.

The list of those within the blood-warrior community is short. Army representatives include the Special Forces, Rangers, and Delta Force. The navy has its SEALs, and the marine corps has the lesser-known Force Reconnaissance. Others share many of the characteristics of the blood warriors. The air force's combat control teams and pararescue specialists deserve an honorable mention, as do paratroopers and snipers who receive special skills training.

The following is their story.

CHAPTER 1

✳✳✳✳✳✳✳

Overview

*E*LITE combat units are not an innovation of the American military. Since the dawn of warfare, commanders have assembled special men into special units to perform special missions. According to legend, English King Arthur surrounded himself with a few dozen carefully selected armed soldiers who become known as the Knights of the Round Table.

The earliest commander for whom reliable records of military operations survive took advantage of the skills of elite* warriors. In 539 B.C. Cyrus the Great, while king of Persia, combined small units of archers and cavalry to defeat larger units armed with pikes and swords. By the time of his death ten years later Cyrus controlled much of the civilized world and ruled over history's first great empire.

Two centuries later Alexander the Great of Macedonia conquered the Persian Empire. His elite *sarissas* units fought with pikes twice the length of ordinary spears and established the tradition for the next fifteen hundred years whereby military elites were those employing innovations in weaponry. Fernandez Gonzalo de Cordoba used a small, elite unit of infantrymen armed with heavy, shoulder-fired muskets known as arquebuses to gain a Spanish victory over the French on April 28, 1498.

---

* The English word *elite* comes from a similar French word meaning "the choice" or "the most carefully selected." Historically its most common use has been in reference to social classes. Its military usage has occurred only in the past one hundred years.

Elite units with superior weapons and equipment again proved successful a short time later. Hernán Cortés, with fewer than six hundred Spanish soldiers supported by twenty horses and ten small cannonlike muskets, conquered an Aztec Empire populated by more than five million people in 1519, giving Spain claim to all of Central America. In 1531 another Spaniard, Francisco Pizarro, defeated the Incas with an elite force of only two hundred men. In addition to spears and swords Pizarro's warriors carried three arquebuses and twenty crossbows.

For a significant span of time special units armed with the most modern weapons and equipment of the day continued to win battles. However, advances in technology and the integration of musket-armed infantrymen, artillery, and cavalry greatly changed the scope of warfare. Kings and commanders discovered that small elite forces, even when properly armed, could not survive against large standing armies, even if the latter were poorly trained and armed. Size and numbers do make a difference; huge armies consistently prove victorious over small forces.

As the scope of warfare changed, the need for more numerous forces followed. Armies of a few thousand men could no longer decide wars with a single battle fought in an area of only a few miles where commanders could see, command, and participate in the entire fight. By the eighteenth century wars were fought on multiple land and sea fronts between armies and navies of tens or even hundreds of thousands. Elite units still guarded their kings, admirals, or generals, but they played less and less of a role in the actual outcome of battles. Instead of designating a single elite knight in shining armor, a dozen special pikemen, or even a company of musketeers, the *elite* title expanded to entire regiments and divisions. Single ships, or fleets of vessels under command of a single captain, also began to be mentioned among the elite.

The record of elite military warriors in America coincides with the arrival of Europeans on the continent. The settlement of colonial America brought a brief return of small elite units as key forces in combat. North America's huge space of uncharted forests and waterways far exceeded the capability of any army or navy of the period to dominate. Its population of Native Americans, loosely organized into more than five hundred tribes, relied on stealth and individual bravery rather than the massing of forces or the sophistication of weapons.

When Native Americans defended their territory against other tribes and the European immigrants, they employed fast actions of short duration. Ambushes, running fights, and brief engagements fought with handheld clubs, spears, and bows and arrows typified Indian warfare. Even after securing muskets and other firearms, Native Americans rarely had the manpower or desire to conduct "conventional warfare."

While Hernán Cortés and Francisco Pizarro easily defeated the dominant tribes of Central and South America in the sixteenth century, other Spaniards, as well as the English and French, found the diverse Indian tribes of North America to be much more difficult opponents. The early European settlers saw the Indians use entirely new battle tactics and, being few in number themselves, adopted the same techniques. Communities and colonies formed, trained, and equipped militia units to defend their property as well as to conduct offensives to destroy the Indians and claim their lands. Some of these units, such as Church's and Rogers's Rangers, became so adept at out-Indianing the Indians that they became the first American military elites.

From the opening shots in 1775 at Lexington Green that started the American Revolution, the rebel colonists discovered that their militias could not fight successfully against the superior numbers of the better-trained British army. As a result, George Washington and his subordinates often formed special units to conduct reconnaissance and raids against the redcoats while generally fighting fixed battles only when no other choice was available. British commanders attempted to form a few elite cavalry and marksmanship units to combat the rebels but usually relied on their superior conventional forces.

Neither could the Americans match the number of British warships, so instead of launching fleets, they manned individual vessels with specially selected crews and officers to engage British merchant ships and single men-of-war. To assist in boarding enemy vessels, and at times to defend captains from their own crews, the Continental Congress authorized the formation of the U.S. Marine Corps in 1775.

The Americans, in both the North and South, eventually discovered the need for larger units of special soldiers during the Civil War. Cavalry increased from small bands to full divisions. Confederates J. E. B. Stuart, John Mosby, and John Morgan led cavalry on reconnaissance and raids that gained the attention of the public as well as their generals. Various infantry brigades on both sides deservedly earned reputations as the elites of their armies. However, other than a few specially equipped marksmen or snipers, few true blood warriors in the modern sense emerged from the war.

During the American Indian wars that prevailed during the three decades following the Civil War, conventional cavalry and infantry bore the brunt of the fighting. The only forces that met the general requirements for identification as warrior elites were bands of Indians briefly assembled against the U.S. Army and several groups of Indian Scouts who fought against their own race in support of the white Americans.

The twentieth century brought even more change to warfare and the influence of warrior elites. Lessons learned in the use of artillery, wire communications, rail support, and massed infantry during the American Civil War, the Crimean War, and other European conflicts of the latter half of the 1800s made combat even more brutal and lethal. Entire nations mobilized, with all their matériel and manpower assets devoted to the conflict. Huge armies of conscripts replaced small professional forces. Heavy artillery, repeating rifles, and machine guns greatly increased the firepower of the infantry and the overall lethality of the battlefield.

By the time the Great War began in 1914, conflict was not among a few countries but rather consumed the entire world. *Total war* became the term for bloody conflict that would kill off an entire generation of young men—especially those of Britain, France, and Germany. By the end of the war in 1918, horse cavalry was basically finished as a means of warfare, and technology began to compete with and even exceed manpower as the dominant combat factor.

The hundreds of miles of trench lines that snaked across Europe in the Great War, however, did not lend themselves to small, specially trained units. Days or even weeks of combat often produced only a few yards of gain and left the no-man's-land between the trenches covered in rotting corpses. Oddly, in a conflict where the infantry of both sides were actually masses of blood warriors, the soldiers who received the most press and public interest, fighter pilots, never even got their boots muddy.

While the Great War involved most of the world, its land and sea battles were limited to a small portion of the earth's surface. It was not until twenty years after the "war to end all wars" concluded that the Second World War truly involved the entire planet and spread warfare across the earth's seas and landmasses. The Second World War added even greater technical advances in weaponry that made trench warfare impractical. The primary tactic became the maneuvering and massing of forces at enemy weak points to break through to rear areas and command centers. Without static trench lines limited to relatively small areas in which to fight battles, the need for intelligence and behind-the-lines operations became much more important.

Early in World War II the Germans led the way in fielding combat elites with airborne units and special raider companies. They also excelled in morale building by naming brigades and divisions after leaders and provinces of the country and awarding them special uniforms and adornments. While not really elite, these units thought they were because of their uniqueness, and as a result often fought beyond their expectations.

The Allies, as well as the Axis, realized the need for blood warriors, but the Americans entered World War II ill prepared in all aspects, including combat elites. Learning from the British, who had formed British Commando units, Americans soon organized Ranger battalions to conduct raids and to lead invasion forces. Interestingly, both the British and Americans took the name for their elites from former enemies. Winston Churchill had fought the Boer commandos in South Africa and personally assigned that name. The Americans had occasionally used the name *Rangers* for special units in previous conflicts, but the moniker originated with British units in North America who first opposed the French and later the American rebels.

Once the Allies had stopped the Axis and begun to retake the European continent and the islands of the Pacific, the need for another warrior elite became apparent. The Axis powers, particularly the Germans, reinforced their beach defenses with a great variety of obstacles. These had to be cleared before the army infantry and marines could assault the beaches. The U.S. Navy's underwater demolition teams (UDTs) became the first to land so that they could clear the way for those who followed.

Beach landings at Sicily, Anzio, and Normandy were key to the eventual Allied victories in Europe, while dozens of amphibious attacks in the Pacific led the island-hopping campaign that defeated Japan. The marine corps, not large enough to take on all the amphibious responsibilities, relied on army divisions to help gain beach footholds and then to exploit the advantage. In Europe particularly, while the beaches were being at least partially cleared by the navy frogmen, army paratroopers struck behind the lines to destroy command and communications centers, while Rangers neutralized the most critical enemy defenses. In the Pacific the marines formed special raider and reconnaissance units that performed duties similar to those of the army paratroopers and Rangers.

At the conclusion of World War II, America drastically reduced the number of combat elites or disbanded them altogether. Blood warriors were a breed whom the American public and military leaders welcomed in time of war, but whom neither group wanted or appreciated in time of peace. However, navy UDT personnel did assist in the few amphibious operations during the early part of the Korean conflict, and the army reorganized Ranger companies to replace the battalions that had served in World War II. Korea, however, soon bogged down into trench warfare similar to World War I, eclipsing the need for the elites.

Another important factor influenced the regression of the combat elites in the post–World War II and Korea period. The United States alone possessed atomic weapons, and some analysts predicted that no nation would challenge its power. A small fleet of long-range bombers armed with a few atomic bombs would be all the military power needed to sustain a viable threat against any opponent. When the Soviet Union fielded its own atomic weapons a few years later, many feared that the next war would result in the end of the world.

More logical thinkers understood, or at least hoped, that the potential of mutual destruction would prevent a global nuclear war, but they also knew that tactical nuclear weapons would change future battlefields. Many believed that the plains of Europe that bordered the Iron Curtain between East and West would be the trigger point. Because air and artillery units could deliver small nuclear weapons, ground troops would have to be widely dispersed and highly mobile to survive. Killing would be done at a distance. There would be no place for blood warriors and their up-close-and-personal combat techniques.

The United States and Soviet Union built and fielded their mechanized armies and deployed their missiles and long-range bombers, but the threat of total destruction discouraged the superpowers from going to war. However, this state of affairs did not deter power seekers from overthrowing their own or other governments to increase their territory and influence.

In the Balkans, Central America, Southeast Asia, and other locations, a series of conflicts began. Guerrilla* tactics, including terrorism, prevailed. Conventional forces generally were not effective in combating guerrillas, and the American public hesitated to support the commitment of its sons to remote fights that seemed to have no direct effect on national interests or security.

As early as 1953 U.S. military commanders recognized the need to organize guerrilla or counterguerrilla units by forming the army Special Forces. It was not until President John F. Kennedy became convinced of the country's need for them in 1961, however, that they gained acceptance and became a major part of the U.S. Army. Wearing their green berets, as authorized by the president, Special Forces increased their operations, especially in Vietnam where they had been assisting the South Vietnamese against communist guerrillas since 1957.

Vietnam ultimately became America's largest counterguerrilla war and the longest conflict in its history. During the more-than-a-decade-long war the United States dropped 6,161,000 tons of bombs on North and South Vietnam and along the Ho Chi Minh Trail in Cambodia and Laos—more than three times the amount of explosives dropped on the Axis powers during World War II.

Bombs, however, had little effect against the highly mobile Vietcong guerrillas and North Vietnamese regulars, who used darkness, mountains, and jungles to mask their movement and hide their camps. Conventional American infantry experienced difficulties in finding and destroying the guerrillas, yet not a single U.S. Army brigade or division arrived in Vietnam with any long-range reconnaissance patrol personnel or Ranger units. The marine corps came with a limited

---

* The term *guerrilla* is from the Spanish for "little wars."

reconnaissance capability, and the navy did deploy a few hundred SEALs, who had evolved from the World War II UDT units.

Where it lacked political and conventional warfare focus in Vietnam, the United States did succeed in advancing old concepts of blood warriors and in developing or expanding special elites who soon were outguerrillaing the guerrilla. More important, the marine Force Reconnaissance, army Special Forces, army LRRPs (later redesignated *Rangers*), and navy SEALs performed well in Southeast Asia. As a result, following the war's conclusion the American leadership for the first time in history agreed to maintain a formidable force of blood warriors in the peacetime force.

The United States was not alone in fielding elite combat units during the Cold War and its aftermath. Great Britain, Australia, Germany, France, the Soviet Union, and other countries maintained elite units capable of reconnaissance, raids, and other special missions. However, these forces focused on "conventional" guerrilla and counterguerrilla operations, leaving themselves ill prepared to face what soon became a worldwide problem.

Instead of hit-and-run guerrilla warfare, terrorism became the order of the day. Terrorists hijacked airplanes, bombed public places, murdered political and military leaders, and took hostages to free imprisoned comrades, gain profit, or avenge past wrongs.

A failed counterterrorism operation by the Germans ultimately influenced the United States and other countries to adapt their elites to the new threat. On September 5, 1972, eight Arab terrorists invaded the Olympic Village in Munich, taking Israeli athletes and coaches hostage. When the German police and military attempted a rescue, eleven Israelis, one policeman, and five terrorists were killed.

In the aftermath of the unsuccessful operation the West Germans formed a special unit, Grenzschutzgruppe 9 (GSG-9), to carry out counterterrorist activities. During its formation the GSG-9 worked closely with the British Special Air Service, which had begun training for similar missions of rescuing embassies, aircraft, and buildings and protecting high-ranking officials. Both groups also monitored terrorist organizations and developed intelligence on their activities.

The Germans faced the first test. In October 1977 terrorists hijacked a German commercial airliner and forced its pilots to fly to Mogadishu, Somalia. In the midst of negotiations, GSG-9 teams stormed the plane, killed or captured the hijackers, and freed the passengers without friendly casualties.

In the aftermath of the successful rescue, American political leaders turned to the military, asking if the United States possessed such a capability. The negative response led to the approval on November 19, 1977, for the establishment of the ultrasecret Delta Force. Authorization for the formation of an elite unit, however, does not an instantly prepared force make. Manning and training an elite counterterrorism squad takes time, not enough of which was available before Delta faced its first challenge. Developments in Iran—where revolutionary "students" stormed the U.S. embassy in Tehran and took American officials and military personnel hostage— soon tested Delta and exposed its weaknesses.

On April 24, 1980, Secretary of Defense Harold Brown informed President Jimmy Carter, "I think we have an abort situation." The president responded, "Let's go with his [the ground commander's] recommendation." Colonel "Chargin' Charlie" Beckwith, founder and leader of the Delta Force, on the ground at a desolate site known as Desert One in Iran, relayed his recommendation to abort. A few minutes later the force assembled to rescue the fifty-three American hostages held by the Iranians lifted off from the desert to return to friendly territory, leaving behind burning aircraft, abandoned helicopters, and the bodies of eight American dead.

Delta Force, supported by Rangers and personnel from the air force and marine corps, had failed completely in its first significant counterterrorism operation. The failure diminished America's prestige among allies and enemies alike and further eroded the confidence of the American public in its government and military.

Within the armed forces some commanders expressed concerns about whether or not the military was getting what it paid for. Such negative evaluations were not surprising. Throughout history both civilian and military leaders have opposed the formation of special or elite units. Civilian governments have faced the quandary of how to maintain a standing army large enough for protection while at the same time keeping that armed force from taking over the leadership of the country. Dictatorships as well as democracies have fallen to dissatisfied military commanders who conducted coups with small, elite forces that could maintain secrecy and exert power beyond their numbers.

Many other military commanders also oppose elite forces, but for completely different reasons. The basic concept in the training of all successful combat forces is the "deindividualizing" of the recruit. Uniformity, from shorn hair and uniforms to repeated drills, turns the comfort-loving, self-oriented civilian into an order-following, teamwork-dedicated soldier. This time-proven, universal requirement of consistency demands that no one person or unit stands out above another. When certain individuals or units receive special attention as elite or superior to the remainder of the force, resentment arises and morale declines. Special headgear and/or other uniform adornments simply inflame the situation.

Officers and noncommissioned officers are not immune to resentment of men and units who receive special benefits and publicity. Many traditional-minded officers and sergeants dislike the break in uniformity that these units create. Their perception is that many volunteers for the elites are misfits or malcontents who cannot succeed in traditional units; they see the special organizations as being full of "undisciplined renegades" or "prima donnas" who disregard the rules and orders of conventional leaders.

More prevalent among officers and NCOs is the opinion that elite units drain other forces of much-needed leadership.

Nearly all of the men who eventually join the elites initially belong to conventional units. When they join elite units, their replacements lack equal training, skills, and abilities.

Superior soldiers, marines, and sailors who might lead squads or sections in conventional units fill the ranks as individual team members within the elites. A Special Forces A-Team or a Delta squad may have more senior NCOs than an entire infantry company. Many of the lower enlisted ranks on SEAL teams and in Ranger platoons would be wearing additional stripes and taking charge of sections or squads in the conventional forces.

A third common complaint about the elite units is the enormous amount of personnel, equipment, and financial assets they require. Their frequent behind-the-lines operations require intensive logistic and combat service support. In many situations, additional ground and air combat forces must be on standby to ensure the successful egress of the elites from enemy territory.

These objections to the elites confronted decision makers in the aftermath of the disaster in the Iranian desert, but wise generals, commanders, and civilian leaders recognized the proficiency of these men and, more important, continued to acknowledge the need for their existence. They understood that it was not the quality of the elites that had caused them to fail in the Iranian desert; instead, it was a matter of organization, command, and control problems.

However, changes did not occur quickly. Individuals who opposed elites as well as traditional interservice rivalries and competition for assets stalled the formation of a joint counterterrorism task force. Initially only the army made some progress by combining its Special Forces, Ranger, Delta, and supporting assets into the 1st Special Operations Command in 1982.

The terrorist explosion that killed 237 marines in their Beirut barracks on October 23, 1983, and the successful but flawed U.S. invasion of Grenada two days later again brought the need for a joint counterterrorist command to the forefront.

After extensive political maneuvering by Congress and the Pentagon, the Department of Defense established the U.S. Special Operations Command (USSOCOM) on April 16, 1987.

Today USSOCOM contains the special operations forces of the army, navy, and air force. This includes the Special Forces, Rangers, Delta Force, and SEALs as well as extensive air and other support units. With the exception of the USMC Force Reconnaissance companies, the SOCOM commander now heads all U.S. special operations forces.

CHAPTER 2

✳✳✳✳✳✳

U.S. Army Rangers: History

*R*ANGERS played an important role in gaining and maintaining the independence of the United States. From the first English colony in North America in the seventeenth century until the twentieth century, Rangers set the standard for future elites both within and outside the U.S. Army.

The English who arrived in North America to establish colonies in the early part of the seventeenth century initially confronted the hazards of disease and starvation. After a brief period of peace, the colonists also faced the threat of annihilation by the Native Americans. With primitive muskets as well as pikes and swords, and some prior training as soldiers, the colonists encountered military challenges in the New World not known in the Old.

These difficulties included their own small population, the harsh unmapped terrain, and the numbers and tactics of the Native Americans opposing them. Dense, virgin forests covered the eastern seaboard where the English established their first colonies. Only a few game trails and occasional Indian pathways penetrated the deep woods. Roads capable of carrying an army of any size were nonexistent.

Colonists who had military training were experienced in the conventional form of warfare that had evolved on the open European plains where standardized long lines of infantry, supported by cavalry and artillery, faced each other across open ground. Armies in which they had served were composed of professional soldiers who limited attacks to the battlefield so there would be few civilian casualties and little property damage.

Native American techniques could not have been more dissimilar. Indians ambushed their enemy and rarely stood to fight a sustained battle. Extremely knowledgeable of the forests and quick to move by foot, the Indians operated from temporary rather than permanent bases. Instead of attacking fortified areas or local militias, the Indians raided isolated communities and individual cabins, not discriminating among men, women, or children as enemies.

With their own limited manpower the colonists had to adapt to the terrain and the enemy to survive. They formed loose organizations of local militias for defense, but the colonists knew that the only way to defeat the Native Americans, or at least to force a peace, was to take the offense and to learn to out-Indian the Indians.

Small groups of the most proficient frontiersmen were soon scouting the forests using the same tactics as their enemy. On their return these men frequently filed reports with their community or colonial leaders stating they "had ranged" certain distances in pursuit of the Indians. As these reports evolved, the soldiers began calling themselves Rangers and named a legend born on the American frontier. The term was not new to the English language, however: As early as 1455 forest officers and gamekeepers in England were occasionally referred to as raungers.

The first official mention of American Rangers appears in a Massachusetts Colonial Archives note from 1670, which briefly marked the arrival of "one of Captain Willet's rangers coming on post on horseback." In fact, Thomas Willet of Rhode Island is credited with organizing the first Rangers when he formed his fellow frontiersmen into a company that scouted against an uprising of the Wampanoag tribe.

Five years later the first sustained action by a Ranger unit occurred during the King Philip's War. In 1675 the Wampanoag's King Philip, known to his Indian allies as Metacom, sided with the Narragansett tribes to raid the areas that are now Massachusetts and Rhode Island.

Philip and his allies destroyed twelve towns and killed more than a thousand white men, women, and children before the colonists could organize an effective resistance. Benjamin Church, born in Plymouth, Massachusetts, in 1639, fought against the Indians in several skirmishes in mid-1675. Based on his combat experiences, Church formed a company of Rangers who employed scouts from other Indian tribes and adapted their tactics to those of their enemy. On December 19, 1675, Church's Rangers participated in the destruction of the principal Narragansett village in the Great Swamp Fight near present-day South Kingston, Rhode Island.

Although the primary Indian resistance ceased with the Rangers' victory, Philip survived and continued to conduct raids against isolated settlements. Church and his Rangers pursued the Indian leader and his followers and on August 1, 1676, captured most of Philip's family. On August 12 the Rangers sneaked into Philip's refuge, where one of the Ranger marksmen shot the chief. King Philip was dead, the war named after him was over, and the American Rangers had their first victory.

For the next three-quarters of a century American colonists continued to develop small-unit tactics and skills to protect their homes and families from the Indians. Some—particularly in New York, New Jersey, and the Carolinas—adopted the title *Rangers*. Most of these groups were loosely organized, and they varied greatly in their effectiveness. It was not until the French and Indian War of 1754 through 1763 that the colonists formalized the Ranger concept and tactics to begin building the reputation that endures to this day.

Despite the early efforts of Willet and Church, the title *Father of the American Rangers* belongs by all rights to Robert Rogers. Born on November 7, 1731, in Methuen, Massachusetts, Rogers grew up in the New Hampshire forest, where his education came not in the classroom but from his fellow frontiersmen and local Indians. Most descriptions agree that he was a stocky, powerful man of medium height with dark hair and eyes. Rogers, with little tolerance for authority, had his first confrontation with law officials at age twenty-four when they accused him of counterfeiting. His reaction to the problem became the model for more than one Ranger in future generations. Rogers volunteered for a dangerous military mission rather than face judgment by the courts.

Instead of jail, Rogers chose to join an expedition commanded by British General William Johnson against a French fort at Crown Point, New York. Rogers made such a favorable impression with his bravery and his abilities as a scout that Johnson promoted him to captain and gave him command of a company in March 1756. Two years later Rogers advanced to the rank of major and command of nine Ranger companies.

Major Rogers recruited his own men and developed new training procedures. He composed and published a list of commonsense rules for operations, security, and tactics that still serves as a guide to special unit operations today. The earliest existing record of this guide, called the "Rules of Discipline," is in Rogers's *Journal*, published in 1766. These lengthy rules have reappeared over the years in several forms. The nineteen orders that have evolved and that are still relevant today cover barracks walls of Rangers and other elite units around the world. These savvy orders include "Don't forget nothing," "Never take a chance you don't have to," and ". . . Finish him off with your hatchet."

Rogers was one of the first commanders to train his men under realistic conditions, including using live ammunition during practice maneuvers. He continued these innovations during actual operations against the enemy. Instead of employing the normal tactics of the British army, Rogers copied the tactics of his Indian opponents, using scouting patrols, ambushes, and deep penetration behind the lines.

When campaigns by regular troops ceased during the cold and deep winter snowfalls, Rogers's Rangers continued their reconnaissance patrols and raids, sometimes operating on snowshoes and, on occasion, deploying scouts across frozen lakes on ice skates. Neither the French nor their Indian allies knew when or where to expect an attack by the Rangers, forcing them to deploy additional defensive forces that they could otherwise have used in offensive operations.

Although the Rangers were enormously successful in their unprecedented operations—or perhaps *because* of their success—many regular British and colonial officials disdained the special unit. Rogers was aware of these low opinions, and he often invited the officers along on operations to observe his Rangers. Few left unimpressed. The Rangers produced most of the successes against the French and Indians early in the war, becoming heroes of the colonists. Rogers persevered, and for the first time in American history the term *Ranger* became well known and highly respected.

Their success was due in part to Rogers's techniques of engagement. To gather information he deployed the Rangers in small, four- to eight-man scout teams prior to action. When the battle actually began, the Rangers often assembled into companies and fought as regular infantry. Rogers and his men saw action in most of the war's major fights, including Halifax in 1757, Ticonderoga and Lake George in 1758, and Crown Point in 1759.

While the Rangers accounted well for themselves during prebattle reconnaissance and fighting as infantry in the engagements that followed, their best-known and most successful action occurred as a result of a raid against an Abenaki Indian camp at St. Francis, about forty miles south of Montreal. The Abenaki, part of the Algonquin tribe, were fierce warriors who surrounded their lodges with poles adorned with scalps of English colonists they had tortured and killed.

Rogers had wanted to attack St. Francis for several years, but his superiors thought the village was too strong and too far behind the lines for a successful strike. Finally in 1759, in need of a victory that would end the Abenaki reign of terror across the countryside, officials granted Rogers permission to raid the village.

Rogers departed Crown Point with 180 of his most proficient Rangers. Traveling by boat and foot, they spent nearly six weeks covering the four hundred miles to their objective. Along the way disease and skirmishes with the enemy reduced their number to 142. Avoiding trails and using stealth, the surviving Rangers finally approached the village undetected. In the darkness shortly before dawn on October 5, the Rangers poured into the village and used shot, bayonet, and hatchet to rout the unsuspecting enemy. By seven in the morning two hundred Indians lay dead amid their burning lodges and scalp poles. The Abenaki were never an effective force again and played no further role in the war.

While the Abenaki were out of the fight, other Indians and French regulars, enraged that the Rangers had been able to penetrate so deep into their territory, made every effort to gain revenge. Multiple columns pursued or tried to block routes back to Crown Point. Greatly outnumbered, the Rangers nevertheless fought their way back through dense terrain and harsh weather.

Although Rogers achieved a great victory in the raid against St. Francis, the operation demonstrated the price future elites would often have to pay for such success. By the time the Rangers made their way back to friendly lines, they numbered ninety-three.

Despite their losses, the Americans welcomed the Rangers back as heroes while colonists celebrated their victory and the end of the Abenaki. The Ranger legend quickly became larger than life. Stories even circulated that the Rangers, out of either need or sheer bravado, had turned cannibalistic during their long march home. Although these rumors are likely false, they added to the Rangers' fierce reputation, which would grow with each succeeding conflict.

Within a year the Rangers faced another situation that would occur over and over in future wars. At the height of their success, several of the Ranger companies were disbanded in September 1760, and the last of Rogers's units were broken up the following January. The British and colonial commanders justified this move by pointing out that St. Francis was no longer a threat and that a need for the Rangers no longer existed. The true reason was more likely internal politics. Regular British troops and colonial militias resented the fame and admiration that the Rangers had achieved. Rangers, therefore, transferred to regular units, where they continued to use their leadership and fighting abilities.

Rogers himself left the Rangers in November 1760 to travel to Detroit to negotiate and accept the surrender of the French on the western frontier. At the conclusion of the war the colonial governments of New York and South Carolina awarded him several administrative positions as rewards for his faithful service. Unfortunately, Rogers was as inept at peacetime administration as he was proficient in wartime leadership. Already in debt from the use of his own money to raise Ranger companies during the war, Rogers continued to make poor financial decisions. When officials discovered in 1765 that he was illegally trading with the Indians to pay off some of his debts, he once again fled the law—this time to England.

Rogers was a hero in London and within a year had published his *Journal* and the *Concise Account of North America*, as well as a play, *Ponteach: or the Savages of North America*. These writings helped Rogers's financial situation but included little accurate history about his Rangers' exploits. As with many war stories told by later elite military commanders and members, the books and play exaggerated what actually occurred. The reaction to these stories by the public also closely resembled that in the future to overblown war stories. Safe in their favorite fireside reading chair, those who had never experienced the acrid smell of gunpowder and stench of rotting flesh on the battlefield took Rogers's stories to heart and felt they knew by association what close combat was really like.

More popular than ever, Rogers was able to get the English authorities to overlook his administrative problems in favor of his reputation and abilities as a battle leader. In 1766 he secured a commission in the 60th Foot Regiment, the "Royal Americans," and returned to the colonies as the commander of Fort Maclanec in present-day Michigan. Rogers, unable to get along well with his superiors, was soon again engaged in illegal trading. General Thomas Gage brought charges of graft and treason against him only two years after the Ranger leader's return to the colonies. Although acquitted because of a lack of evidence, Rogers lost his command and in 1769 once again returned to England. This time, however, instead of a hero's welcome and eager readers, Rogers faced debtors' prison.

After his release from jail Rogers disappeared from history for a few years. He later claimed to have served as a mercenary in Algiers in 1774, but there is no evidence to substantiate this claim.

At the beginning of the American Revolution in 1775 Rogers left England and returned to North America. He initially offered his services to George Washington, but the American general did not trust the former Ranger and at one time even imprisoned him as a spy. Upon his release Rogers turned to the British army and used his combat record in the French and Indian War to secure a commission as a lieutenant colonel. As such he commanded two companies of Loyalists—American colonists who remained loyal to the Crown—first called the King's Rangers, later renamed the Queen's Rangers. Rogers attempted to train his new command using his proven rules. However, in battles against the rebel colonists near White Plains, New York, in October 1776, the new British Rangers failed.

For several years Rogers served as a recruiting officer for the Loyalist forces, but he never regained the confidence of his senior commanders. His home life suffered as well. In 1778 the New Hampshire legislature granted his wife's petition for divorce and granted her the custody of their only child.

In 1780 Rogers returned to England, where he lived austerely on a half-pay pension. He wrote no more books or plays and his last great battle, which he lost, was against the bottle. Rogers died in a cheap London hotel on May 18, 1795, and was buried at St. Mary's in Newington.

Although Rogers had little personal impact on the American Revolution, his Ranger concept and tactics did. Even before the outbreak of the Revolution, the Continental Congress recognized the need for elite units. On June 14, 1775, the Congress resolved that "six companies of expert riflemen be immediately raised in Pennsylvania, two in Maryland, and two in Virginia."

In Virginia officials of Frederick County appointed Daniel Morgan as captain in charge of raising a local company. Morgan, a thirty-nine-year-old veteran Indian fighter originally from Hunterdon County, New Jersey, took only ten days to assemble ninety-six local marksmen. Instead of militia uniforms, the newly formed company wore buckskin hunting jackets and trousers along with leather moccasins. Like Rogers's Rangers they carried knives and hatchets, but more important, they adopted the much more accurate Pennsylvania long rifle as their primary weapon.

Morgan and his company participated in the invasion of Canada in late 1775 where the British captured the rebel leader during the raid on Quebec on December 31. Although his attack failed, he had so impressed his superiors that upon his exchange he was promoted to colonel and ordered to organize a corps of sharpshooters. Morgan's command varied from two hundred to five hundred men during the remainder of the war as the unit combined Ranger tactics with expert marksmanship. They participated in almost every major battle. George Washington called them his Corps of Rangers and relied upon them in the most difficult circumstances.

Morgan's Rangers also impressed their British opponents. At Saratoga the Rangers contributed so much to the American victory that British General John Burgoyne remarked, "Morgan's men were the most famous corps of the Continental Army. All of them crack shots."

Morgan relied upon more than just superior weapons and

tactics to achieve battlefield success. He was a master of motivation. In October 1780 Washington promoted Morgan to brigadier general in command of continental and state infantry units. Prior to the Battle of Cowpens in South Carolina on January 16, 1781, Morgan assembled his command and pronounced, "On this ground, I will defeat the British or lay down my bones."

In a lighter vein, Morgan addressed his North and South Carolina volunteer militiamen who were nearing the end of their brief enlistment. "Just hold up your head, boys, three fires [musket shots]," he said, "and you are free, and then when you return to your homes, how the folks will bless you, and the girls will kiss you for your gallant conduct."

Just before the fight began, Morgan took off his shirt and showed his men the scars left from a whipping administered by the British after he struck an officer while serving as a teamster in 1756. His orders that followed may have been as much for revenge as revolutionary zeal: "Shoot for epaulettes [officers], boys," he shouted.

Morgan's men heeded his advice. In a battle that lasted less than an hour Morgan's Corps killed more than 100 British soldiers, wounded 230, and captured 830 with the loss of only a dozen dead and 60 wounded. Morgan later attributed his success that day "to the justice of our cause and the bravery of our troops."

Unlike Rogers, Morgan proved successful after the war during his retirement at his Virginia estate. From 1797 through 1799 he served a term in the House of Representatives, dying in Winchester, Virginia, on July 6, 1802.

Other Ranger units formed during the American Revolution did not experience the successes of Morgan's Corps. Much of Morgan's success came from his abilities to select his men and their arms, but more important, he also had the time to train his corps to develop the skills and discipline necessary to survive and achieve victory.

Thomas Knowlton was a thirty-six-year-old native of West Boxford, Massachusetts, and one of the most experienced officers in the Continental army when George Washington selected him to form a unit of Rangers in late August 1776. Knowlton, a veteran of the French and Indian War, had already fought at Bunker Hill where, as a captain, he held the rebels' defenses on the left and later covered their withdrawal under withering British musket fire and bayonet assaults. Promoted to major in the 20th Continental Infantry, Knowlton exhibited more bravery as well as a knack for behind-the-lines operations on January 8, 1776, when he led a raid against a British headquarters on the outskirts of Boston.

Washington was well aware of Knowlton's talents when he ordered the newly promoted lieutenant colonel to form a unit of Rangers. Washington and his army were not faring well in the battles around New York, and the general realized that he needed intelligence from patrols and prisoners.

Unfortunately Washington did not give Knowlton sufficient time to train his company of 120 Rangers before committing them to the fight. On September 16, 1776, less than two weeks after the formation of the Rangers, Washington ordered them to scout the British positions at Harlem Heights, New York; to circle the enemy in order to disrupt their rear; and to capture prisoners. During their movement the inexperienced Rangers rode too close to the British center. A superior British force attacked and cut them off from retreat to friendly lines. In minutes Knowlton and most of his command lay dead. Knowlton's Rangers—or Knowlton's Connecticut Rangers—ceased to exist except as a footnote to history.

Rangers in the southern colonies were much more successful. Although greatly outnumbered by British and Loyalist troops, the rebels had the advantage of the vast theater of operations and their knowledge of the terrain.

Despite their advantages the British soundly defeated the rebels at Camden, South Carolina, on August 16, 1780. The rebel army needed time to regroup after their loss. Francis Marion formed a small band of guerrillas, who struck isolated British outposts, couriers, and supply columns while living off the land. A South Carolina native, Marion knew the territory, especially the coastal swamps where he hid and from where he launched his raids. Marion's group rarely exceeded one hundred men and usually operated in much smaller groups, coming together only to make joint attacks. In addition to his prewar and pre-guerrilla-combat experience in conventional units, Marion apparently was knowledgeable of Robert Rogers's rules and adopted them for his own use.

Marion so confounded the British command that they dedicated most of their Loyalist forces under command of Colonel Banastre Tarleton to tracking down the guerrilla leader. Tarleton failed and, in frustration, declared, "As for this damned old fox, the devil himself could not catch him." Tarleton's statement provided the nickname Swamp Fox for Marion.

By the end of the war Marion was a brigadier general and second only to Washington as the best-known and most popular officer in the army. Following the war he served several terms in the South Carolina senate and for six years as the commander of Fort Johnson in Charleston harbor. He died at his plantation home in Berkeley County on February 27, 1795.

It is noteworthy that service with Rangers also influenced several other American commanders who significantly contributed to the success of the Revolution. Generals John Stark and Israel Putnam, both of whom commanded at Bunker Hill and other subsequent battles, learned their war-fighting skills as junior officers with Rogers's Rangers in the 1750s. Yet lasting fame went not to these conventional force commanders but to Rogers and Marion, who have lived on in the history of Rangers and in the minds of the public through books, motion pictures, and television series.

Surviving Ranger units, along with most of the rest of the army, were disbanded shortly after the British surrender at Yorktown in 1781. State and community militias in the post-

Revolution years occasionally used Ranger tactics to combat local Indian uprisings, but these soldiers reverted to civilians as soon as the threat ended.

The official name *Ranger* did not appear again in the U.S. Army until a congressional directive ordered the formation of six Ranger companies on January 2, 1812, for a period of service of one year. Between that date and March 3, 1815, Congress authorized eleven additional Ranger companies for similar periods of active service. In later years, when the United States became more urban, an enlistment for only twelve months would not offer sufficient time to train an effective elite force. In the nineteenth century, however, most Americans were familiar with current firearms, and their marksmanship often meant the difference between a full and an empty dinner pot. Many potential Ranger recruits also lived in isolated villages and on farms where diligence and preparedness meant the difference between survival and becoming an Indian scalp pole adornment.

Most of the Ranger action in the War of 1812 focused on fighting Indians rather than the British. Rangers under command of Colonel John Coffee made their most significant contribution during the final months of the war. Coffee's Rangers, mostly from Tennessee, supported General Andrew Jackson in his Southern Campaign against the Creek Indians and then in the war's final battle at New Orleans. Like Morgan in the Revolution, Coffee saw that his men were armed with the most durable and accurate rifles available. In addition, he adopted Morgan's buckskin uniforms, and many of his men copied former Rangers by carrying hatchets for close-in fighting. Coffee also hired Choctaw Indians to fight against their traditional Creek enemies.

In eastern Alabama, Coffee's Rangers and Indian scouts conducted a careful reconnaissance of the Creek primary camp at Horseshoe Bend on the Tallapossa River. Using information provided by the Rangers, Jackson overran the village on March 27, 1814, killing 900 and capturing 500 with the loss of only 51 killed and 148 wounded.

With the Creeks neutralized, Jackson turned to the defense of New Orleans as Coffee's Rangers kept the general informed about the British advance. They also, on occasion, sneaked near the British lines and shot stragglers or pickets. Coffee's Rangers' final fight was part of Jackson's victory over the British at Chalmette just east of New Orleans on January 8, 1815. Although the battle is often listed as the most significant American victory of the war, it was actually important only for Jackson's political future. Unknown to the participants because of slow communications, the war had officially ended two weeks earlier with the signing of the Treaty of Ghent.

After the War of 1812 Jackson continued to use Rangers to combat the Native Americans. In May 1818 he recruited two companies under Captains McGrit and Boyle to pursue Seminole Indians in the panhandle of Florida. In addition to its captain, each company had two lieutenants and seventy enlisted men, most of whom were woodsmen from Tennessee and Georgia. In the field the companies received no administrative or logistical support other than a single medical specialist, who assisted both companies.

The most significant action by the Rangers occurred during a patrol in the fall of 1818. Boyle's Ranger company, while attached to the 4th Infantry Regiment, paddled up the Yellow River and then marched undetected overland to attack and destroy a Seminole village on Choctawhatchy Bay on October 8. Today's Rangers train on the same waterways and in the woodlands where Boyle's men fought more than a century and a half ago. The water move up the Yellow River and then the cross-country patrol to the Indian camp occurred on what is now Eglin Air Force Base—home of the current Florida Ranger camp, which conducts the third phase of the modern Ranger School.

As the American frontier expanded westward, the combat techniques honed by Rogers, Morgan, Marion, Coffee, and

Boyle proved successful in fighting the numerically superior Indians. These early Rangers, like those who would follow, learned that small groups using aggressive patrolling followed up with swift, violent attacks could easily defeat larger forces.

When the few American colonists attempted to settle the vast Spanish territory of Texas a decade after the War of 1812, they faced opposition from Mexicans as well as Indians. Colony leader Stephen F. Austin established a company of ten Rangers shortly after his arrival in Texas in May 1823. Austin initially paid the Rangers out of his own pocket, but, as it grew, the entire colony assumed responsibility for the support of additional "ranging companies." Landowners provided men for limited time periods and contributed to the pay of captains, who occupied the only permanent Ranger positions. These early Texas Rangers wore no uniforms, served under no flag, and functioned at best as loosely organized paramilitary units. Yet by the time Texas declared its independence from Mexico in 1836, the Rangers had won a place in folklore and in fact for their effectiveness as fighters. For the next decade, until Texas joined the Union in 1845, its history was little more than the story of Rangers protecting the property, lives, and sovereignty of the Lone Star State.

T. E. Fehrenbach, in his masterful book *Lone Star*, wrote of the Rangers, "Throughout his whole existence as a fighting man, the Texas Ranger was outnumbered by his foes. This produced not caution but canniness and an almost incredible aggressiveness. The Ranger found his best defense was to attack, dominate, subdue." These comments would prove equally true for future Rangers.

The Texas Rangers learned from predecessors like Morgan to arm themselves with the best weapons. Despite U.S. Army Ordinance Corps officers' rejecting Sam Colt's six-shot revolver, the Texans adopted it as their primary weapon. Fighting mostly from horseback, the Rangers needed the advantage of the Colt's firepower—six times greater than that of their Comanche and other foes, who carried single-shot weapons.

After statehood the Rangers remained as a military force that reported directly to the governor. During the Mexican War of 1846, several of the Ranger companies were attached to regular U.S. Army units and served as scouts behind the lines. After the war they returned to state control, occasionally joining the army against the Indians.

In 1854 the Rangers were relieved of military responsibilities and became the state's law enforcement agency. Today they number only sixty total active Rangers, but their reputation for solving crimes and keeping the peace still earn them the highest respect. The Texas Rangers have always been known for their toughness.

Perhaps the best example of this characteristic, which would not differ much from future Rangers, occurred during major labor riots by Mexicans in the Rio Grande Valley in the early part of the twentieth century. With part of their town in ashes and their local law officers ineffective, city officials requested that the governor send the National Guard to restore order. When the officials met the train carrying the promised reinforcements, only a single individual wearing the badge of a Texas Ranger stepped down on the platform. In response to the local officials' surprise and rising anger, the lone Ranger calmly declared, "One riot, one Ranger."

The single Ranger then proceeded to the headquarters of the labor organizers, pistol-whipped their leader, arrested him, and departed with his prisoner on the next train. No more rioting took place; one Ranger had indeed been sufficient. Today a monument to the "one Ranger" stands in the lobby of Dallas's Love Field Airport.

The American Civil War provided opportunities for Rangers to serve the North and the South. In a war where both sides spoke the same language, shared ethnic origins, and knew the terrain, Ranger units could operate with ease behind enemy lines.

Each southern state fielded at least one Ranger unit during the war, as did nearly all those in the North. The designation *Ranger*, however, was liberal and often taken by units that were not true to the term. By the war's conclusion, more than four hundred units from both sides had fought under the title.

The few commands that employed the traditional Ranger tactics of reconnaissance and raids behind the enemy lines made significant contributions and became some of the most popular and best-known soldiers of the long conflict. In addition to gaining fame, the Civil War Rangers shared other characteristics of future blood warriors. Military and civilian leaders on both sides equated the Rangers' behind-the-lines operations with guerrilla warfare. To many it lacked the nobility of conventional combat.

The North and South debated the issue of Ranger or partisan units and even at times dictated that captured soldiers from such units be hanged or shot. To provide a veil of legitimacy the South went as far as to legislate the approval of Rangers. On March 27, 1862, the Confederate Congress passed the Partisan Ranger Act, which, in addition to making the units official, also authorized them to live off the land and to keep a share of captured booty during operations. This caused officials on both sides to brand the Rangers as outlaws and renegades—titles that at times future generations of Rangers would also share.

The South fielded more Ranger units during the war. This was partially because of the tradition of unconventional warfare in the region, which dated back to Francis Marion in the American Revolution. A more dominant factor, however, was a matter of resources. The South, always short on manpower and equipment, had to maximize whatever it had available to meet the stronger northern army. Rangers, in addition to providing intelligence through reconnaissance, could tie down large enemy forces with raids in the rear areas. The mere threat of Rebel Ranger operations behind the lines kept thousands of Union infantrymen guarding headquarters, supply points, and transportation centers rather than fighting on the front lines.

John Singleton Mosby, the Gray Ghost, led the most famous of the Confederate Rangers. While Mosby ultimately set the example for many latter-day Rangers to follow, his advancement to the leadership position was not easy. Born in Edgemont, Virginia, in 1833, Mosby entered the University of Virginia at the age of fifteen. Soon thereafter, Mosby shot and wounded a fellow student following a brief argument. Only a special act sponsored by friends in the state legislature prevented his serving six months in jail and paying a thousand-dollar fine after the courts found him guilty of the crime.

Mosby read law books while in jail awaiting his trail. After being freed by the legislative act, he returned to the university and graduated in 1852. Three years later he was admitted to the Virginia bar. Within days of the outbreak of the Civil War, Mosby enlisted as a private in the Confederate cavalry and participated in the first Battle of Bull Run on July 21, 1861. A year later Mosby served as one of the advance scouts for General J. E. B. Stuart during the famous ride around General George McCellan's Union army during the Peninsular Campaign.

The lawyer-turned-cavalry-scout so impressed Stuart that in December 1862 he placed Mosby in charge of nine men and ordered them to conduct guerrilla warfare in Loudoun County, Virginia. Mosby's successful attacks on isolated Union outposts and supply lines earned him a lieutenant's commission the following February. He soon built his force to a group of three hundred men who, in June 1863, were designated the 43rd Virginia Cavalry, often referred to as the 43rd Virginia Ranger Partisan Battalion.

Mosby, schooled in law rather than military science, learned quickly on the battlefield and from the writings of the great commanders. He particularly liked books about Napoleon and adopted many of the French leader's tactics of mobility and concentration of firepower. Mosby also copied the ideas of the Texas Rangers in that he secured the fastest horses, armed his men with the best revolvers, and eschewed the traditional cavalry sabers.

Mosby's most spectacular raid occurred on March 9, 1863, when he led twenty-nine men ten miles into Union-held territory. Entering an enemy camp at Fairfax Court House, Virginia, under the cover of darkness and a driving rainstorm, the Rangers captured Brigadier General Edwin H. Stoughton, commander of the 5th New York Cavalry, along with thirty of his men and fifty-eight horses. Mosby and his Rangers withdrew without a single casualty and turned their prisoners over to regular Confederate troops at Culpeper, Virginia.

The raid against Fairfax Court House earned Mosby a promotion to captain and additional fame among the Rebels. It also spread his reputation in the North, where commanders increased their guard detachments at the expense of frontline units. Even President Lincoln expressed concern about the Fairfax raid, saying, "I can make another brigadier general, but I can't make a horse."

Mosby continued to advance in rank, and by the summer of 1863 was an important reconnaissance asset of J. E. B. Stuart's cavalry. In a report about activities leading up to the Battle of Gettysburg, Stuart proclaimed, "Mosby was particularly active and efficient. His information was always accurate and reliable."

Over the next year Mosby's men raided throughout northern Virginia, often the only opposition to free movement by the northern army. Union commanders became so infuriated at the lightning-quick raids that cost them men and supplies that they began to refer to the partisans as bandits and promised to execute any prisoners taken from Mosby's band. On September 23, 1864, elements of George A. Custer's command carried out this promise by hanging or shooting six captured Rangers. Custer would later deny that his men were responsible.

Over the next six weeks Mosby took his revenge. On October 14 he stopped a Baltimore & Ohio passenger train and removed $173,000 from its mail car. Later, when asked how he supplied and paid his soldiers, he replied, "By the courtesy of the United States Army Quartermaster General."

Mosby also sought more direct revenge for the execution of his men. During October his patrols captured twenty-seven cavalrymen from Custer's division. On November 6 Mosby had the prisoners draw lots and then hung three and shot three. He then sent word to the Union commanders that in the future he would treat prisoners well—unless more of his men were executed.

The raids and harassment by Mosby's Rangers did not cease in the war's concluding months. In fact, they carried out their final raid on the same day that General Lee surrendered at Appomattox Court House, April 9, 1865. When President Lincoln was assassinated five days later, many in the North, including U. S. Grant, initially thought Mosby was somehow responsible. One of the plotters had briefly ridden with the Rangers, but Mosby had nothing to do with the killing.

At the time Lincoln was shot, Mosby, then a colonel, was dodging the many Union patrols still trying to capture him. After Appomattox, Mosby conferred with Union officers but refused to surrender his command. Stealing away, he assembled his men one last time and spoke to them briefly, stating, "I disband your organization in preference to surrender. I part from you with pride in the fame of your achievements and grateful recollections of your generous kindness to myself."

Mosby was as successful as a civilian as he had been a warrior. He soon put old hatred aside as he reestablished his law practice and supported Grant for the presidency. By presidential appointment Mosby served as U.S. consul general to Hong Kong from 1878 to 1885. In addition to publishing two books on his wartime experiences, Mosby went on to serve in the Department of Justice from 1904 to 1910. He died on May 30, 1916, still revered as the Gray Ghost of the Confederacy and one of the great role models for future Rangers and special operators.

*   *   *

Much less famous but equally as effective were Confederate Rangers under the command of John H. McNeill. After brief service in Missouri as a cavalryman, McNeill returned to his Virginia family home, where he recruited a company of partisans in September 1862. For the next year McNeill and his men operated as a part of larger cavalry units. In the spring of 1863 McNeill's Rangers began to ride independently, conducting raids and reconnaissance missions similar to those of Mosby.

McNeill's Rangers frequently acted as scouts on the flanks of movements by the Army of Northern Virginia, but behind-the-lines raids is where they made their most significant impact. The Rangers attacked supply points and brought back much-needed provisions for the Confederate army. Often the raiders captured more than they could carry and destroyed the rest. In May 1864 McNeill and his men burned an entire train of six locomotives and one hundred cars in northwestern Virginia, depriving the Union army of supplies and equipment valued at more than a million dollars.

On October 2, 1864, Union troops killed McNeill during a raid on Mount Jackson, Virginia. His son Jesse assumed command of the Rangers and continued his father's operations. The following February, McNeill's Rangers made their most spectacular raid when they crossed into Maryland. Using the password they had secured from a prisoner, the Rangers rode to Cumberland, where they captured two generals and then safely made their way back to Confederate lines. Even Mosby, who had conducted a similar operation, praised the raid as surpassing anything his Rangers had ever accomplished.

Less than two weeks before the war concluded, McNeill's Rangers destroyed still another railroad train and depot. Like Mosby's, McNeill's Rangers never surrendered but disbanded and returned to their homes.

Ranger units also were home to other Confederates. Colonel Turner Ashby, another Virginian, conducted successful Ranger operations similar to those of Mosby and McNeill. General

John Hunt Morgan, a Mexican War veteran from Kentucky, commanded a conventional cavalry division during the war but frequently led his command deep into northern territory on raids. During twenty-four days in August 1862, Morgan's Raiders rode more than one thousand miles behind enemy lines, where they captured and paroled twelve hundred prisoners.

A year later, after several small raids into northern Kentucky, Morgan led his largest operation northward. Morgan's more than two thousand cavalrymen averaged twenty-one hours a day in the saddle from July 2 to July 26, 1863, covering up to fifty miles a day. The raid captured Corydon, Indiana, and threatened Cincinnati, Ohio, before far larger numbers of Union troops cut off their escape routes and captured most of the command, including Morgan.

The raids eroded the morale of the Union army as well as of civilians, who were not accustomed to having the war take place on their home territory. Morgan eventually escaped and assumed command of the Department of Northwest Virginia. He died in battle at Greenville, Tennessee, on September 4, 1864.

William C. Quantrill was another Confederate who proved to be extremely successful at guerrilla warfare. However, Quantrill and his raiders also demonstrated that Americans could see those who conducted Ranger-type operations as bandits as readily as heroes.

Born in Dover, Ohio, in 1837, Quantrill worked as a schoolteacher until 1857, when he moved to Kansas and joined the pro-slavery faction. He participated in at least two skirmishes with abolitionists, and authorities suspected him in several robberies and murders before the outbreak of the Civil War. Early in the conflict Quantrill led a small group of guerrillas who supported the Confederacy. After assisting in the siege of Lexington and the capture of Independence, Missouri, Quantrill's company was formally mustered into the Confederate army.

Despite receiving a captain's commission on August 11,

1862, Quantrill continued to operate independently from any Confederate command. Many of his activities seemed directed more at settling old scores from the prewar anti-slavery skirmishes in Kansas and Missouri than in contributing to any military campaign.

On August 21, 1863, Quantrill led his most notorious raid when he and 450 men slipped through the Union lines along the Missouri River and rode undetected for more than sixty miles to Lawrence, Kansas. Quantrill's men sacked and burned the defenseless town, killing 180 men, women, and children. Lawrence had no particular military value, and Quantrill claimed the attack was in revenge for the Union destruction of Osceola, Missouri, a year earlier. It is more likely, however, that the guerrillas destroyed Lawrence to enact revenge against its citizens for previous actions against Quantrill and his men.

Quantrill won a conventional battle against Union soldiers at Baxter Spring, Kansas, on October 6, 1863, but tarnished his victory by shooting his prisoners. A short time later Quantrill's Raiders disbanded because of internal strife among the group's leaders. Quantrill accomplished little more in the war than escaping capture by the Union forces, who had declared him a bandit and labeled him "the bloodiest man in America." On May 10, 1865, a Union patrol finally succeeded in tracking down the guerrilla leader at Taylorsville, Kentucky. Quantrill was mortally wounded and died a few weeks later in a prison hospital.

While Quantrill's motivation is extremely suspect, and his lack of attention to the rules of warfare is criminal, he nevertheless was a master at Ranger-type tactics. His abilities to conduct raids far behind enemy lines matched those of any leader on either side during the war. What Quantrill taught his command they used after the war—but in criminal rather than military pursuits. Frank James, Cole Younger, and a host of other outlaws, including possibly Jesse James and even Belle Starr, saw their first action under the black flag of Quantrill's Raiders. In fact, a copy of that simple pennant with stitched letters spelling out QUANTRILL hangs today on the wall of the boyhood home of the James brothers, which is now a museum, in Kearney, Missouri.

Individual Union Ranger units were neither as successful nor as well known as their Rebel counterparts. The North had fewer Rangers and fewer reasons to organize more. Since most of the war's activities occurred in the South, the Rebels had the advantage of local population support. Also, the size and resources of the Union army precluded the need for behind-the-lines reconnaissance.

Samuel C. Means led the most effective unit of Union Rangers. Means, a Virginia businessman who remained loyal to the Union, served as an enlisted scout during the first months of the war. In June 1862 the U.S. secretary of war, Edwin M. Stanton, awarded Means a commission and ordered him to recruit a company of his fellow Loudoun County Virginians to fight the Rebels.

For the next two years the Loudoun Independent Rangers conducted scouting missions for the Union army around Harpers Ferry, as well as limited raids on Confederate supply trains. In their most successful mission they destroyed an ammunition convoy belonging to General James Longstreet. Means's Rangers also had several confrontations with Mosby's Rangers in which they generally held their own.

In March 1864 the U.S. Army ordered Means to consolidate his Rangers with the 3rd West Virginia Cavalry. Means refused, stating that his Rangers, by orders of Secretary Stanton, were for "special service" and subject to his—and only his—command. Stanton agreed that the Rangers were to remain independent, but Means resigned nevertheless. The Rangers, however, continued under its junior officers until they mustered out of the service on May 30, 1865.

Although Means's Rangers served throughout most of the war, they are not as well known as a group of Union raiders who performed only one daring mission. On April 12, 1862, James J. Andrews and twenty-one volunteers slipped behind

Confederate lines and hijacked a locomotive at Big Shanty (now Kennesaw), Georgia. Andrews's plan was to run the stolen locomotive, the General, to Chattanooga and destroy the rail line, bridges, and telegraph line as they went.

Shortly after they hijacked the locomotive, the Confederates took up pursuit on the train engine Texas. Ninety miles later the General ran out of fuel and the Union raiders fled into the countryside, ending what became known as the Great Locomotive Chase. The Confederates captured all the raiders and then executed Andrews and seven of his men. Eight of the raiders escaped their prison cells and made their way back to Union lines. The Confederates later paroled the remaining six. These survivors, as well as those executed, received the first Medals of Honor ever presented.

The end of the Civil War brought peace to the North and South but not to the expanding American borders in the West. While the U.S. Army and local militias had neutralized the horseless eastern tribes by midcentury, the proud Indian horsemen of the Great Plains were not yet willing to surrender their homelands. For the next thirty years the U.S. Army faced determined enemies who employed their own brand of Ranger-type tactics.

Indians fought on territory they had been born to—land where no stream, valley, or ridgeline was a stranger. They lived off the land and fought only when all odds were in their favor. Time was no factor in Indian tactics, as they fought not for victory but for survival.

Initially the U.S. Army established forts and dispatched cavalry and infantry patrols in pursuit of the remaining nomadic Native Americans. The Indians rarely stood and fought, preferring to slip away in small groups and reassemble later to attack isolated outposts or unprotected civilians. Years of experience in the huge clashes of infantry and artillery at bloody battlefields such as Bull Run, Antietam, and Gettysburg did little to prepare soldiers for the hit-and-run tactics of the Indians.

The need for the army to employ men who understood the enemy and who had knowledge of the vast western terrain was evident. Scouts, both white and Indian, soon rode in front of the regular troops. Whites such as Kit Carson, Al Sieber, Bill Cody, and many others whose names have been linked with the myths and legends of winning the American West earned their early fame scouting for the army. Indian scouts stepped forward to fight against other tribes who were traditional enemies.

The use of civilian scouts was formalized in 1868 when Major George A. Forsyth presented to General Phil Sheridan a plan for harassing the Indians without using the already shorthanded regular army garrisons. Forsyth proposed that a small, highly mobile group of experienced frontiersmen be formed to fight the Indians using their own tactics. They would track, attack when possible, and keep the enemy from the safety of their sanctuaries.

Sheridan approved the plan, and Forsyth quickly recruited fifty scouts. Forsyth, who had risen from private to brevet brigadier general in the Civil War, had no trouble finding volunteers. The promise of a dollar a day to fight Indians without formal enlistment into the army was an attractive offer. After all, most of the volunteers had been fighting the Indians for a long time with no reward whatsoever except keeping the hair on their heads.

It did not take much training for the experienced Indian fighters to be ready to begin operations. Less than a month after their formation, Forsyth's scouts were on patrol in eastern Colorado. They soon discovered, as would future Rangers, that experience and fighting ability are sometimes no match for sheer numbers. On September 17 a band of more than a thousand Cheyenne, Sioux, and Arapaho warriors under the leadership of Roman Nose surprised the fifty scouts near the Arikaree Fork of the Republican River.

The scouts retreated to an island in the river and for four days held off the Indians before black soldiers of the 10th Cavalry rescued them. Several of the scouts were killed, including Lieutenant F. H. Beecher, the second in command of the expedition. Forsyth suffered serious wounds, as did his concept of patrolling scouts.

The fight at what became known as Beechers Island discouraged civilian volunteers and forced General Sheridan to look for new ways to combat the hostiles. Instead of volunteer white units, he recruited more Native Americans to scout against neighboring tribes. When these Indian Scouts discovered the hostile camps, he committed regular cavalry and infantry units to destroy them. Sheridan was particularly successful at campaigning in the dead of winter when the Indians were less mobile. He also used the modern technology of the telegraph and rail lines for communications and mobility. These improved tactics resulted in the destruction of many villages—some critics preferred to call them massacres—and the Indians' surrender to reservations.

With the neutralization of their own tribes, even more Indians sought to become army Scouts. By the mid-1880s only the Apache in the Great Southwest continued to resist the whites' settlement of their territory. In the last major campaign of the Indian wars, General George Crook used Native American Scouts with the utmost efficiency. When 150 Apaches under the leadership of Geronimo killed several settlers in May 1883 and escaped to the Sierra Madre of Mexico, Crook assembled 250 men, 193 of whom were Indian Scouts, and pursued the renegades.

Crook caught up with the Indians and returned them to the United States. Except for a brief escape by Geronimo and a few followers, all of whom the Indian Scout–led U.S. Cavalry again captured, the war whoops of the Apache were silenced.

Captain John G. Bourke of the 3rd U.S. Cavalry accompanied Crook's expedition. In a book about his adventures Bourke recorded a description of the Indian Scouts, a depiction that would include many important characteristics of future Rangers and special operators. Bourke wrote in *An Apache Campaign in the Sierra Madre,* "The two great points of superiority of the native or savage soldier over the representative of civilized discipline are his absolute knowledge of the country and his perfect ability to take care of himself at all times and under all circumstances. . . . Every track in the trail, mark in the grass, scratch on the bark of a tree explains itself. . . . He can tell to an hour, almost, when the man or animal making them passed by, and, like a hound, will keep on the scent until he catches up with the object of his pursuit. . . . Approaching the enemy his vigilance is a curious thing to witness. [He] has no false ideas about courage; he would prefer to skulk like the coyote for hours, and then kill his enemy, or capture his herd, rather than by injudicious exposure, receive a wound, fatal or otherwise. But he is no coward; on the contrary, he is entitled to rank among the bravest."

America's nineteenth century ended in the Spanish-American War, a conflict begun in 1898 that produced neither elite units nor advances in Ranger operations. Theodore Roosevelt's 1st U.S. Volunteer Cavalry, composed of a few former Indian fighters and many adventurers—ranging from Ivy League college students to working western cowboys—gained much fame. While the soldiers fought bravely, they did so without their horses, which had been left behind in Florida, and would have taken even more casualties if the black 9th and 10th Cavalry regiments had not come to their aid at San Juan Hill.

The most successful Ranger-type operations of the war occurred during the efforts to neutralize Filipino rebels after Spain surrendered the Philippines. On February 4, 1901, Colonel Frederick Funston learned the location of guerrilla leader Emilio Aguinaldo's jungle headquarters. Funston, fluent in Spanish from his service in Cuba, gathered a force of ninety soldiers and native Filipinos. Disguised as prisoners and guards, he and his men entered Aguinaldo's camp and captured the rebel leader.

Once again a small group of dedicated soldiers, under superior leadership and using Ranger tactics, proved successful where a larger conventional force had failed. From the time the first English colonists arrived in the New World until the beginning of the twentieth century, Rangers established their value and fighting abilities. Warfare, however, like the nation itself, was changing, and it would be decades before the modern battlefield would experience modern Rangers.

CHAPTER 3

✳✳✳✳✳✳✳

U.S. Army Rangers: Modern

No formal or informal Ranger units existed in the U.S. Army during the first four decades of the twentieth century. Commanders saw no need for behind-the-lines operations during the trench warfare that dominated World War I. By the time the United States entered the conflict, the war was a series of campaigns where each side competed for yards of territory rather than miles. Some believed that the newly developed airplanes could provide reconnaissance with no risk to ground troops.

The global, multifronted aspects of World War II presented new challenges to American commanders. The British, Soviets, and Germans had already used special operations forces to great advantage before the Americans entered the war. U.S. Chief of Staff George C. Marshall recognized a need for a similar capacity. In the spring of 1942 Marshall sent Brigadier General Lucian K. Truscott as his official representative to the British Combined Operations Staff in Northern Ireland, where Americans assembled and trained after their arrival from the United States. Marshall's instructions to Truscott were to integrate American troops into conventional and Commando-type operations as soon as possible.

On May 26, 1942, Truscott requested permission to form the 1st Ranger Battalion along the lines of the British Special Service Brigade. Marshall immediately approved the plan. Truscott chose the name *Ranger* as a tie to American historical units and in consideration of the British. According to Truscott, "Rangers was selected because the name Commandos rightfully belonged to the British and we sought a name that was more typically American. It was therefore fit that the organization destined to be the first American ground forces to battle Germans on the European continent should have been named Rangers in compliment to those in American history who exemplified such high standards of individual courage, initiative, determination, ruggedness, fighting ability, and achievement."

Although *Ranger* was a term first used by British and colonial officers, such as Church and Rogers, for their units in the French and Indian War, the English never considered adopting the term for their modern elite units. Instead, *Commando* was the personal choice of Winston Churchill, who admired the mounted Boer guerrillas of South Africa. So the Americans became Rangers and the British, Commandos—both oddly adopting names for their elites from former enemies.

Truscott turned to Major General Russell P. Hartle, commander of all U.S. Army units in Northern Ireland, to secure volunteers for the 1st Ranger Battalion. Hartle supported the formation of the new unit and recommended his own aide-de-camp, William O. Darby, as its first commander. Darby, a newly promoted thirty-one-year-old artillery major and graduate of West Point, seemed an unusual choice with his noninfantry background and current assignment as a general's "horse holder." But he was the right man for the job. Truscott described him as "outstanding in appearance, possessed of a most attractive personality . . . and filled with enthusiasm."

Darby fully met his superior's expectations. While Robert Rogers rightfully held the title *Father of the American Rangers*, Darby soon established himself as the *Father of Modern Rangers*. Darby had free rein in manning, arming, supplying, and training his force. He personally interviewed each volunteer, selecting only the most motivated and physically and mentally fit. Darby openly warned soldiers not to join the Rangers, telling them there would be no privileged individuals and that no unit would have it tougher. Reality in training was Darby's goal. He used live ammunition, resulting in the death of one Ranger and the wounding of several others during the realistic exercises.

Darby accepted only seven hundred of the two thousand volunteers. He then led these men through a British Commando course that usually lasted seven weeks. The Americans took only thirty-one days to complete the training, and by the end of the course Darby had reduced the original 700 volunteers to 520 men. On the parade field of Carrickfergus, Northern Ireland, these men were activated into the 1st Ranger Battalion on June 19, 1942.

Two months later, on August 19, a detachment of forty-two Rangers commanded by Captain Roy Murray accompanied seven thousand British and Canadian Commandos on a raid against German defenses at the French port of Dieppe. The attack failed, but the modern American Rangers experienced their combat baptism. Although their role had been minor, the detachment from the 1st Ranger Battalion did fire America's first shots against the Nazis. Three Rangers died in the raid and several others were captured. The American press, desperate for heroes in the trying times of the war's first months, reported the Ranger participation as larger and more significant than it actually was, helping advance the public's admiration for the elites.

Darby, now a lieutenant colonel, used the lessons learned to continue the rigorous training. He then led his Rangers in their first battalion-sized action as they spearheaded the Allied invasion of North Africa. The 1st Battalion went silently ashore at night and destroyed two artillery gun batteries to clear the way for the 1st Infantry Division to capture the port of Oran on November 10.

A few weeks later the Rangers conducted their first behind-the-lines raid when they attacked an Axis position at Sened, Tunisia. In addition to killing many enemy soldiers, the Rangers captured ten with only one killed and ten wounded. On March 31 the 1st Ranger Battalion conducted a twelve-mile night march across desert and mountains to surprise the Italian garrison guarding the El Guettar Pass. In addition to capturing two hundred prisoners, the raid opened the way for General George Patton's troops to take the surrounding heights. For their action at El Guettar the 1st Ranger Battalion earned its first Presidential Unit Citation and Darby received the Distinguished Service Cross, second only to the Medal of Honor for combat bravery.

Near the end of the successful North African campaign, the ranking military leadership recognized the need for additional Ranger units. In April 1943 Darby transferred officers and sergeants from the 1st Battalion to form the 3rd and 4th Ranger Battalions. Major Roy Murray, who had led the Rangers into action at Dieppe, assumed command of the 4th Battalion, while Major Harman Dammer took charge of the 3rd. Darby remained in command of the 1st Battalion but also assumed control of all three battalions in what became known as Darby's Rangers.

Darby's Rangers spearheaded the Seventh Army's invasion of Sicily at Gela and Licata in July 1943. They then led Patton's drive on Palermo. Their hit-and-run tactics were so successful that they captured more than four thousand prisoners in a single day—more than twice the total number of Rangers in the command.

The three Ranger battalions again led the Allies ashore in their next invasion at Salerno the following September. They seized the important heights on both sides of the Chinuzi Pass and then, with help from infantrymen from the 36th Division and paratroopers from the 82nd Airborne, staved off eight German counterattacks.

All three Ranger battalions fought, mostly as conventional infantry, in the bitter winter mountain battles at San Pietro, Venafro, and Cassino. The lightly equipped Rangers were neither trained nor organized for conventional combat but performed well nevertheless. It would not be the last time that senior commanders misused the Rangers in World War II and later.

After a brief period to rest and train new volunteers, the three Ranger battalions led the amphibious attack seventy miles behind German lines at the port of Anzio. On January 22, 1944, the Rangers seized two gun batteries that dominated the port, captured the city of Anzio, and pushed inland to secure the landing site for the follow-on forces. It was a classic Ranger operation and successful in every aspect.

The string of Ranger victories, however, was about to come to a disastrous end. Only a week after their capture of Anzio, the 1st and 3rd Battalions led the 3rd Infantry Division off the beach to attack German positions at Cisterna. Unaware that the Germans had heavily reinforced the area, the Rangers approached the village along a flooded irrigation canal, where the Nazis launched a devastating ambush.

German artillery, tanks, and machine guns fired point-blank into the Rangers from the surrounding heights. Badly outnumbered and totally outgunned, the Rangers fought gallantly. Back at the beach, Darby quickly assembled the 4th Battalion and attempted to break through the German encirclement to reinforce his beleaguered Rangers. The 4th Battalion failed and turned back only after all its company commanders were dead and half of its Rangers were casualties. The other two battalions fared even worse. Of the 767 Rangers in the 1st and 3rd Battalions who advanced on Cisterna, only 6 safely made their way back to friendly lines.

Darby's Rangers virtually ceased to exist overnight. The survivors fought in several German counteroffensives against the Anzio beachhead in February before being transferred to Civitavecchia, Italy, to man a scouting and patrolling school for infantrymen assigned to the Fifth Army. On May 6 the newer Rangers were reassigned to other units and the remaining one hundred surviving veterans transferred to Camp Butner, North Carolina. The 1st and the 3rd Battalions were officially deactivated on August 15, 1944, and the 4th Battalion followed on October 26.

Darby survived the battle but not the war. After Cisterna he assumed command of a regiment in the 45th Infantry Division. Later, as a colonel with the 10th Mountain Division, he was killed by German artillery at Torbole, Italy, on April 30, 1945, in one of the final actions of the war. At the time of his death, Darby was on the promotion list for brigadier general. On the recommendation of Secretary of War Stimson and President Harry Truman, the army posthumously promoted Darby to the one-star rank. Darby was dead at the young age of thirty-four, but his reputation would live on as the *Father of the Modern Rangers* and one of the few American officers whose command was better known by its leader's name than its numerical designation.

While Darby's Rangers were fighting and dying in Italy, two more battalions were organized in the United States with the specific mission of preparing to lead the Allied invasion of Europe. The army activated the 2nd Ranger Battalion on April 1, 1943, at Camp Forrest, Tennessee, and formed the 5th Battalion the following September 1. Both battalions were organized into a task force under the command of Lieutenant Colonel James Earl Rudder.

Rudder's Rangers spent nearly one year training for a specific mission. On June 6, 1944, the Rangers waded ashore at Normandy. "Never has any commander been given a more desperate mission" was the way General Omar Bradley described the task.

Using grappling hooks and guts, the Rangers scaled the sheer two-hundred-foot cliff walls of Point de Hoc to neutralize German positions overlooking Omaha Beach. The Rangers accomplished their mission but paid a high price. Of the 355 Rangers who scaled the cliff, 197 became casualties.

Rangers of the 5th Battalion and a company of the 2nd on the flank suffered nearly 50 percent casualties but still managed to climb the ninety-foot-high cliffs at Vierville and silence still more German defenses. It was on these bitterly fought cliffs and beaches that the modern Rangers earned their unofficial motto. When the main body of the invasion was pinned down, Brigadier General Norman Cota, assistant commander of the 29th Infantry Division, realized that the

Americans had to advance inland or they would die at the water's edge. Cota turned to Lieutenant Colonel Max Schneider, commander of the 5th Battalion, and ordered, "Lead the way, Rangers."

Schneider led his Rangers forward and a breakout soon occurred, allowing the invasion to pour into Europe. From that time to the present Rangers have accompanied their salutes with a proud "Rangers lead the way, sir."

Schneider, Rudder, Cota, and other leaders at Normandy learned lessons that would last for the remainder of the war—especially that of demanding that their soldiers unquestionably follow their orders and do their duty. By late 1944 Cota, promoted to major general, was in command of the 28th Infantry Division. Rudder, still a lieutenant colonel, commanded the division's 109th Infantry Regiment.

These heroic, example-setting Ranger leaders were deadly serious about the importance of discipline and loyalty. When one of Rudder's men in the 109th Regiment, Private Eddie D. Slovik, deserted and was later apprehended, the former Ranger commander recommended a court-martial. Cota, the division commander, convened a trial that found Slovik guilty and sentenced him to death. Cota and his senior commander, General Dwight D. Eisenhower, approved the punishment.

Rudder and Cota witnessed the execution of Slovik, the first and only soldier executed for desertion in the U.S. Army since the Civil War, on January 31, 1945, at St. Marie aux Mines in eastern France. Later that day Rudder sent a written message to his soldiers of the 109th Infantry: "I pray that this man's death will be a lesson to each of us who have any doubt at any time about the price that we must pay to win this war. The person that is not willing to fight and die, if need be, for his country has no right to live."

The lesson Rudder learned from his Rangers at Normandy stayed with him for the rest of his life. When he became president of Texas A&M University in the 1960s, he lectured the Corps of Cadets, many of whom would soon be on their way to Vietnam, in every speech about the dedication, tenacity, loyalty, and teamwork that his Rangers had exhibited "on the cliffs of Normandy."

Both Ranger battalions continued to serve in the European Theater until the end of the war. The 2nd fought in the battle for Brest, France, and the 5th saw extensive action in the Huertgen Forest and at the Battle of the Bulge. After the Normandy invasion, however, the units rarely conducted the Ranger-type missions for which they existed. Most of the time they supported conventional combat forces in traditional infantry missions. At times they participated in mop-up operations and even guarded headquarters and prisoner compounds.

At the end of the war the 5th Battalion performed occupation duty in Reid, Austria. The unit then returned to Camp Miles Standish, Massachusetts, where it was deactivated on October 22, 1945. The 2nd Battalion finished the war at Grun, Czechoslovakia, and then, after several months of occupation duty, returned to Camp Patrick Henry, Virginia, where it was deactivated on October 23, 1945.

One other Ranger battalion operated against the Germans in the European Theater although never organized as an authorized unit. On December 20, 1942, the 29th Infantry Division formed a Ranger battalion from its internal assets at Tidworth Barracks, England. The battalion's commander, Major Randolph Millholland, organized and trained his Rangers in a fashion similar to Darby's. Upon completion of their training, the 29th Rangers, while attached to the British Special Service Brigade, participated in two raids and one reconnaissance against German positions in Norway.

In their final mission they destroyed a German radar station on the small island of Ile d'Ouessant just off the Brittany peninsula, killing more than twenty of its crew. The Rangers withdrew but not before deliberately leaving behind a cartridge belt and helmet clearly marked MAJ. R. MILLHOLLAND,

U.S. RANGERS so the Germans would know who had done the damage.

Despite the success of the 29th Rangers, all efforts to gain official recognition for the unit from the War Department failed. On October 15, 1943, the battalion was disbanded and its members returned to other infantry elements within their division.

Rangers also led the way in the Pacific Theater. On September 26, 1944, the 6th Battalion was formed at Port Moresby, New Guinea, as a part of the Sixth Army with Colonel Hank Mucci in command. Its mission was to support the invasion of the Philippine Islands. On October 17 and 18, with only three weeks of training, the 6th Battalion destroyed Japanese positions on the islands of Suluan, Homonhon, and Dinagat. It then established signal lights that guided the Sixth Army invasion force ashore on Leyte.

The 6th Battalion next moved to the island of Luzon, where it performed what many consider the most daring and successful behind-the-lines raid in U.S. history. On January 30, 1945, the Rangers, aided by native Filipino guerrillas, penetrated thirty-five miles behind the Japanese lines to rescue more than five hundred emaciated veterans of the Bataan Death March who had been imprisoned at Cabanatuan for nearly three years. Attacking at night, the Rangers killed more than two hundred Japanese soldiers and liberated the POWs, carrying many of the former prisoners on their backs as they evaded enemy patrols and safely made their way back to friendly lines. General Douglas MacArthur would one day say, "No incident of this war has given me greater satisfaction than the Ranger rescue of these Americans."

Later commanded by Colonel Robert Garrett, the 6th Rangers played an important role in the capture of Manila and Appari. In training to lead the invasion of mainland Japan when the war ended, the unit remained in the Philippines until December 30, 1945, when it was deactivated.

*   *   *

While the Rangers of World War II played an important role in the development and traditions of their modern brothers, the official lineage of the current battalions derives from still another special operations unit. In August 1943 President Franklin Roosevelt met with Prime Minister Winston Churchill and other Allied leaders at a conference in Quebec. One of their recommendations led to the formation of an American special unit capable of penetrating far behind Japanese lines to assist the Chinese army in its efforts to capture Burma. The unit's specific mission was to destroy Japanese communications and supply lines.

A call for volunteers for "a dangerous and hazardous mission" produced nearly three thousand willing soldiers, most of whom were veterans of jungle combat in the Guadalcanal, New Georgia, and New Guinea campaigns. Officially activated on October 3, 1943, the 5307th Composite Unit (Provisional), code-named Galahad, became better known as Merrill's Marauders in honor of their commander Brigadier General Frank D. Merrill, after *Time* magazine correspondent James Shepley published an article about the unit.

After extremely tough training in the jungles of India, the Marauders joined General Joseph Stilwell and his command in northern Burma on January 8, 1944. In February the 5307th penetrated the enemy lines and engaged in the first ground combat by Americans against the Japanese on the Asian continent. Over the next six months the Marauders led the attacks for the Chinese 22nd and 38th Divisions' recovery of northern Burma and cleared the way for the construction of the Ledo Road, which linked the Indian railhead at Ledo with the Burma Road to China.

The Marauders fought in high mountains and through dense jungles from the Hukawny Valley in northwestern Burma to Myitkyina on the Irrawaddy River. They marched more than one thousand miles and participated in five major engagements and thirty skirmishes. During these fights the 5307th virtually destroyed the much larger Japanese 18th

Infantry Division that had participated in the victories at Singapore and Malaya.

Using Ranger tactics, the Marauders operated deep in enemy territory without the benefit of fixed resupply lines or artillery support. They fought with what they carried on their backs and on a few pack mules that accompanied them. On August 3 the Marauders culminated their operations with the capture of the only all-weather airfield in northern Burma at Myitkyina.

The success of the 5307th earned it the Presidential Unit Citation, but the fight at Myitkyina was its last. Originally organized as a provisional unit for a three-month mission, the Marauders had spent more than double that period in the world's harshest jungle fighting against the best of the Japanese army on Stilwell's insistence. But casualties from combat and jungle diseases had decimated its ranks.

Like other Ranger units, the Marauders were a hastily assembled and trained organization of tough soldiers assigned an extremely difficult mission. Provisional and expendable, the unit was disbanded once it accomplished its mission.

On August 10, 1944, the survivors of the 5307th were reorganized into the 475th Infantry Regiment subordinate to the 5332nd Brigade, known as the Mars Task Force. The brigade continued actions in Burma until February 1945, when it defeated the remaining Japanese.

In March 1945 the 475th was airlifted to China, where it spent the remainder of the war equipping and training the Chinese army. The regiment was deactivated on July 1, 1945. The 475th remained on the nonactive rolls until June 21, 1954, when it was again activated, redesignated the 75th Infantry Regiment, and posted to duty in Okinawa.

Although the 475th Infantry Regiment participated in little combat, it carried the honors and lineage of the 5307th that then passed to the 75th Infantry. From this complex series of activation, deactivation, reactivation, and reorganization moves came the unit designation for the current Rangers.

The six Ranger battalions and Merrill's Marauders of World

War II also left other legacies for current Ranger organizations. The history of such things as unit insignia is complicated. Initially the official authorized shoulder patch was a blue-and-yellow diamond-shaped field with RANGERS stitched across it. Unfortunately the patch closely resembled the logo worn on the uniform of Sunoco gas station employees across the United States. The Rangers did not like the patch but defended it in brawls with other soldiers and civilians who asked for a "fill-up" or "tire check."

Another problem with the blue diamond patch was that the Rangers in the field were already wearing a completely different design. While recruiting the first Ranger battalions and far ahead of stateside bureaucracy, Darby sponsored a contest for a patch design. The one selected, submitted by Sergeant Anthony Rada of Flint, Michigan, featured a scroll with a black background trimmed in red bearing IST RANGER BATTALION stitched in white letters, a design similar to the insignia of the British Commandos who had assisted in the initial training of the Rangers.

In usual Ranger fashion, all five of the Ranger battalions in the European Theater took matters into their own hands. They ignored the blue diamond patch and proudly wore the scroll on their left shoulders. The 6th Battalion in the Pacific, despite the fact that there was no official link to the European battalions, learned of the scroll through the Ranger grapevine and also adopted it as their preferred shoulder insignia. Although it would not become official for another forty years, the black, red, and white scroll remained the patch of choice for the Rangers.

Merrill's Marauders also wore unauthorized insignia later adopted by Rangers. The 5307th wore a blue, red, green, and white shield-shaped patch adorned with a star, a sun, and a lightning bolt. After several changes over the next three decades, two of which added and then deleted the Confederate flag in recognition of Mosby's Rangers, the Marauder patch became the official regimental shield of the 75th Regiment.

Although it took many years and several wars, today's Rangers wear Darby's patch and Merrill's shield.

Patches, shields, and other uniform adornments are important to history and morale, but the real business of Rangers is on the battlefield. While the much smaller post–World War II military had no place for the elite Rangers, the army once again sought special skills when it faced a determined enemy on the frozen mountainsides and mud-filled rice paddies of Korea.

Two months after North Korea invaded the South, Army Chief of Staff General J. Lawton Collins ordered that Ranger units be established, with one company assigned to each infantry division. Collins, aware of the misuse of Ranger battalions in World War II, specifically outlined the mission of the new companies. In a memorandum dated August 29, 1950, Collins ordered that Ranger companies be used "to infiltrate through enemy lines and attack command posts, artillery, tank parks, and key communications centers or facilities."

Collins also directed that the new Ranger companies be organized and trained at Fort Benning, Georgia, under the command of Colonel James G. Van Houten. Each company would contain three platoons, each of these having three squads of ten men. Five officers and a few logistic and administrative personnel brought each company's strength to 113 men.

Requests for volunteers produced immediate results. Because Van Houten intended for his Rangers to be paratrooper-qualified, most of the volunteers came from the 82nd and 11th Airborne Divisions. Interest in the new Ranger companies was so high that nearly five thousand men volunteered from the 82nd alone. With fewer than five hundred men needed to man the first four Ranger companies, Van Houten and his officers could be aggressively selective. Van Houten chose his officers and then allowed his captains, who would lead the companies, to pick their own men.

The Ranger companies differed little from their predecessors in that dedicated volunteers who were extremely physically fit and seeking challenges manned them. However, there was one great difference between the Korean Rangers and those of previous conflicts: For the first time the Ranger elite units allowed African Americans to volunteer.

Although President Harry Truman had issued Executive Order 9981 on July 26, 1948, declaring the end of segregation and guaranteeing the "equality of treatment and opportunity" in the armed forces, the military had done little to integrate its ranks by the outbreak of the Korean War. African Americans could become Rangers, but despite Truman's order, they served in their own segregated unit.

Van Houten established his Ranger training headquarters at Harmony Church, several miles from the main Fort Benning facilities. The first volunteers arrived on September 20, 1950, and the rigorous training began on October 9. Training mostly at night, the Rangers learned demolitions, sabotage, map reading, land navigation, hand-to-hand combat, and communications. They also familiarized themselves with all U.S. weapons as well as those used by the enemy. They learned to control artillery, naval, and air support. In addition to low-level parachute operations, the Rangers practiced amphibious assaults.

By mid-November the four companies had completed their training. The 1st, 3rd, and 4th Ranger Companies were officially "white," while the 2nd was "black." As the first and only black Ranger unit in U.S. history, the 2nd Ranger Company would distinguish itself on the battlefield.

The only Korean War–era Ranger company formed outside the United States organized at Camp Drake, Japan, with three officers and seventy-three enlisted soldiers selected from volunteers from units throughout the Far East. The 8213th Army Unit, otherwise known as the Eighth Army Ranger Company—or simply "Raiders"—became official on August 24, 1950. Rangers from the 8213th joined the 25th Infantry Division in Korea in mid-October and saw action almost immediately. The Eighth Army Rangers conducted extensive behind-the-lines reconnaissance missions and raids before they were officially disbanded on March 28, 1951. The 5th Ranger Company, which had arrived from the States, replaced them three days later.

By the time the 5th Company arrived in Korea, other Rangers were already fighting throughout the peninsula. The 1st Ranger Company landed on December 17, 1950, attached to the 2nd Infantry Division. In addition to the 5th Company with the 25th Infantry Division, the 2nd, 3rd, 4th, and 6th Ranger Companies served with the 1st Cavalry and 3rd, 7th, and 24th Infantry Divisions.

These six Ranger companies fought in almost every major battle from their arrival until late 1951. Many Korean War Ranger veterans recall that fighting outnumbered and surrounded was routine during this time. In addition to their usual reconnaissance and raids, the 2nd and 4th Companies participated in the first Ranger combat airborne operation when they jumped with the 187th Regimental Combat Team at Munsan-ni on March 23, 1951.

Of the fourteen Ranger companies organized and trained at Fort Benning, only six made it to Korea before officials reversed themselves and began disbanding the units. Although no one doubted the fighting abilities of the Rangers, not all of the army's senior leaders were completely satisfied with the concept of Ranger companies. Several of the division commanders who had Rangers attached complained that the companies' organization was so austere that they could not feed or supply themselves and required other units to provide this support. Another widespread complaint was one heard in previous wars. Commanders protested that the Ranger companies drained desperately needed elite soldiers from their units. In the combat environment, where there was always a shortage of small-unit leaders, many commanders believed that the concentration of superior soldiers into a few Ranger companies was a luxury the army as a whole could not afford.

Another strike against the Rangers was the high rate of

casualties they sustained. Although many of their casualties were the result of their misuse as conventional infantry against superior numbers of enemy, the fact remained that in less than a year of combat, 146—one in every nine—had died.

Yet another negative often mentioned, including in official documents, was that white and black Rangers could not effectively operate behind the lines where both the enemy and the civilian population were Asian. Of course, the Rangers had already proven this theory invalid in Korea and would again show its lack of merit during the Vietnam War.

Perhaps, though, the most important factor ensuring the demise of Rangers in Korea was that by the summer of 1951, they were no longer needed. The lines had became fairly static near the original boundary between north and south along the thirty-eighth parallel, making the conflict resemble the First World War rather than the Second.

On July 10, 1951, the Department of the Army ordered the deactivation of all Ranger companies. On August 1 the six companies in Korea ceased to exist, and their former members transferred to the 187th Regimental Combat Team. The remaining Ranger companies back in the States also began to deactivate; by December 1 there were none remaining on active duty.

Although no longer needing Ranger units, the army leadership recognized that the elite fighters were not a concept that could be put on the shelf until the next war. On October 3, 1951, General Collins directed that "Ranger training be extended to all combat units of the Army in order to develop the capability of carrying out Ranger-type missions in all Infantry units of the Army."

The chief of staff's instructions also authorized the Infantry School at Fort Benning to establish a Ranger Department capable of training and maintaining one Ranger-qualified officer per company and one Ranger-qualified NCO per platoon throughout the Army's infantry units. Ranger School graduates were, therefore, to be spread throughout the army, providing each infantry company with expertise while not concentrating the elite troops in their own units.

On October 10 the U.S. Army Ranger School officially opened under the authority of General Order 113. Members of the Ranger Training Command, who had trained the Korean War Ranger companies, were reassigned as instructors to the new school.

The Ranger School, like its Harmony Church headquarters, has remained fairly consistent over the years. Basic conditioning and combat and reconnaissance patrolling instruction take place at Fort Benning locations. Mountain training occurs in northern Georgia near Dahlonega, and amphibious and jungle training tests the students in the Florida panhandle at Eglin Air Force Base. Ranger training camps at Benning, north Georgia, and Florida bear the names of Darby, Merrill, and Rudder, respectively.

From its beginnings the school has been the most physically and mentally demanding of all the armed forces training courses. The school lasts a little more than eight weeks; however, if the training were scheduled on the basis of a forty-hour week, it would take more than twenty-six weeks to complete.

Graduates of the Ranger School receive the coveted black-and-gold tab. Originally the plan was for each man who successfully completed the course to be awarded a black-and-red tab with white letters spelling RANGERS. The design was an adaptation of the Ranger scroll patch, intended to recognize those who completed the training for the Ranger companies of the Korean War. By the time the Department of the Army finally authorized the tab, the colors had mysteriously changed to black and gold. Although no official explanation has ever been given, many Rangers noticed that the new colors closely resembled those of the U.S. Military Academy at West Point and noted that many of its graduates were in decision-making positions in the Pentagon. Regardless, the Ranger tab soon became one of the most respected uniform adornments.

High-level discussions about reestablishing Ranger units in the years following the Korean War recognized that only men on the ground could gather timely battlefield intelligence. While NCO and officer graduates of the Ranger School returned to their units to train squads and platoons in the basic techniques of combat and reconnaissance patrolling, thereby developing a general knowledge of Ranger-type operations, the army neither organized nor trained units for specific reconnaissance missions.

Ultimately, Ranger units remained deactivated for two primary reasons: First, developing ordinary infantrymen into teams capable of handling traditional Ranger-type missions required more time and resources than were available. The other barrier was the age-old problem of the army's preparing to fight the last war instead of focusing on the next possible conflict. Since Rangers had generated much controversy in Korea, few leaders were willing to advocate reactivating the elite units—especially in the limited-resource environment of post–Korean War America.

The army progressed, and in some instances regressed, through several reorganizations during the late 1950s. None of these changes, however, included officially adding any type of Ranger organization to the force structure. Still, several unofficial attempts to form Ranger-type units did occur. The only one to carry the actual title *Ranger* was a provisional platoon in the 8th Infantry Division that existed for nearly two years beginning in 1959. Two additional experimental scout companies emerged about the same time in the V and VII Corps in Germany, but they did not carry the name *Ranger*.

It was not until December 1960 that the army took its first steps in a long, involved process that eventually resulted in the current Ranger organization. At that time the Department of the Army directed the Continental Army Command (CONARC) headquarters at Fort Monroe, Virginia, "to reevaluate the current organization and to make recommendations for necessary changes."

CONARC's study called for a major armywide restructuring labeled Reorganization Objective Army Division (ROAD), which soon became ROAD-65 to include its planned date of implementation. Under the new organization each division would have a common fixed base of support with varying numbers and types of infantry and armored battalions. Rather than one official division structure, the army would now have a flexible template from which units could be structured to specifically meet the requirements of different missions, terrain, and tactical situations.

Although ROAD-65 was not intended to tailor a force specifically to meet the upcoming challenges in Southeast Asia, it did provide the flexibility for units to adapt to a new and different kind of war. More important, at least in Ranger history, ROAD-65 defined the need for and the composition of Ranger-type units in the modern army.

Even though the Ranger School had been in operation for a decade and Rangers had proven their worth in both World War II and Korea, army planners remained careful in their use of the term *Ranger*. Resentments lingered about the Korea Ranger companies, and during the austerity of the peacetime military few were willing to concentrate elite soldiers in a few units. Also, many of the planners thought the army needed a special reconnaissance force more than the raid-oriented Rangers.

As a result, the planners avoided the term *Rangers*, a decision that ultimately caused ongoing confusion for special operations units. The history of renaming the special units without using the term *Ranger* reads like a study of the war in Vietnam itself—convoluted, confusing, and unclear.

CONARC began by publishing a series of directives to assist all agencies "in the timely preparation of training literature" for all aspects of ROAD-65 reorganization. On May 25, 1961, CONARC published Directive 525-4 titled "Combat Operations, ROAD-65 Training Literature, Long Range Reconnaissance Patrolling." This five-page directive, classified Confidential until three years after its publication, provided the first official use of the term *LRRP*, commonly pronounced as *lurp*. More important, this directive, signed by Brigadier General James R. Winn, became the "birth certificate" of the Vietnam War–era LRRPs, which led directly to the establishment of the Ranger battalions that exist today.

The directive's "Concept" paragraph stated that LRRPs should normally work in teams of four to six men, operate at night or under conditions of limited visibility, and assume concealed positions during daylight to observe specific targets or routes. Suggested missions included locating and identifying enemy formations and dispositions, adjusting air and artillery strikes on these positions, and performing bomb damage assessments. The directive recommended the uses of LRRPs on a conventional battlefield; however, except for its failure to mention the capture of prisoners, it outlined the exact missions that members of these units would perform in Vietnam.

CONARC Directive 525-4 did mention the *R* word in recommending that personnel selected for LRRP units have previous Ranger or Special Forces training. It also recommended that special equipment and weapons be provided the reconnaissance units.

A year later the directive evolved into CONARC Regulation 525-4. The elevation from a directive to a regulation meant that instead of offering guidance, the document now required implementation. The Infantry School staff at Fort Benning took the lead, and on June 18, 1962, the Department of the Army published its results as Field Manual 31-18, "Long Range Patrols: Divisions, Corps, and Army." FM 31-18 expanded CONARC Regulation 525-4 to include details on missions, organization, training, and conduct of operations.

Along with the new FM came the Table of Organization and Equipment (TO&E) 7-157, which called for two hundred enlisted men and nine officers organized into a company headquarters and three patrol platoons capable of fielding twenty-four teams of five men each. In an effort to make each

LRRP company independent rather than reliant on the unit to which it was attached, the TO&E also included transportation, communications, and operations sections.

On January 12, 1965, the Department of the Army published an updated copy of FM 31-18 that differed little from the previous edition except for its title, "Infantry Long Range Patrol Company," the first deviation of the name. Everything was now in place for the formation of the LRRPs—except for one major factor. While FM 31-18 provided what LRRPs were supposed to do and TO&E 7-157 outlined the personnel and equipment required, the field manual contained the guidance that the units were not to exist until specifically authorized by the Department of the Army.

As the slow, formal process of writing manuals and orders in the peacetime army crawled forward, actual combat once again accelerated the process. At the same time that staff officers at Fort Benning and in the Pentagon were forming Ranger-type units on paper, battlefield commanders in Vietnam were finding an immediate need for the elite blood warriors.

General William C. Westmoreland assumed command of the Military Assistance Command—Vietnam (MACV) in June 1964. He later recalled that he knew he would need LRRPs "shortly after [he] arrived in Vietnam."

Although the need was apparent to the MACV commander, no formal LRRP units existed, and conventional U.S. infantry divisions had not yet arrived in-country. Westmoreland turned to members of the Special Forces, who had been in Vietnam since 1957 providing training for the South Vietnamese army and organizing paramilitary units of tribesmen such as the Montagnards to fight the communists.

Following Westmoreland's orders the Special Forces organized Project Delta in October 1964 and began conducting long range reconnaissance patrols a few months later. The Special Forces subsequently fielded Projects Omega and Sigma before turning all three "Greek" projects over to the MACV Studies and Observation Group (SOG), which was formed on June 16, 1964.

When regular U.S. infantry units began arriving in Vietnam in 1965, most of their commanders shared Westmoreland's vision of the need for ground reconnaissance units. It was not, however, their highest priority. American infantry arrived in Vietnam trained and equipped for a land war on the European plain, anticipating that battles would be fought with conventional tactics in a mechanized and tank-heavy environment. Americans had not faced a guerrilla enemy since the Philippine Insurrection and the Indian wars.

This need to adapt the entire army to a counterguerrilla war in terrain that varied from open rice paddies to thick jungles and steep mountain ranges was the primary reason in the delay for forming Ranger-type units. Compounding this factor was the traditional anti-Ranger reasoning that the elite units drained conventional units of badly needed leaders and also that the morale of the whole decreases when some soldiers receive special treatment. Many senior commanders also remembered the independent nature of World War II and Korean Rangers and their reluctance to follow orders from those outside their own chain of command.

Of the fifteen U.S. Army divisions and separate brigades that served in Vietnam, not a single one arrived in-country with a LRRP unit in existence. Only one had laid sufficient groundwork and conducted adequate training so that it could quickly organize reconnaissance units.

The 173rd Airborne Brigade was the first U.S. Army ground unit to arrive in Vietnam and also the only one that had done any prearrival preparation for the fielding of LRRPs. Formed two years previously on the island of Okinawa, the 173rd was the "fire brigade" in the Pacific and the only American infantry unit assigned to Vietnam that had previously focused on jungle operations.

During training, the brigade used the island of Iriomote, south of Okinawa, as an area for patrolling and reconnaissance. Units as small as three men and as large as a company were inserted on the island by parachute and boat to remain for a month with their only resupply coming from airdrops.

Although he has received little credit, Brigadier General Ellis W. Williamson, who commanded the 173rd both on Okinawa and in Vietnam for a total of three years, deserves recognition as the founder of LRRPs in Southeast Asia. Within a few days of the brigade's arrival in-country, Williamson had deduced that small units could penetrate the jungle and gather information much better than large search-and-destroy-type operations.

Williamson claimed, "I believe that I personally organized the LRRP; however, we did not call them by that name at the time. When we first started using them in Vietnam they were known as Delta Teams."

Here another convolution began. The 173rd Airborne Brigade Delta Teams had no link with the Special Forces Project Delta except for the similarities in the names. Others also used *Delta* for special units in Vietnam. Some claimed that was because Delta followed Alpha, Bravo, Charlie in the military phonetic alphabet, and the various projects just happened to be the fourth in a series. Others note that cavalry units responsible for reconnaissance that were attached to infantry units were usually designated Delta Troop. Still others claim that Delta merely stood for *D*, which meant "death." To further confuse things, the army later named its supersecret elites Delta Force, though it had no linkage to any Vietnam unit.

Neither Williamson nor any of his staff recall where they got the name *Delta Teams*, but they do remember that they had a lot to learn about their most advantageous employment. According to Williamson, "We immediately formalized the approach to small patrols by having each infantry battalion organize five special patrol units that were manned by specially selected personnel. We experimented quite a bit with respect to size, mission, armament, communications, and survival."

Other units arriving in Vietnam also quickly saw the need and began to form their own special reconnaissance units. The names for these units varied at first. In addition to the

173rd's Delta Teams, the 101st Airborne Division fielded recon elements named Hatchet and Hawk Teams and Tiger Forces. As timed passed and more divisions arrived in-country, however, the designation *LRRP* became the preferred title.

While the arriving units in Vietnam formed Ranger-type units they called LRRPs, there is no evidence that they referred to any of the training directives, field manuals, or the authorized TO&E that had already been published. In every case units arrived in-country, recognized the need for reconnaissance groups, and formed them to meet the needs as observed by the ground commanders. Some LRRP leaders did have access to FM 31-18, but there was no implementation authorization or guidance from the Department of the Army, MACV, or from the newly organized U.S. Army, Vietnam (USARV), which had been formed on May 15, 1965, to command the rapidly increasing number of American units.

General Westmoreland, now "dual hatted" as the commander of both MACV and USARV, maintained his interest in LRRPs and often sent commanders of newly arriving units to observe the reconnaissance units of the 173rd. On July 8, 1966, Westmoreland formalized LRRP units already in existence and ordered those units that did not yet have recon units to immediately organize them. The Secret message released by MACV operations officer Major General John Tillson III and titled "Long Range Patrols" stated, "COMUSMACV [Westmoreland] had directed that a comprehensive Long Range Patrol program be developed in SVN [South Vietnam]. In order to establish an interim MACV capability until sufficient TO&E Long Range Patrol units can be authorized, organized and become available in country, a provisional organization will be required from assets available in country. A Long Range Patrol (LRP) is defined as 'A specially trained unit organized and equipped for the specific purpose of functioning as an information gathering agency responsive to the intelligence requirements of the tactical commander.' These patrols consist of specially trained personnel capable of performing reconnaissance, surveillance, and target acquisition within the dispatching unit's area of interest."

The USMACV message made it clear that major units were to take immediate action, but at the same time it proved confusing. The message referred to a *Long Range Patrol* or *LRP*, making it clear that Westmoreland preferred this term for the new units. The designation *Long Range Reconnaissance Patrol* or *LRRP* that had begun with the CONARC directives of 1961 evolved to *LRP* with the publication of FM 31-18 in 1965. Many units, however, as well as military personnel at all levels continued to use the term *LRRP*.

Throughout the war official documents, unofficial correspondence, and even unit signs in front of headquarters and uniform patches used the terms *LRP* and *LRRP* interchangeably, with the occasional *LURP* thrown in for good measure. The best explanation for the official use of *LRP* rather than *LRRP* is that the only official reference, FM 31-18, clearly established the former as the correct name. The writers of both the FM and the July 8 MACV message were officers who were true to their longtime army mission orientation of "closing with and destroying the enemy." The idea of forming units strictly for reconnaissance was foreign to their training. Many of those who served as LRPs, LRRPs, LURPs—or whatever you choose to call the elite warriors—laugh at the confusion and offer the suggestion that the reason *reconnaissance* was not used in the message or the official unit designations was that it simply was too difficult to spell.

In his July 8 message Westmoreland provided a means for the training of the special skills, but the action added still another twist to the name confusion. On September 15, 1966, he directed Colonel Francis J. Kelly, commander of the 5th Special Forces Group at Nha Trang, to establish a Recondo School to train LRP volunteers. At least *Recondo*'s origins were trackable. A combination of the words *recon* and *commando*, *Recondo* was Westmoreland's choice for the Nha Trang school because during the general's prewar command of the 101st Airborne Division at Fort Campbell, Kentucky, from 1958 to 1960, he established a similar training program. In fact, the 101st maintained its Recondo School after the departure of Westmoreland and reestablished the training for its soldiers after their arrival in Vietnam.

Colonel Kelly used many Project Delta veterans as instructors in the Recondo School. Graduates compare the tough Recondo course with the Fort Benning Ranger School, noting that their graduation exercise of actually patrolling in enemy-held territory exceeded the Infantry School's requirements.

By late 1966 most of the U.S. divisions and separate brigades in Vietnam had some form of provisional LRRP unit. These varied in size and support depending on their senior commander's feelings toward elite units and on the needs in his area of operations. The 4th Division experienced particular success with its LRRPs, and Westmoreland often had its commander, Major General William R. Peers, brief the USARV staff and subordinate commanders.

The primary reason LRRPs were provisional rather than regular units was a matter of counting personnel. Congress and the media closely monitored the total number of soldiers assigned to Vietnam. Until sufficient numbers were authorized, commanders had to form their LRRPs from their infantry units. Every man who went to the LRRPs meant that his infantry platoon was left one man short with no official means of gaining a replacement.

By the summer of 1967 Westmoreland was well aware of his subordinate commanders' complaints about this provisional manning process. He was confident that LRRPs had proven their worth and that the need for their skills was increasing. More important, the escalation of the war had won him the approval of additional authorized soldiers. As a result, Westmoreland ordered the formal activation of LRP units with separate companies assigned to the corps-sized field forces and to divisions. Platoon-sized detachments were authorized for the separate brigades.

Those units already in Vietnam quickly formalized their LRP companies and detachments. Units brought in later also added LRPs to their troop lists. During the next year nine companies of the 20th, 50th, 51st, 52nd, and 58th Infantry Regiments were attached to the field forces and divisions. Five infantry detachments—the 70th, 71st, 74th, 78th, and 79th—joined the separate brigades. A National Guard LRP company from Indiana also briefly joined the force structure.

The designation of these numerical units resulted not from tradition or history but rather from availability. Since separate companies were a rarity in the U.S. Army, there was no precedent for their assignment and use. Neither the LRRPs nor their commanders were really concerned, for they were now official and had authorized manning slots. As for history, they figured they could write their own.

However, an important aspect was missing from the authorized separate companies and detachments. The LRRP units lacked a central headquarters to provide them overall command and support. Neither Westmoreland nor his staff provided any further guidance for LRRP employment. The LRRPs were to be completely under the command and control of whatever field force, division, or separate brigade they were assigned to.

This lack of command unity was not an inadvertent omission but rather an intentional decentralization. Each LRRP area of operation varied in terrain and level of enemy activity. What worked in one region might prove deadly in another. This lack of overall guidance allowed the flexibility needed for the LRRPs to perform successfully. It also, however, provided the disadvantage of offering little opportunity for the sharing of lessons learned among units.

Back in the States, where the military bureaucracy moved much slower than it did in the combat zone, staff officers attempted to keep written doctrine reasonably current with what was occurring on the battlefield. On August 23, 1968, the Department of the Army published a revised edition of FM 31-18. The primary difference between the new and old manuals was the addition of a chapter titled "Stability Operations," which was the military buzzword for the warfare taking place in Southeast Asia. The back of the new manual also included two woefully inadequate appendixes, one on patrol steps and the other on tactical standard operating procedures.

While the revised FM acknowledged and somewhat clarified LRRP operations in an unconventional environment, it further muddled the official name of the recon men. The new edition had yet another title—"Long-Range Reconnaissance Patrol Company." No explanation for the reemergence of *reconnaissance* accompanied the manual. Perhaps it was in recognition of what the recon men had been calling themselves all along, or maybe the authors of the manual finally learned to spell *reconnaissance*. Whatever the reason, the unit designations as *LRP companies* and *detachments* remained unchanged.

Outside forces joined the fray over the proper name of the units. Rangers of World War II and Korea, having formed veterans organizations after returning from their wars, were greatly interested in seeing that Rangers would also have a role in the Vietnam conflict. These veterans, as well as Ranger advocates on the active army staff, lobbied that LRRPs in Vietnam were performing traditional Ranger missions and should be so designated.

Two primary factors delayed action on redesignating LRRP units as Rangers. First, the war itself offered more pressing priorities than name changes. Second, the official lineage of battle honors and campaign participation had already been assigned to the Special Forces. Finally, after effective lobbying efforts by former members of Merrill's Marauders, the army selected the 75th Infantry Regiment as the parent organization of Vietnam LRRPs.

On January 16, 1969, the Department of the Army dispatched Message Number 893755, "Redesignation of Long Range Patrol (LRP) Units." Provisions of the message authorized the change of names of the separate LRP units to letter companies of the 75th Infantry Regiment effective on February 1. The message also provided guidance for the establishment of two new stateside Ranger companies, with A Company at Fort Benning and B Company at Fort Carson, Colorado.

A Company moved to Fort Hood, Texas, shortly after its organization. Neither company ever went to Vietnam, as their primary mission was to train to deploy in case of emergency in Europe, where they would support the two forward-deployed U.S. corps in Germany.

On February 1 the thirteen LRP companies and detachments in Vietnam assumed the letter designations of 75th Regiment companies—C, D, E, F, G, H, I, K, L, M, N, O, and P. Neither the Pentagon nor officials in Vietnam offered an explanation about the absence of the J Company. Some veterans speculate that the military phonetic pronunciation of *J* is *Juliet*, and that perhaps no one wanted a Ranger company with such a feminine moniker. A better explanation is that the military had avoided the use of the letter *J* since the nineteenth century, when telegraph and semaphore signalers confused the letters *I* and *J*.

On March 7, 1969, the Department of the Army tied up another loose end by issuing Change Number 1 to FM 31-18, which stated, "Title is changed to read Long Range Reconnaissance Ranger Companies." However, the text did not use the term *LRRRP* or *Ranger* anywhere.

The redesignation had little impact on operations in Vietnam. Units changed names and began to call themselves Rangers in addition to LURPs. The old official names of *LRP* and *LRRP* continued to be used along with *Ranger* in official and unofficial reports and documents.

Prior to the redesignation, the LRRPs wore the patch, often with an added airborne tab, of the unit to which it was attached. With the redesignation, the Rangers simply ignored the order to continue wearing the unit patch and, without exception, began wearing the black-and-red scroll previously worn by World War II and Korean Rangers. The Vietnam Rangers also unofficially adopted the motto "Rangers Lead the Way" as well as the 75th Infantry Regiment's official motto, "Sua Sponte." The additional motto was appropriate for the volunteer recon men, as it means "Of Their Own Accord."

The Vietnam Rangers also adopted the unofficial headgear that would eventually become their most recognizable uniform adornment. Although it would not be officially sanctioned until the publication of Army Regulation 670-5, the black beret had a long history. As early as 1756 many of Rogers's Rangers had worn a Scottish cap, similar to a beret, known as a tam-o'-shanter. During World War II several of the airborne regiments copied the British paratrooper maroon beret for occasional wear.

Modern Rangers first began wearing black berets during training at Fort Benning prior to deployment to the Korean War in 1951. Colonel Van Houten, the Ranger Training Center commander, liked the beret, and he and his staff were the first to wear it as their daily headgear. The 10th Ranger Company, activated on October 15, 1951, was the first active unit to wear the black beret.

After the Korean War ended, the Ranger School staff continued to wear the black beret, but the army's leadership, at best, only tolerated its wear. In Vietnam some LRRP units adopted the black beret, while a few wore the traditional maroon berets of the airborne and some even secured tan versions from allied Australian special operations forces. Not until 1969, when the LRRPs were redesignated Rangers, did the black beret become standard.

Just why black became the preferred color for the Ranger beret is not known. Maroon had long been the color for the berets worn by airborne units, including those of the South Vietnamese army. Commandos from Great Britain, France, and other European nations had long worn green berets, while their armored units wore black.

It would appear that the Rangers did not select green as their beret color because President John F. Kennedy had already awarded it in 1961 to his pet project, the Special Forces. This theory falls apart, however, with the realization that the Rangers at Fort Benning had selected black a decade before the president's decision.

Although no official decision paper remains in the files, or perhaps ever existed at all, the veterans of the early Ranger Training Center recall that black represents the color of the night. Since much of their training occurred at night, the black beret represented the time when the Rangers were at their best.

While the Rangers were able to take the initiative in selecting patches, mottoes, and head covers, some things were beyond their influence. Despite the new company designations, the Department of the Army did not authorize a regimental headquarters. Ranger companies continued to operate under the command of their parent field force, division, or separate brigade. Because there was no overall headquarters for the 75th in Vietnam, the Department of the Army designated the Ranger Department at Fort Benning as the custodian of the regimental colors. This was a formality only, as even the department's director, Colonel Y. Y. Phillips, acknowledged in a March 7, 1969 memo: "The Department will not function as an 'active' headquarters."

Less than a year after the redesignation of LRP companies to Rangers, the U.S. began to turn more of the fighting over to the South Vietnamese. As the American war effort wound down, combat units and their assigned Ranger companies were withdrawn. Several of the divisions and separate brigades, as well as their Rangers, were disbanded. Divisions that did return to the States reverted to peacetime organizations that did not include Ranger units.

By the end of 1970 only six of the original thirteen Ranger companies that served in Vietnam were still in existence. Further unit withdrawals and stand-downs reduced the number of Ranger companies to one by early 1972. On August 15, 1972, this last Ranger unit, H Company, assigned to the 1st Cavalry Division, folded its flag and ceased operations.

In nearly every war in which the United States had fought prior to Vietnam, Ranger units had been formed to accomplish the most difficult missions, only to be disbanded as soon as the country returned to peace. Although all thirteen Ranger companies that served in Vietnam ceased to exist after the end of U.S. involvement in the conflict, A Company at Fort Hood, Texas, and B Company, now at Fort Lewis, Washington, remained on the active rolls with a strength of 198 men each. For the first time in its history the U.S. Army had Ranger units in its ranks during peacetime.

The two Ranger companies continued to train for deployment to Europe in support of the two forward-deployed U.S. corps. Many LRRP/Ranger veterans from the Vietnam units served in the companies, which frequently participated in field exercises in Germany. The two stateside companies added to the reputation of the Rangers as highly trained and motivated soldiers.

The need for additional Rangers in the post-Vietnam army soon became apparent. At the outbreak of the Middle East war of 1973, senior officers in the Department of the Army became concerned that the post-Vietnam force had concentrated too much on heavy mechanized and armored divisions. With the exception of the 82nd Airborne Division, the army had no light, mobile forces that could quickly deploy to world hot spots.

As a result, Army Chief of Staff General Creighton W. Abrams sent a message to the field the following January directing that a Ranger battalion be formed, the first since World War II. As an armored-battalion commander in that war and during his command of MACV/USARV in Vietnam, Abrams had become well acquainted with Rangers. He knew the positive and negative aspects of the units, and he was familiar with the old objections about the elites.

General Abrams considered all these factors in his charter

authorizing the first peacetime Ranger battalion in U.S. history. He declared, "The Ranger battalion is to be an elite, light, and most proficient infantry battalion in the world; a battalion that can do things with its hands and weapons better than anyone. The battalion will not contain any 'hoodlums' or 'brigands' and if the battalion is formed of such persons, it will be disbanded. Wherever the battalion goes, it will be apparent that it is the best."

While Abrams made it clear what kind of men he wanted—and did not want—in the new Ranger units, he also made it clear it was to be an infantry battalion. Its organization would center on companies and platoons rather than patrol teams. The battalion would serve as the premier American strike force with the ability of deploying anywhere in the world within eighteen hours, its mission to stand ready to conduct special military operations in support of the policy and objectives of the United States of America. This included airborne and airmobile operations as a part of conventional forces, strikes against targets deep inside enemy territory, rescue operations, safeguarding U.S. citizens and property abroad, and deployment worldwide as a show of force.

On January 25, 1974, the headquarters of the U.S. Army Forces Command published General Order 127 directing the activation of the 1st Battalion, 75th Infantry (Ranger), with an effective date of January 31. Worldwide recruitment began immediately. Personnel assembled at Fort Benning and training began in March. On July 1, 1974, men of the 1st Battalion flew from Fort Benning and parachuted into their new home at Fort Stewart, Georgia.

On October 1, 1974, the 2nd Ranger Battalion was activated at Fort Lewis, Washington. Both battalions trained rigorously at their home stations and in Europe, Korea, the Mideast, North Africa, Canada, and Central America. Replacement volunteers had to attend a four-week Ranger Indoctrination Program (RIP). Only about half of the Ranger volunteers successfully completed RIP and were assigned to the battalions' companies. A year later, if they proved their leadership skills, the replacements were allowed to attend the formal Ranger School at Fort Benning.

The members of the new Ranger battalions understood the traditions of the elite soldiers who had preceded them. They quickly adopted a creed and recited it in unison at every ceremony and important event. "Never shall I betray my comrades," they swear in the Ranger Creed. They also promise never to leave a fallen comrade behind and to fight on "though I be the lone survivor."

The creed, while certainly in line with the standards of past Rangers, was new. Written by Neil R. Gentry, the command sergeant major of the 1st Battalion and a veteran of the Vietnam LRRP company of the 101st Airborne Division, the creed was quickly adopted by the 2nd Battalion and is still recited by all current Ranger units.

The first real combat operation by the modern Ranger battalions was in support of the abortive hostage rescue operation in Iran in 1979. Eighty-three men from Company C, 1st Ranger Battalion, under the command of Captain David L. Grange, deployed to the Desert One staging area and other Mideast airfields. The Rangers were to provide security for the Delta Force operators who were to conduct the actual rescue of the American hostages. Although the operation proved disastrous as a mission because of flawed planning and a lack of command unity, the fiasco in the desert provided the impetus for the eventual formation of the Special Operations Command, which controls current Rangers and other elite units.

The ultimate validation of the effectiveness of the Ranger battalions in combat came during the liberation of the Caribbean island of Grenada during Operation Urgent Fury. On October 24, 1983, the 1st and 2nd Battalions led the American attack with a daring, low-level parachute jump from a mere five hundred feet to seize the Cuban-held airfield at Port Salines. At that altitude the Cubans could not depress the trajectory of their anti-aircraft guns to engage the Rangers or their aircraft. Lieutenant Colonel Ralph Hagler, commander of the 2nd Battalion, later explained, "Since the drop was too low to have time to deploy a reserve chute, we discarded them and carried more ammunition instead." After securing the airfield the Rangers rescued isolated American medical students at the True Blue campus and later conducted heliborne assaults to eliminate pockets of resistance.

The success of the Rangers in Grenada convinced the army to increase the size of the Ranger force and to establish an overall headquarters. On October 3, 1984, the Department of the Army activated the 3rd Battalion as well as a regimental headquarters at Fort Benning to command all three battalions. The two thousand men of the new Ranger Regiment were the largest peacetime force of the elite warriors in American history. Also, for the first time, Rangers had an authorized official parent headquarters.

A final step in the evolution of the modern Rangers occurred on February 3, 1986, when Secretary of the Army John O. Marsh ordered the redesignation of the 75th Infantry (Ranger) as the 75th Ranger Regiment. Rangers were no longer parenthetical. Marsh also directed that the lineage and honors of former Ranger units be transferred from the Special Forces to the 75th Regiment. The modern Rangers then formally carried the honors of Merrill's Marauders, World War II and Korean War Rangers, as well as those of the LRRPs and Rangers of Vietnam.

It was not long before the regiment faced its first combat test. The entire regiment participated in Operation Just Cause to restore democracy to the Central American country of Panama. Early in the morning of December 20, 1989, the 1st Battalion conducted an airborne assault to seize Omar Torrijos International Airport and Tocumen Military Airfield. Meanwhile, the 2nd and 3rd Battalions parachuted onto the airfield at Rio Hato to attack a concentration of Panamanian Defense Forces and to seize a home belonging to General Manuel Noriega.

Following these successful assaults the Rangers conducted follow-up operations to neutralize further resistance. In less than a week the Rangers had captured more than a thousand prisoners of war and eighteen thousand weapons at a cost of five dead and forty-two wounded.

The conventional nature of the war in the Persian Gulf in 1993 did not readily lend itself to Ranger operations. Most of the Ranger Regiment remained in reserve, but Company B and the 1st Platoon of Company A of the 1st Ranger Battalion did join Operation Desert Storm on February 12, 1991. These Rangers conducted raids and assisted in the search for Iraqi Scud missiles. They returned home on April 15 having sustained no casualties.

A short time later Company B, 3rd Ranger Battalion, deployed to Mogadishu, Somalia, to support a United Nations peacekeeping mission. The Rangers, along with Delta Force operators and special operations force aviation assets, were to capture key leaders in order to stop clan fighting in and around the city.

On October 3 the Rangers participated in a daylight raid against targets in the center of Mogadishu. After several of their helicopters were shot down, the Rangers, who numbered fewer than a hundred, became involved in a fierce battle against a least a thousand well-armed fighters. The Rangers, true to their creed, stayed to fight rather than leave behind their fallen brothers. For eighteen hours the Rangers fought in what has been called the fiercest battle by Americans since the Vietnam War.

The Battle of Mogadishu cost the special operations force eighteen dead and seventy-six wounded. Among the dead were six Rangers. Estimates placed the enemy body count at more than three hundred, with twice that many wounded.

From their first raids against Indians in pre-Revolutionary America to the battlefields of the Civil War, World War II, Korea, Vietnam, and the hot spots of the past decade, the Rangers have indeed led the way. Their history is written in the blood of their ranks and they stand today, as they repeat in their creed, to "uphold the prestige, honor, and high esprit de corps" of the Ranger Regiment. For two centuries the

Rangers were the only true American blood warriors. No
study of today's American military elites can begin or is
complete without a thorough understanding of the evolution
of the Rangers.

CHAPTER 4

✳✳✳✳✳✳✳

U.S. Army Rangers: Today

*T*ODAY'S 75th Ranger Regiment is a highly trained and rapidly deployable light infantry force. With specialized skills that enable it to be effective against a diverse variety of conventional and special operations targets, the regiment is America's premier strike force and stands alone as the most elite light infantry battalion in the world. In the past, Rangers led the way and fought in nearly every U.S. conflict. At present they are the force best prepared to perform worldwide missions in the interests of the United States. Their actions against the Taliban and other terrorists are as current as the front pages of today's newspapers.

These missions include deep raids, airfield or other transportation center seizures, reconnaissance, and recovery or rescue of personnel and equipment. The Rangers also serve as an important aspect of diplomacy in their capacity to deploy almost immediately worldwide as a "show of force." The arrival of the Rangers is an absolute indicator of U.S. resolve.

Today's Rangers may deploy into any type of terrain, from desert sands to Arctic ice floes. They are thoroughly trained for missions on land, sea, and air. Professionalism, shock action, and surprise are the Rangers' greatest assets.

The headquarters of the 75th Ranger Regiment, commanded by a full colonel, remains at Fort Benning where it was originally established in 1984. Its three battalions, each commanded by a lieutenant colonel, are also firmly established at posts from which they have operated for more than a decade—the 1st Battalion at Hunter Airfield on Fort Stewart,

Georgia; the 2nd Battalion at Fort Lewis, Washington; and the 3rd Battalion at Fort Benning.

Each battalion has 580 volunteers organized into three combat companies and a headquarters company, each commanded by a captain. Each combat company is organized into four platoons led by lieutenants—three rifle and one weapons—totaling 175 men. Three infantry squads and a machine-gun squad are assigned to each rifle platoon. Along with the battalion command element, the headquarters company contains fire support, communications, medical, and logistic elements.

The majority of the more than two thousand men (women are not permitted to join) assigned to the Ranger Regiment are infantrymen. There are slots, however, for more than twenty other military occupation specialties (MOS). In addition to fire direction, medical, and communications specialists, the regiment actively recruits mechanics, personnel clerks, intelligence analysts, and even cooks and chaplain's assistants. Volunteers for the regiment must first successfully complete basic and advanced individual training. Each must be a U.S. citizen, capable of qualifying for a Secret clearance, and either airborne-qualified or willing to attend the U.S. Army Basic Airborne Course before assignment to the regiment.

Merely volunteering for the regiment does not mean a soldier instantly becomes a Ranger. All soldiers in the rank of E-4 (specialist) or below must complete the Ranger Indoctrination Program (RIP) in order to receive the beret* and assignment to a battalion. All soldiers above the rank of E-4,

* To unify their image and to increase morale Army Chief of Staff General Eric Shineki announced in October 2000 that the black beret would become the standard head wear for all soldiers. Despite tremendous objections from Ranger veterans organizations as well as some political leaders, who noted that Rangers exclusively had worn the black beret for half a century, the army adopted the change on June 14, 2001. On that date the Ranger Regiment, with permission from Shineki, began wearing tan berets. Regardless of the controversy, time has proven that a beret of any color is just a hat and that the Rangers continue to be the world's best infantry.

including officers, must pass the Ranger Orientation Program (ROP) before they join the regiment.

The mission of the three-week-long Ranger Indoctrination Program is to select and prepare candidates for service in the regiment. Activities include physical training, Ranger history instruction, map reading, airborne operations, day and night land navigation, combatives, knot and rope skills, water survival, road marches, and combat lifesaving. To successfully complete RIP the candidates must score 70 percent or more on all tests, run five miles in forty minutes or less, swim fifteen yards in full uniform and equipment, and complete a twelve-mile road march.

The Ranger Orientation Program for sergeants in the grade of E-5 and above, as well as officers, includes physical conditioning, road marches, weapons familiarization, fire support, antiterrorism, urban warfare, airborne operations, regimental standards, water survival, and communications. Successful candidates must score 70 percent on all graded exercises and tests, complete a twelve-mile road march carrying a forty-five-pound rucksack within three hours, run five miles in forty minutes or less, and swim fifteen yards in full uniform and equipment.

An additional requirement of all NCOs and officers in ROP is a psychological assessment. Candidates must also receive a positive recommendation following a Ranger staff interview.

Successful graduates of RIP and ROP receive their scroll patch, tan beret, and assignment to one of the three Ranger battalions. There they join their companies, platoons, and squads in training for future contingencies.

While the new volunteers are now officially Rangers, except for officers and the senior NCOs, they likely have not attended the U.S. Army Infantry School Ranger Course before joining their units. The highly coveted slots in the Ranger School are few. Members of the regiment must prove themselves and exhibit exceptional leadership and physical skills before the units sends them to the formal Ranger course.

Those who are selected face what is undoubtedly the most difficult training in the U.S. Armed Forces. According to Pamphlet SH 21-75, the purpose of the Ranger course is "to teach and develop Combat Arms Functional Skills relevant to fighting close combat, direct fire battle. Leadership development is a tertiary benefit to the student—not the course purpose. Selected officer and enlisted personnel will be challenged by requiring them to perform effectively as small unit leaders in a realistic tactical environment under mental and physical stress approaching that found in combat. It provides the student with practical experience in the application of the tactics and techniques of Ranger operations in wooded, lowland swamp, and mountainous environments. Emphasis is placed on development of fundamental individual skills through the application of the principles of leadership while further developing military skills in the planning and conduct of dismounted infantry, airborne, air assault, and amphibious squad and platoon size combat operations."

Before beginning the Ranger course, prospective students must successfully complete Zero Week, which begins seven days prior to the formal course. During Zero Week candidates accomplish administrative processing tasks and become acclimated to both the Georgia weather and the extreme standards required by the Ranger cadre. During this phase students must pass the physical fitness and water survival tests.

Zero Week is physically and mentally taxing, but training really becomes tough when the course actually begins. The Ranger School consists of sixty-one days, in which training occurs for an average of 19.6 hours per day, seven days a week. The training takes place in three distinct geographic locations. The first, or Benning Phase, is twenty-one days in length and is conducted by the 4th Battalion, Ranger Training Brigade, at Fort Benning, Georgia. The second, or Mountain Phase, also lasts twenty-one days and is taught by the 5th Battalion, Ranger Training Brigade, at Camp Frank D. Merrill in northern Georgia near Dahlonega. The third, or Florida Phase, is seventeen days and is led by the 6th Battalion at

Camp James E. Rudder at Eglin Air Force Base in the Florida panhandle. Travel, maintenance, and administrative processing occupy the other two days of the course.

During the entire two months of training, Ranger students face constant pressures accentuated by hunger, lack of sleep, and the need to be prepared to assume a leadership position at any moment. These harsh mental and physical conditions often mimic those found on the actual battlefield. It is not unusual for a student who has had no sleep and only a single ration for more than twenty-four hours to be crossing an icy swamp in the middle of the night—only to be approached by a Ranger cadre who says, "The patrol leader is dead, you are in charge. Where are you? What are you going to do now, Ranger?"

During the course Rangers are paired in buddy teams and are responsible for each other's welfare, morale, and safety. What little they have, they share. It is not unusual for a Ranger to send his buddy half a candy bar years or even decades after they shared the hunger and hazards of the mountains and swamps together.

Throughout the course the Ranger cadre emphasize small-group instruction techniques. This is conducted through practical, realistic, and strenuous field training that focuses on current tactical doctrine. These exercises last from one to twelve days and require the Ranger students to cover distances of one to nineteen miles per day over all types of terrain in all kinds of weather conditions.

During the two months many students quit on their own accord. Injuries reduce the class size even more as those who are hurt or become sick are recycled into subsequent classes or returned to their units. Occasionally the training is so realistic that Ranger students, despite strict safety regulations, are fatally injured.

Completion of the course does not mean that all students receive the black-and-gold Ranger tab. If their various scores, especially those while in leadership positions, are unsatisfactory, the tab is not awarded. These students, the dropouts, and the injured often total more than half of those who began the training. The 50 percent failure rate is even more significant when you consider the number turned away from ever beginning the training during Zero Week and other preliminary training conducted by the units of potential students.

Successful graduates of the Ranger School sew the black-and-gold tab above their unit patch on their left uniform shoulder. Those who then report to the Ranger Regiment join the most elite light infantry strike force in the world today. Rangers assigned to other units wear the tab that immediately marks them as leaders with special skills and dedication. All go forward aware that the marching jody call is no exaggeration, for indeed, "If you are brave and bold, you too may wear the black and gold, for danger is no stranger to an airborne Ranger."

CHAPTER 5

✷✷✷✷✷✷✷

U.S. Army Special Forces: History

O_F all the modern military elites, perhaps the best known and least understood are the Special Forces or Green Berets. While they share experiences and skills with their peers in other elite units, the Special Forces alone focus on organizing, teaching, and building indigenous populations to conduct guerrilla or counterguerrilla operations.

Much of the blood-warrior history of the modern Rangers is also a central part of the heritage of the Special Forces. Although the Rangers deserve their claim to direct linkage to Rogers, Marion, and Mosby, these early role models certainly played a pivotal role in the development of the modern Special Forces as well. Rangers and Green Berets also rightly share the accomplishments of Darby, Merrill, Rudder, and others during World War II.

Prior to the Second World War, the United States had little experience in unconventional warfare. The American military mostly used the conventional tactics of the time. Any efforts to secure assistance from allies or from factions inside the enemy territory were diplomatic rather than military issues.

The most significant efforts prior to World War II to organize indigenous forces occurred during the Indian wars of the last half of the nineteenth century. Field commanders in the West, faced with huge spaces and few friendly troops, frequently solicited Indians from opposing tribes or clans to fight against their traditional enemies.

While encouraging intertribal warfare reduced the burden

of Indian fighting on the American army, the victors of these skirmishes came out better armed and prepared to fight their benefactors. As a result, the army made efforts to more directly involve Native Americans in the military and to make their roles official. In 1866 the U.S. Army implemented General Order 56 to recruit one thousand Indians into the regular force.

The primary mission of the Indian Scouts was to serve as guides, provide reconnaissance, gather intelligence, and fight when necessary. They also maintained order on the reservations.

Most of the Indian Scouts initially came from the Pawnee, Navajo, and Seminole tribes. Some of the latter were multiracial because of the intermarriage of Indians and escaped black slaves prior to the Civil War. In the latter part of the Indian wars, Apache from various clans of the tribe also joined the Scouts and were instrumental in General George Crook's capture of Geronimo in 1886.

Despite the support of Congress and the success of the Native Americans in the field, the Indian Scouts never numbered more than two hundred at any one time. Language and cultural barriers, compounded by racial prejudice, hindered their acceptance. Many senior commanders, including General Philip Sheridan, believed that the purposes of the Indian campaigns were subjugation and annihilation, not assimilation.

Those commanders, like Crook, who did encourage the use of the Scouts found them helpful because of their knowledge of the land and the enemy. They also proved themselves to be resourceful and brave in combat. Between 1869 and 1890 a total of fifteen Scouts earned the Medal of Honor.

Local commanders used Indian Scouts in various capacities, depending on their own agendas. Neither their uniform nor name was official until near the end of the Indian wars. In 1890 Army Circular 10 provided the initial official guide to Scout uniforms, including the first authorization of the crossed-arrow insignia that would later become a part of modern Special Forces. A year later General Order 28 made the name *U.S. Scouts* official.

U.S. Scouts participated in their last combat operations as a part of General John J. Pershing's expedition into Mexico in 1916. After their return the Scouts performed routine garrison duty at remote posts in the Southwest. On November 30, 1943, the few remaining veterans were transferred to regular units when the Scouts were disbanded. The last three U.S. Scouts retired from active duty in 1947.

Except for the limited use of Indian Scouts, the United States did not formally initiate widespread efforts to conduct unconventional warfare until World War II. The breadth and magnitude of that war called for two different aspects of unconventional warfare—direct guerrilla action behind the enemy lines and the arming and training of local forces to conduct sabotage and resistance against their occupiers.

The initial World War II unit in the Special Forces lineage ultimately performed missions different from those for which it had originally been organized. Shortly after the United States entered the war, British Admiral Louis Mountbatten suggested that the Allies form a joint American-Canadian force to conduct deep, behind-the-lines raids. These attacks were to destroy power stations, communications centers, and fuel refineries in Nazi-occupied regions of Norway and Romania.

On July 9, 1942, the 1st Special Service Force (1st SSF) was activated at Fort William Henry Harrison, Montana, under the command of Colonel Robert T. Frederick. As a War Department staff officer, Frederick had helped in the preplanning of the unit with Mountbatten. While enthusiastic about commanding the force, Frederick did not agree with its proposed missions, believing along with others that the behind-the-lines raids would place too many innocent civilians in harm's way and that Nazi retaliation would endanger even more.

When the army decided in September 1942 not to participate in the raids, the 1st SSF was already well on its way to achieving combat readiness. Rather than disband it, General George C. Marshall, the army chief of staff, assigned the unit to direct combat with a limited mission to perform behind-the-lines raids.

Frederick recruited his American volunteers from army units throughout the Pacific and western United States. He also scoured the enlistment centers for woodsmen, hunters, trail guides, and others familiar with the outdoors. Frederick soon discovered that many units sent him malcontents and discipline problems. Some of the "volunteers" were out-and-out criminals pending charges.

Frederick accepted all of the volunteers regardless of their past. Most of the men welcomed a second chance and relished in the idea of joining an elite unit. Frederick sent those who did not conform back to their original units or to the stockade if appropriate. The Canadians arrived at Fort Harrison more organized and disciplined. After a few confrontations, however, the soldiers from neighboring countries blended into a motivated, well-trained team.

When fully manned, the 1st SSF contained 2,194 enlisted men led by 173 officers. Its three regiments had enlisted men from both countries, with two commanded by Americans and one by a Canadian. Each of the American commanders had a Canadian executive officer, while an American was second in command of the regiment led by a Canadian.

Training for the force was similar to that for Army Ranger battalions. All members were airborne-qualified and spent extensive periods practicing hand-to-hand combat and developing skills in mountaineering and explosives. Much of this training took place during harsh winter conditions.

After amphibious training at Norfolk, Virginia, the 1st SSF sailed to Alaska in August 1943 to join the invasion of the Aleutian island of Kiska. By the time the invasion force went ashore, the Japanese had evacuated the island. The 1st SSF returned to Fort Ethan Allen, Vermont, and, after a brief period of training and refitting, sailed for the Mediterranean Theater on October 27.

Following a brief stay in Casablanca, the force landed at Naples on November 19. On December 3 the force assumed its first combat mission of attacking enemy positions along the German Winter Line guarding the Liri Valley. By scaling a two-hundred-foot cliff in the German rear, the 1st SSF was able to neutralize the enemy positions after a fierce two-hour battle—much faster than the three days anticipated by Allied planners. Over the next six weeks the force conducted a series of operations to seize key German positions on mountain peaks along the way to Cassino and northward.

On January 17, 1944, the 1st SSF was withdrawn from the front lines for rest and reorganization. The unit then joined a detachment of Rangers near the Anzio beachhead on February 2. Operating mostly at night, the force conducted raids against German outposts and also established artillery forward observer positions to call in fire on the main enemy units.

By May 9 the 1st SSF had been back on the front lines for nearly one hundred days. With no rest they joined the offensive toward Rome, reaching the city on June 4 and immediately securing the important bridge crossings over the Tiber River. By this time the 1st SSF had earned the title of *Devil's Brigade* because of its fierce fighting ability.

On August 14 the force joined Operation Anvil in southern France. Approaching the enemy shore in small rubber boats at Ile d'Hyères, the SSF surprised several German artillery positions to secure the invasion's left flank. The force then pushed inland to cut off enemy escape routes.

Over the next three months the force continued operations along the French-Italian border. Casualties mounted, and the men were finally withdrawn from the front line on December 5. Securing and training replacements for the elite unit was difficult in the midst of combat operations, and with the battle lines fairly stable, the army's leadership decided the special skills of the 1st SSF were no longer needed. On December 5 the army disbanded the unit at Menton, France. Its surviving veterans were reassigned to the 474th Regimental

Combat Team and to the 82nd and 101st Airborne Divisions. On January 6, 1945, the 1st SSF was officially deactivated.

The Devil's Brigade demonstrated the merits of special soldiers performing difficult tasks in direct combat. However, another World War II organization did far more in establishing methods and procedures for special warfare, becoming an even greater influence on modern blood warriors.

Before the United States joined the Allies in World War II, President Franklin Roosevelt had become concerned about the lack of any means to coordinate the tremendous amount of information and intelligence flowing into Washington. Roosevelt dispatched William J. "Wild Bill" Donovan, a Columbia University graduate and Wall Street lawyer who had earned the Medal of Honor in World War I, to England to study the British intelligence organization.

Upon his return Donovan recommended that a single central agency be formed to control all foreign information. Roosevelt agreed and on July 11, 1941, authorized the Office of the Coordinator of Information (COI) with Donovan at its head. On June 13, 1942, the COI became the Office of Strategic Services (OSS), with the overall responsibilities for intelligence, propaganda, sabotage, subversion, and other clandestine activities.

None of the armed services welcomed a separate command with these missions. Career military officers looked at the OSS as misfits led by socially elite graduates of Ivy League schools who sought special treatment as they avoided the regular infantry and navy. General Douglas MacArthur, as the senior army commander in the Pacific Theater, refused any OSS support in his area of operations. MacArthur claimed he needed immediate help and could not wait for the OSS to train and be deployed. He also questioned how the OSS could be effective with its headquarters remaining in Washington.

MacArthur did not trust elite units not directly under his command and disliked anything or anyone that distracted from his own presence and fame. Some accounts state that when MacArthur received his initial briefing on the subject, he became angry when he noticed that the OSS briefer wore nonregulation argyle socks.

Whatever his reasons, MacArthur never allowed the OSS to operate in his region of command in the Pacific. Only outside his area of operation, primarily in Burma and China, and only by providing advice to the navy underwater demolition teams (UDTs) did the OSS contribute in the war against the Japanese.

Two of the primary activities of the OSS in Europe played a significant role in the future of Special Forces. Organizational groups (OGs) composed of teams of about fifteen men with special weapons and language skills parachuted far behind enemy lines to conduct direct action against the enemy. Smaller three-man teams called "Jedburghs" also jumped into enemy territory to provide assistance to resistance groups.

Volunteers for the OGs and Jedburghs came from many sources. In addition to Ivy League graduates, the two OSS groups attracted professional athletes, ex-patriots, big-game hunters, and a variety of individuals with not-so-glamorous backgrounds such as bartenders, jewelers, union organizers—some only marginally legal.

The OSS formed its first OGs in late 1942 with teams specifically targeted against the Axis in France, Norway, Greece, Yugoslavia, and Italy. Each country OG consisted of four officers and thirty enlisted men capable of fielding two fifteen-man teams. Training for the teams included parachute school and language instruction for targeted regions.

The first OGs entered enemy territory in April 1942. Although they were capable of independent operations, the teams provided arms and ammunition to resistance groups and joined them on raids against enemy supply and communications lines. In addition to direct combat the OGs provided other types of support. Teams in Greece helped partisans build an airstrip for the evacuation of downed Allied aircrews. They also helped another group establish a mule-mobile field hospital that went from village to village in Greece treating partisans and civilians.

As the war progressed, the OSS committed more and more OGs to the European Theater. Most were extremely successful in destroying the enemy with minimum losses of their own. Near the end of the war, Donovan claimed in a report to the Joint Chiefs of Staff that nineteen OG teams in France had killed or wounded 928 Germans at the cost of only seven Americans killed and six wounded.

Not all teams were so fortunate in other countries. In March 1944 an entire OG team, "Ginny II," was captured shortly after their infiltration into northern Italy. Despite the fact that they wore uniforms and carried U.S. military equipment, the Germans shot them all as spies.

By the summer of 1944 more than eleven hundred men made up OG teams all across the European Theater. To ease the administrative requirements of such a large organization and to reinforce the chain of command, the army redesignated the OGs in August as the 2761st Special Reconnaissance Battalion, Separate (Provisional). Their original country focus carried on to the different company organizations within the battalion. OG teams targeted against Italy and Germany made up Company A, OGs in France became Company B, and OGs operating in Greece, Albania, and Yugoslavia formed Company C.

When the war in Europe finally came to an end, four hundred of the OGs assigned to the 2761st transferred to Kunming, China—outside MacArthur's area of command. There they established a paratrooper school and training base for Chinese commandos.

One significant OSS operation took place in Asia. In northern Burma, which was also outside MacArthur's area of operations, Colonel Ray Peers commanded OSS Detachment 101, whose mission was to organize Kachin tribesmen against the Japanese. Peers—with only 131 officers and 553 enlisted men—recruited, organized, armed, and trained 11,000 Kachin guerrillas. Operating in small groups and in units as large as battalions, the Kachins and their OSS advisers conducted ambushes, raids, and other harassing activities against the Japanese occupiers. They also provided surveillance that produced target information for 85 percent of the American air strikes in the region.

With the loss of only 22 Americans and 184 Kachins, OSS Detachment 101 claimed an enemy body count of 5,428. When General Joseph Stilwell, commander of the China Burma India Theater, questioned how the Kachins accounted for such an exact number of enemy kills, Peers and a subordinate produced bamboo tubes and dumped their contents on a table. As the general observed the pile of rotting ears, the OSS men recommended that he divide by two to confirm their count.

In all likelihood the number of claimed enemy deaths was extremely conservative. Adding unconfirmed deaths to Detachment 101's total would easily have doubled its claim.

The Jedburghs were the other primary OSS operators; they served in the European Theater and contributed to the historical lineage of the modern Special Forces. Allied planners recognized the need for teams that could infiltrate behind the German lines prior to the invasion of France. In addition to directly disrupting German communications and supply lines, these teams could organize local resistance and establish communications to provide intelligence to the invasion force.

The OSS began recruiting men for the Jedburghs in August 1943. Each team contained an American or British officer, a French officer, and an enlisted radio operator. The recruiting process and all aspects of their training remained Top Secret. Even the source of their name has never been officially revealed, or perhaps it has been lost with the passage of time. Originally, the teams were to be called Jumpers, but this proved unpopular with both the teams and the Allied intelligence staff. Most accounts claim that *Jedburgh* was ultimately selected from a list of "preapproved" code names. More likely, however, the name came from the Scottish Highland twelfth-century burgh, or walled town, on the Jed River, where the initial team training occurred.

Whatever the source of their name, the Jedburghs trained hard for their unique missions. The first phase of their training included many of the same skills taught to the OGs: unarmed combat, the use of explosives, and communications. A second training phase took place at Ringway, England, where the Jedburgh candidates learned how to use parachutes. Since it was anticipated that Jedburgh teams would only use the skill once or twice, the airborne school lasted only three days.

The final Jedburgh training phase was at the transformed aristocratic family estate of Minton Hall. There the Jedburghs continued their training while forming their own teams based on trust, ability, and friendship. They then practiced additional sabotage skills as well as escape and evasion techniques. During this period each group received its designation—either a male or female first name, such as Team Andy or Team Wanda.

The first Jedburgh teams jumped into France on June 6, 1944, in support of the D-Day invasion at Normandy. Other teams joined the Operation Dragoon landings in southern France in August. In September still more Jeds participated in the Operation Market Garden airborne invasion of occupied Holland. Between June 6 and September 16 a total of 276 Jedburghs organized into ninety-nine teams jumped into France, Belgium, and Holland.

By the fall of 1944 the Allies were prepared to invade Germany itself. The Jedburghs returned to Britain on October 13, 1944, where they disbanded. The Jedburgh veterans joined the OGs or transferred to other positions. Some later joined the OGs at the training center in China.

"Wild Bill" Donovan maintained a close relationship with President Roosevelt and encouraged him to retain the OSS after the war. The OSS commander, however, had few supporters outside his own command. Most military leaders firmly believed that intelligence and special operations forces should remain a part of the uniformed services rather than be a separate agency working directly for the president. Many also expressed reservations about elite units in general and particularly disliked what they perceived as arrogance and superiority on the part of the OSS personnel in particular.

Two primary factors ultimately doomed the continuance of the OSS. In February 1945 members of the U.S. press learned that Roosevelt was seriously considering maintaining the OSS after the war concluded. Several major newspapers carried editorials condemning the concept and referring to a peacetime OSS as an "American Gestapo."

The death of Roosevelt was the second and final blow to the future of the OSS. Harry Truman did not share Roosevelt's support of the organization. He, like many others, believed that peace would prevail after the defeat of Germany and Japan and that the proposed United Nations could handle future disputes. Only a month after the surrender of Japan, Truman signed an executive order terminating the OSS effective October 1, 1945. The few OGs and Jedburghs still on active duty transferred to regular units. Donovan, relieved from active duty, returned to his prewar law practice.

The postwar euphoria of peace did not last long. While the United States could deter large-scale conventional warfare with its threat of atomic bombs, it had completely dismantled its ability to combat unconventional forces. Both the Soviet Union and the People's Republic of China overtly and covertly supported the expansion of communism throughout the Third World in what they called "national wars of liberation."

The ashes of World War II had not yet cooled before the Soviets began to implement their plans to dominate Europe. From the heat of the Second World War the United States entered what became known as the Cold War with the Soviet Union and its communist allies.

One of the first "hot spots" in the Cold War occurred in Greece, where communist guerrillas attempted to topple the government. On March 12, 1946, President Truman, in an

address to Congress requesting funds to assist the Greek government, announced the policy known as the Truman Doctrine, which would remain the cornerstone for U.S. foreign
policy throughout the Cold War. The policy of the United
States, the president stated, would be "to support free peoples
who are resisting subjugation by armed minorities or outside
pressure."

On June 24, 1948, the Soviets imposed a road, rail, and
water blockade of Berlin, causing the Cold War to very nearly
become hot. Only aerial supply of the free sector of the city
prevented it from falling to the Soviets. A divided Berlin and
Germany resulted.

A year later the Soviets exploded their first atomic device.
The United States no longer had a monopoly on the super-
weapon. The awareness of the U.S. and Soviet Union that
they possessed the capability of mutual destruction prevented total war but did nothing to stop the smaller conflicts.

After the communist North Koreans failed to conquer
South Korea in a conventional, non-nuclear war, China and
the Soviet Union realized that they could better use their resources in guerrilla warfare. They were soon supporting
"wars of liberation" by communist guerrillas in Asia, Latin
America, Africa, and the Middle East.

Initially the United States had no capacity to directly
combat the wars of liberation and to enforce the Truman Doctrine. Since the end of World War II most of the army's
leaders had focused on large-scale conventional battlefields
with the potential of escalation to nuclear warfare. Only a few
officers—mostly OSS veterans—continued to support the
idea of unconventional forces. Two colonels, Aaron Bank and
Russell Volckmann, veteran OSS operators who remained on
active duty following World War II, were the leaders of the efforts. In 1952 they gained the support of Brigadier General
Robert McClure, who headed the psychological warfare staff
in the Department of the Army.

Bank and Volckmann, with the support of McClure, lobbied the army staff. They argued that there were areas

throughout the world where conventional warfare would be unlikely but where communist-supported guerrilla activities found ideal targets. They recommended the formation of a special unit that would provide small advisory forces to assist established governments in defending against communist insurgent threats. These teams could also take direct action in enemy-held areas through sabotage, raids, and intelligence-collection operations.

Bank and Volckmann were well qualified to lead the way in establishing the modern Special Forces. Volckmann had evaded capture following the surrender of U.S. forces in the Philippines in 1942 and escaped to the mountains of northern Luzon, where he organized a twelve-thousand-man guerrilla force of local Filipinos, who fought the Japanese for the remainder of the war.

Bank had followed a more conventional route into unconventional warfare. In 1944 he volunteered for the OSS Jedburghs and joined Team Packard in organizing resistance in southern France. In early 1945 Bank formed a team of one hundred German prisoners of war who professed to be communist and anti-Nazi. The team, code-named Iron Cross, trained to capture or kill high-ranking Nazi leaders, including Hitler, Goebbels, Bormann, and Göring. However, the war ended before the team could be deployed. Bank then joined the OSS in China and later went into Laos seeking to liberate Allied POWs. After the war Bank served in counterintelligence in Europe and commanded the 187th Regimental Combat Team in Korea before joining Volckmann in encouraging the formation of the Special Forces.

By 1952 the lobbying efforts, strongly influenced by communist aggression in Korea and around the world, yielded dividends. In June the Department of the Army authorized the formation of the 10th Special Forces, which would be subordinate to the command of McClure's Office of the Chief of Psychological Warfare. Many officers, including Volckmann, objected to this command relationship because they were opposed to the Special Forces being associated with the "dirty tricks" for which psychological operations were known throughout the military. They silenced their objections, however, when they learned that the decision had been made and the command structure was the best they were going to achieve.

Possibly because of Volckmann's objections, he was not selected for command of the new unit. That position went to Bank, who more likely won out because of his direct OSS experience in World War II.

On June 20, 1952, Bank assumed command of the 10th Special Forces Group (Airborne) at Smoke Bomb Hill, Fort Bragg, North Carolina. Although the Department of the Army authorized twenty-three hundred men for the new unit, on its activation day its personnel totaled only ten—Bank, a warrant officer, and eight enlisted men. Bank immediately began recruiting and found volunteers from the former ranks of the OSS and Rangers as well as the paratrooper units. Many of the volunteers were immigrants who had come to the United States after their countries came under the control of the Soviet Union following World War II.

While veteran World War II special operators and recent arrivals from Europe were anxious to fight communism, the majority of regular army officers avoided the newly formed Special Forces. Most officers believed the future of the army, and their careers, lay in conventional forces, which were becoming more mechanized and oriented to the possible nuclear battlefield. Some of this attitude proved favorable to the new unit. Instead of "spit and polish, by the book" officers and NCOs, the 10th Group attracted imaginative individuals who were innovators. They liked the idea of a new approach to warfare and the independence it granted to its operatives.

Volunteers for the 10th Group had to meet strict standards. All volunteers had to be airborne-qualified or willing to attend the training before reporting for duty. Each had to pass rigorous physical fitness and intelligence tests and exhibit the ability to teach the skills he mastered. Psychological exams also tested the Special Forces candidate, with particular emphasis on abilities to endure long periods of isolation and to adapt to foreign locations and cultures.

Bank and his staff generally looked for men who were team players. Other important characteristics included physical stamina, dependability, adaptability, enthusiasm, self-discipline, loyalty, judgment, ingenuity, and moral courage. While modesty was not required, and self-confidence and arrogance were appreciated if not expected, the Special Forces did desire that its volunteers possess a degree of decorum.

Bank began training his volunteers as soon as they reported to the 10th Group. His primary focus centered on the unit's official primary mission as defined by the Department of the Army: "To infiltrate by land, sea, or air, deep into enemy-occupied territory and organize the resistance/guerrilla potential to conduct special forces operations, with emphasis on guerrilla warfare."

While the primary mission was certainly difficult, the Special Forces were also assigned equally complex secondary missions. These included counterinsurgency operations, deep-penetration raids, and reconnaissance or intelligence-gathering missions.

All of the men who began Bank's training had successfully completed the challenging paratrooper course. Still others wore the Ranger tab as graduates of the Fort Benning course.

Bank immediately established that Special Forces missions and training would not duplicate those of the Rangers. The Ranger battalions of World War II and the companies that served in Korea were organized and trained as light infantry to hit hard and fast and then give way to follow-on conventional units. Special Forces would not be light infantry focused on brief missions. Rather, they would train to become capable of self-sustaining missions that might last months, even years, deep within hostile territory. They would have to learn the language of their focus area and survive on their own with little or no supply from the outside.

Bank further defined the differences between Ranger and Special Forces units. According to the 10th Group commander,

"Our training included many more complex subjects and was geared to entirely different, more difficult, comprehensive missions and complex operations."

Bank and the 10th Group initially oriented their training focus on Western Europe. Throughout its early years the Special Forces kept their activities quiet, seeking no notice or publicity. Not everyone on the army staff supported the new unit, but Bank and his men soon proved their professionalism and ability to meet the changing military needs around the world.

After a year and a half the group reached a degree of proficiency that allowed it to transfer half of its strength to Bad Tolz, West Germany, on November 11, 1953. This portion retained the designation of the 10th Special Forces Group, while those who remained at Fort Bragg were renamed the 77th Special Forces Group.

The Special Forces continued to grow during the 1950s as they expanded their focus from Europe to the world. On April 1, 1956, sixteen men from the 77th Group formed the 14th Special Forces Operational Detachment and in June transferred to Hawaii. A short time later they began training activities in Taiwan, Thailand, and Vietnam. During the next year three more detachments—the 12th, 13th, and 16th—were formed from the 77th Group at Fort Bragg. These three were soon reorganized into the 8231st Army Special Operations Detachment. On June 17, 1957, the 14th and 8231st were combined and redesignated the 1st Special Forces Group, with their headquarters on the island of Okinawa and their mission to support operations in the Far East with mobile training teams. On June 6, 1960, the portion of the 77th remaining at Fort Bragg was redesignated the 7th Special Forces Group.

Another reorganization within Special Forces occurred in late 1956. Special Forces training at Fort Bragg originally came under the control of the U.S. Army Psychological Warfare Center. To more closely define just what they were training to accomplish, the command changed its name to the U.S. Army Special Warfare School on December 10.

During their early years the Special Forces experimented with several sizes and types of organizations. Initially they formed groups of fifteen men into Operational Detachments A or "A-Teams," using the model developed by the OSS during World War II. Soon the number was reduced to twelve, consisting of a captain, a lieutenant, and ten experienced enlisted men.

While the Special Forces were expanding and experimenting with different organizations, they also were establishing official and unofficial insignia. As a motto they adopted the Latin phrase "De Oppresso Liber," meaning "To Free the Oppressed" or occasionally interpreted as "To Liberate from Oppression." The motto was integrated into the distinctive black-and-gold Special Forces crest, which also includes two crossed arrows to symbolize their role in unconventional warfare. A fighting knife, a symbol of silent deadly combat and the straight and true qualities of the Special Forces soldier, is attached over the arrows.

For a shoulder patch the Special Forces chose a teal-colored arrowhead shape with gold adornments. Teal blue represents the Special Forces' encompassing all-branch assignments, and gold stands for inspiration. The arrowhead represents the stealth and craft of Indians, America's first warriors, and a gold upturned dagger stands for their unconventional warfare mission. Three lightning bolts cross the dagger represent blinding speed and strength, as well as the three infiltration methods of land, air, and sea. An airborne tab tops the patch.

The crest and patch were official for authorized wear for everyone assigned to the Special Forces. Another uniform item began appearing shortly after the formation of the 10th Group, but it would be nearly a decade before the green beret gained official sanction. There are many stories, some conflicting, on the origins of the green beret. The most accepted, however, is that it began with a drawing by Major

106 *Michael Lee Lanning*

Herbert Brucker in 1952 of a Special Forces soldier wearing a beret.

Lieutenant Roger Pezzelle saw the drawing and liked the idea of a distinctive headgear for his team, which was still undergoing training. In late 1952, after receiving no response to his request through official channels to field-test berets, the young Special Forces officer went into Fayetteville, just outside the Fort Bragg gates. The only suitable berets he could find there were black, but he nevertheless purchased one for each member of his team—and an extra one for Colonel Beck in case his commander liked the idea.

Pezzelle's Operational Detachment FA-32 was by all accounts the first A-Team to wear berets, regardless of color. Beck apparently saw the team's headgear when they completed their training in the spring of 1953 but made no effort either to end or to endorse the wearing of berets. After graduation Pezzelle and his team transferred to Bad Tolz, where he commissioned a German tailor to make green berets for his team.

Nearly a year after Pezzelle's official request to field-test green berets, a box of the headgear arrived at Special Forces headquarters. Neither Pezzelle nor Brucker was at Fort Bragg, but since the berets came through official channels, some of the Special Forces soldiers conveniently assumed they were authorized and began wearing them, though wisely not in official formations. Because there were insufficient numbers of the issue berets for each man in the group, additional ones were finally found in Fayetteville and other off-post sources.

About this same time several of the soldiers observed Canadians wearing a sort of green beret during joint exercises. After a few inquiries the 77th Group began ordering similar berets from the Dorothea Knitting Mills in Canada. The "Rifle Green" model became the true forerunner of today's beret.

A short time later the 77th Special Forces Group published an internal order authorizing the green beret. Members of the 10th Group in Germany also continued to wear the beret sans any internal or external approval. For the remainder of the 1950s the Special Forces wore their berets in the field and anytime senior officers were not around.

During their first decade of growth the Special Forces avoided wearing their berets in public and attracting publicity about their mission and training. Few civilians knew they existed. This was to change with the election of John F. Kennedy.

During his inaugural address on January 20, 1961, President Kennedy noted the changes that had occurred during the twentieth century: "Let the word go forth from this time and place, to friend and foe alike, that the torch has been passed to a new generation of Americans, born in this century, tempered by war, disciplined by a hard and bitter peace, proud of our ancient heritage, and unwilling to witness or permit the slow undoing of those human rights to which this nation has always been committed, and to which we are committed today at home and around the world."

The new president then made it clear that he would support the Truman Doctrine. "Let every nation know, whether it wishes us well or ill, that we shall pay any price, bear any burden, meet any hardship, support any friend, oppose any foe to assure the survival and the success of liberty."

Kennedy was well read in counterinsurgency and counter-guerrilla warfare. Although his military background was in the navy, Kennedy understood that the communist-supported wars of liberation like the one in Vietnam would require an unconventional army. One of his earliest visits as president was to Fort Bragg, where he liked what he observed in the conventional 82nd Airborne Division and the XVIII Airborne Corps. However, it was the 7th Special Forces Group that made the biggest impression on him. The young president saw the Special Forces as his best and most economical means of meeting his promise to "pay any price, bear any burden, meet any hardship . . ." in defense of freedom.

Kennedy also liked the green berets worn by his chosen soldiers. Before going to Fort Bragg on October 12, 1961, the president sent word to the Special Warfare Center commander, Brigadier General William P. Yarborough, asking that group members wear their berets during his visit. Some accounts claim that this order provided the impetus for the official recognition of the distinctive headgear. Actually, the Department of the Army, aware of Kennedy's support, had sent a message to Fort Bragg shortly before the president's visit authorizing the green beret as an official part of the Special Forces uniform.

When Kennedy arrived at Fort Bragg to inspect the assembled Special Forces, Yarborough, wearing his beret, met the president. Kennedy remarked, "Those are nice. How do you like the green beret?"

Yarborough replied, "They're fine, sir. We've wanted them a long time."

At the end of his visit to Fort Bragg, the president again expressed his support for the Special Forces. In a letter to Yarborough he wrote, "My congratulations to you personally for the presentation today. . . . The challenge of this old but new form of operations is a real one and I know that you and the members of your command will carry on for us and the free world in a manner which is both worthy and inspiring. I am sure that the green beret will be a mark of distinction in the trying times ahead."

In a White House memorandum to the Department of the Army on April 11, 1962, President Kennedy again expressed his support for the Special Forces. He also restated his backing for the green beret, calling it "a symbol of excellence, a badge of courage, mark of distinction in the fight for freedom."

The Special Forces never forgot Kennedy's support. To honor his memory, members of the Special Forces pay their respects to the late president by laying a wreath and a green beret on his grave every November 22, the anniversary of his assassination.

Whether or not Kennedy was supportive of the increased U.S. involvement in Southeast Asia before his untimely death remains under debate. Whatever his stance on the escalating war in Vietnam, it is clear that the president was fully aware that the Special Forces would play an important role in "the trying times ahead."

CHAPTER 6

✳✳✳✳✳✳✳

U.S. Army Special Forces: Vietnam to Today

*A*FTER the arrival of the sixteen-man 14th Special Forces Operational Detachment in June 1956, the number of Green Berets in Vietnam increased slowly. Their numbers grew larger after Kennedy's endorsement in 1961 and vastly increased in 1964 when President Lyndon Johnson escalated U.S. involvement in the war.

A-Teams all across Vietnam trained South Vietnamese and other indigenous personnel to defend remote outposts, often in the middle of territory controlled by the local Vietcong and North Vietnamese invaders. Captain Roger Donlon earned the first Special Forces Medal of Honor for his leadership in the defense of the outpost at Nam Dong on July 5, 1964.

By September 1964 there were so many A-Teams in Vietnam that the army formed a provisional group headquarters at Nha Trang to command and control the Special Forces soldiers. Six months later, in February 1965, the 5th Group was officially activated to replace the provisional headquarters and to control most Special Forces activities in Vietnam.

During the long war the A-Teams established a total of 254 outposts throughout Vietnam, most built along the main communist infiltration and supply routes. Some of the war's fiercest battles occurred around these remote camps, where often outnumbered and outgunned Green Berets and their local allies stood fast. At places like Song Zoai, Plei Mei, and Nam Dong the communists made every effort to destroy the Special Forces outposts. By the height of U.S. involvement in

Vietnam in 1969 more that thirty-seven hundred Special Forces soldiers were in action across the country.

The Special Forces armed and trained more than sixty thousand indigenous tribesmen, including Montagnards, Nungs, and Cao Dei, and formed them into Civilian Irregular Defense Groups (CIDGs) to assist in the defense of the outposts. The CIDGs, with Special Forces leadership and advisers, also performed independent missions against the communists and proved to be the A-Teams' staunchest allies.

Other members of the Special Forces formed special reconnaissance teams that joined indigenous personnel scouting deep in enemy-held territory. At times they ignored borders and rescued downed pilots in Cambodia and Laos, as well as conducting surveillance missions along the Ho Chi Minh Trail.

Not all the Special Forces in Vietnam were dedicated directly to fighting the Vietcong and North Vietnamese regulars or to training local forces to defend their outposts and villages. Special Forces medics provided medical support to isolated villages and trained locals to provide further care. A-Teams and support elements built hospitals, schools, roads, and canals. During their more than fourteen years in Vietnam, members of the 5th Special Forces Group performed more than forty-nine thousand economic assistances; thirty-four thousand educational efforts; thirty-five thousand welfare benefits; and ten thousand medical projects. While much of the American effort to win "hearts and minds" during the war paid little or no dividends, the Green Berets were respected and appreciated by most of the people of South Vietnam.

The Special Forces also passed along their expertise to Americans as well as to the Vietnamese and other indigenous personnel. On the orders of General William C. Westmoreland, the 5th Group's commander, Colonel Francis J. Kelly, established the Recondo School at Nha Trang. Veteran Special Forces reconnaissance personnel there trained LRRPs,

Rangers, and other U.S. personnel in how to "outguerrilla the guerrilla."

Special Forces played an important role throughout the Vietnam War, especially considering their small percentage of the overall U.S. force after the arrival of conventional infantry units. At the height of American involvement in Vietnam during 1969 less than 1 percent—about thirty-eight hundred—Special Forces soldiers were among the half million Americans.

This small number of blood warriors earned far more than their share of Medals of Honor with eighteen. Members of the Special Forces in Vietnam also received ninety Distinguished Service Crosses, America's second highest combat award, and 814 Silver Stars, the third highest. They also earned more than twenty-six hundred Purple Hearts for wounds received in direct combat. One other statistic also notes the dangers and hazards of Special Forces operations in Southeast Asia. Although they comprised less than 1 percent of the total number of U.S. forces in-country, eighty—or more than 4 percent—are listed on the rolls of the more than two thousand missing in action.

Despite their small number, the Special Forces made a lasting impression on the American military and public—especially the latter. The Vietnam War, although supported by the majority of the general population for most of the decade-long conflict, was extremely unpopular with those in the media, motion pictures, recording, and literary industries. Where previous American wars had spawned dozens, if not hundreds, of movies, songs, and books that supported the war and its warriors, these outlets were much more likely now to turn out products that protested U.S. involvement in Southeast Asia. At best they portrayed its soldiers, sailors, airmen, and marines as losers duped into fighting for their country; at worst as crazed psychos who murdered, pillaged, and raped their way first across the war zone and through their neighborhoods after they returned home.

Although the Vietnam War was America's longest armed

conflict, it produced only one film, one song, and one book that favorably presented the war and its warriors—and all were about the Special Forces and shared the title *The Green Berets*. In 1963 Robin Moore, a veteran World War II aviator, called upon his Harvard classmate and brother of the president, Robert Kennedy, for permission to observe the Special Forces in Vietnam. Moore trained for nearly a year before going to Southeast Asia. On his return he wrote his observations as a novel, and in May 1965 *The Green Berets* quickly climbed many of the best-seller lists. Although written as fiction, the book is based very closely on what Moore saw and experienced in Vietnam. The book is still in print today.

In 1966 a Special Forces staff sergeant, Barry Sadler, strummed a few chords on his guitar and wrote a simple song about "America's best" who wore a special hat. "The Ballad of the Green Berets" became a chart topper and its lyrics the most sung and best-known refrains about the war.

In June 1968 John Wayne, king of cowboy and war movies but not a veteran himself, filmed his version of the conflict in Southeast Asia with extensive support by the Department of Defense. While the film did fairly well at the box office, no other Hollywood release showed the war and its participants in a positive light. In fact, Hollywood produced at least one antiwar, pro-protestor film for each year of the conflict. Although widely panned by film and war critics alike, *The Green Berets* was positively received by members of the Special Forces and others in uniform, but, as veterans noted, "Like bread to a starving man, hell, it was all we had."

Despite the positive feelings of most of the Special Forces veterans toward the book, song, and film, not all appreciated becoming known as Green Berets. Many were and are today quick to note that the beret "is only a hat," while the Special Forces soldier is a highly motivated and trained warrior who is an expert at both conventional and unconventional warfare.

The widespread attention the Special Forces received in the entertainment media did nothing to change the increasing dissatisfaction of the American people with the prolonged war in Vietnam. Richard M. Nixon ran for president in 1968 on the platform that he would end the war in Vietnam. Shortly after his inauguration in 1969, he announced his plan of Vietnamization—turning the primary efforts of the war over to the South Vietnamese and beginning the withdrawal of American troops.

At the end of 1969 the Special Forces began turning over their camps to their South Vietnamese counterparts. On March 5, 1971, the 5th Group Headquarters moved from Nha Trang to Fort Bragg. A few teams transferred to Thailand, from where they continued limited secret missions into Vietnam, but these teams returned home at the end of 1972, ending Special Forces participation in the Vietnam War.

Despite their courageous and honorable performance during the conflict in Vietnam, the Special Forces received an indifferent welcome home from the American public and faced an uncertain future in the army. The general public had little use for anyone in uniform, particularly blood warriors who had become proficient at outguerrillaing the guerrilla. Many in the uniformed ranks still looked upon the Green Berets as "Snake Eaters" who exhibited little discipline or respect for the regular forces.

In the aftermath of Vietnam the army reduced the Special Forces by more than half and deactivated the 3rd, 6th, and 8th Groups. The 10th Group did its best to find a mission in the armored-oriented European conventional warfare planning. The 5th and 7th Groups took even more desperate measures to avoid additional downsizing. Many of these actions wandered far from the traditional blood-warrior missions of the Green Berets.

In the mid-1970s the 5th and 7th Special Groups initiated Project SPARTAN (Special Proficiency at Rugged Training and Nation-building). SPARTAN projects included building roads, medical facilities, and other public works on Indian reservations in Florida and Montana. Special Forces' medics also provided free medical care to impoverished communities such as those in the isolated counties of Hoke and Anson in North Carolina.

Many veteran Green Berets during this period transferred to conventional infantry units or to the newly formed Ranger battalions. Construction and community planning were not missions desired by all blood warriors. When the Special Forces' morale was at its lowest, another president stepped forward to rebuild the Green Berets and renew their morale and blood-warrior spirit. Ronald Reagan assumed the presidency in 1981 and immediately took measures to bolster the military.

A part of this emphasis included renewing the capabilities of the Special Forces to combat insurgencies in such hot spots as Asia, Africa, and Central America. Special Forces A-Teams deployed worldwide to organize and train allied forces. They also continued their humanitarian aid by providing medical support as well as building roads and schools. Special Forces operations proved particularly successful in Honduras, El Salvador, and Nicaragua.

Members of the 7th Special Forces Group stationed in Panama also supported Operation Just Cause to stabilize that country's government. During the operation Green Berets, designated Task Force Black, gathered intelligence and conducted surveillance. They also took a direct combat role in securing a bridge over the Pacora River where, in an intense firefight, they prevented a much larger number of Panamanian Defense Forces from reinforcing an attack against U.S. Rangers.

During the 1980s the Special Forces continued to base its primary organization around the A-Team. Other than replacing the lieutenant positions with more experienced warrant officers, the A-Team of Vietnam and the 1980s basically remains unchanged today.

Meanwhile, the Department of the Army made several changes to recognize and support the Special Forces. In June 1983 the army authorized a Special Forces tab for the left shoulder of the uniform of those who completed Green Beret training. More important, the army made Special Forces a separate career field for enlisted soldiers on October 1, 1984, and a separate branch for officers on April 9, 1987.

Prior to these actions enlisted men and officers were controlled for assignment and promotions by their original branch, such as infantry, engineers, or medical. Now instead of an A-Team composed of as many as half a dozen or more occupational specialties, each Green Beret, officer and enlisted alike, carries the career management field number of 18. A letter following the number indicates the soldier's specific skill and rank within the 18 Special Forces field.

In addition to providing a separate occupation number for Special Forces, the Department of the Army also authorized the crossed-arrows collar insignia first used by the Indian Scouts in the nineteenth century. Officers and enlisted men who had previously worn the insignia of their original branch now had their own.

During the expansion of the Special Forces in the 1980s, the Green Beret chain of command recognized that a high dropout rate during training was wasting time and resources. After a two-year study Special Forces refined its list of prerequisites for volunteers and organized a three-week assessment course to test the physical and mental condition of candidates.

The fairly simple prerequisites remain in effect today. Volunteers must be male, have a high school diploma or GED, score above average on general intelligence and physical fitness tests, and carry no record of any court-martial or drug-related offense. Enlisted applicants must be in the grade of E-4 or above and officers at the rank of captain or on the captain's promotion list. Each of these ranks normally takes about two years to achieve, eliminating the acceptance of new recruits* and officers. Recruiting bulletins summarize, "Special Forces candidates must be mature and self-

---

* In January 2002 Special Forces, because of recruiting shortfalls, for the first time began accepting men directly from basic training.

motivated; open and humble, particularly with other races and cultures; and better conditioned physically and emotionally than the average soldier. We are looking for NCOs who are a little more aggressive and independent, but able to work well within a small, cohesive team."

In 1989 the Green Berets formally adopted an assessment course for volunteers that, with a few changes, remains in effect today. The Special Forces Assessment and Selection (SFAS) is a twenty-three-day exercise that tests the physical and mental abilities of candidates to see if they are capable of passing the Qualification Course and becoming productive members of an A-Team. During Phase 1 of SFAS, candidates must pass the standard Army physical training (PT) test and a battery of emotional and psychological exams. Phase II concentrates on physical strength, including forced marches, obstacle courses, swimming, and land navigation. Phase III focuses on leadership skills and judges the abilities of each candidate to solve problems, organize, motivate subordinates, and work as a member of a team.

SFAS places the candidate under constant physical and mental pressure to determine how the soldier reacts under stress. One of these tests simulates the rescue of injured downed pilots by requiring a team of candidates to carry two sand-filled duffel bags for more than six miles.

Boards made up of SFAS staff meet after Phases I and II to determine who continues the assessment, and then another board screens each class at the end of Phase III to decide who advances to the Qualification Course. Only about half of each class continues to the actual course.

Officers and enlisted soldiers who pass SFAS must then complete airborne training if they are not already parachute-qualified. They then report to the Special Forces Qualification Course, or Q Course, for training that lasts a year or more. During the first phase of the Q Course officers and enlisted men hone their skills in leadership, land navigation, and patrolling. In Phase II the officers separate for fifteen weeks of indoctrination in Special Forces missions, operations, and specialty skills. Enlisted soldiers divide into their specialty areas, with weapons and engineer sergeants attending thirteen weeks of classes, while communications NCOs go for twenty-one weeks. Medical personnel receive forty-five weeks of additional training.

Special Forces weapons sergeants master all U.S. rifles, pistols, and machine guns as well as weapons from foreign nations. They also train in operating mortar sections and acting as forward artillery observers. Engineer sergeants learn how to build and to destroy bridges, fortifications, and buildings as well as how to arm and disarm more than fifty U.S. and foreign mines. Communications sergeants learn all the current army commo equipment, including clear and scrambled coding systems and satellite communications and digital systems. Each team's communications personnel become capable of maintaining contact with their forward observation base from anywhere in the world.

Special Forces medical sergeants receive the longest and most detailed training. In addition to classroom and hospital training, they spend at least four weeks as ambulance crew members in high-trauma-rate cities including Chicago and New York. Medics perform an additional four-week period as interns at a public health agency. Upon completion of their training, a Special Forces medical sergeant is fully qualified as a civilian emergency room assistant or paramedic.

Upon completion of the first two phases of the Q Course the candidates are reunited at Fort Bragg, where they plan and execute actual missions under circumstances as realistic as possible. After a final three-week exercise is held in the Uwharrie National Forest in central North Carolina, called Operation Robin Sage, the staff evaluates the students on their individual and common skills and their teamwork.

Upon successful completion of Robin Sage, the candidates receive their Special Forces tabs and their green berets. They are then assigned to a specific Special Forces group. Before reporting, however, each new Special Forces soldier must attend language training that lasts up to six months. Specific languages required depend on the area of responsibility of the group to which the soldier is to be assigned.

Training does not end when a Green Beret reports to his A-Team. In fact, training is never-ending for the Special Forces—they constantly practice their specific skills while also cross-training in those of their team members. Opportunities are also available for acquiring additional individual skills at schools that specialize in water operations, diving, sniping, high-altitude low-opening (HALO) parachute operations, Pathfinder operations, and escape and evasion.

Exceptional Special Forces NCOs may volunteer for warrant officer status. Those accepted attend the army's warrant officer training program and then return to Fort Bragg for the eighteen-week Special Forces Warrant Officer Basic Course, where they learn additional leadership and management skills. Upon completion of the course they are reassigned to A-Teams as executive officers.

These direct training programs and the coordination of specialized schools operated under the U.S. Army 1st Special Operations Command until November 27, 1990, when the unit was redesignated the U.S. Army Special Forces Command (USASFC). From that date to the present, the USASFC has been responsible for training, validating, and preparing Green Berets to deploy and execute all operational requirements for subordinate commands around the world.

A major general (two stars) commands the USASFC that is headquartered at Fort Bragg, North Carolina. The USASFC, like the other army blood-warrior units, is subordinate to the U.S. Army Special Operations Command (USASOC), also headquartered at Fort Bragg, which is commanded by a lieutenant general (three stars).

As of the beginning of the twenty-first century the USASFC commands and controls five active duty Special Forces groups and two groups assigned to the National Guard. The 1st Special Forces Group, positioned at Fort Lewis, Washington, provides support to the Pacific and eastern Asia with one battalion detached for duty on Okinawa, Japan. The 3rd Special Forces Group, based at Fort Bragg, North Carolina, supports the Caribbean and western Africa, while the 5th Group, headquartered at Fort Campbell, Kentucky, supports southwest Asia and northeastern Africa. The 7th Group serves Central and South America from Fort Bragg, and the 10th Group supports operations in Europe and western Asia from Fort Carson, Colorado, along with a battalion stationed forward in Stuttgart, Germany. Two additional National Guard Special Forces groups—the 19th in Draper, Utah, and the 20th in Birmingham, Alabama—are also subordinate to the USASFC.

Today, as in the past, the Special Forces are unique in that they are fully deserving of the title of *blood warriors*—while at the same time they stand as the finest teachers, trainers, and nation builders in the U.S. armed forces. They are the most widely deployed of any of the elite forces, with A-Teams assigned either full time or temporarily in hot spots and remote locations around the world. No other group of American soldiers covers such a wide range of missions. Because their operations often take place in isolated locations with limited communications, the Green Berets operate with a tremendous amount of independence.

Today the Special Forces are ready to follow their creed of doing "all that their nation requires" while being prepared to "succeed in any mission, and live to succeed again." Around the globe they remain the last, best chance of many peoples to ever experience basic human rights and freedom. The blood warriors of the Green Berets remain dedicated "to free the oppressed."

CHAPTER 7

****

U.S. Army Delta Force: History

DURING the first two centuries of its independence, the United States of America had its military elites concentrate on behind-the-lines operations and special strikes against specific targets. Opponents were other military forces who generally fought as honorable soldiers battling for their cause or country. While air forces of opposing sides often indiscriminately dropped bombs and missiles, producing "collateral damage" of thousands of innocent civilians, the true blood warriors—both friendly and enemy—focused on eliminating their uniformed opponents rather than noncombatants.

Some armies, however—particularly those who could not compete on the conventional battlefield—employed terrorism to advance their cause. Sun-tzu, the Chinese writer of the epic *On War*, wrote in 500 B.C., "Kill one, terrorize a thousand." Bombings, kidnappings, and murders have long been tools of the terrorist, but only with recent advancements in communications technology have these tactics threatened world stability and security. Individuals and small terrorist groups not only wreak havoc with minimum assets, but also fill live television screens around the world to promote their cause.

During the Vietnam War, the Vietcong and their supporters from the north spread terror across the country with bombings, booby traps, and assassinations. These communists routinely tortured and murdered village leaders (and their families) thought to be supportive of the Saigon government.

They bombed public facilities and vehicles to inflict death on those near the blast and to instill fear in others.

Terrorism in Vietnam played a role in escalating the war. A lone man with a single bomb could blow up a restaurant, kill and maim a few soldiers and innocents, and be on the nightly news around the world within hours. Fanatics, despots, crazies, and loyal followers of causes—both obscure and prominent— saw that terrorism could bring attention, and even legitimacy, to their agendas. By the 1970s religious, political, and criminal groups began to bomb, hijack, and kidnap to further their objectives and philosophies. Terrorists around the world learned much from their bloody kin in Vietnam.

Ultimately, however, in a theater of more than one million uniformed combatants, it was not the terrorists who ruled the day. Conventional North Vietnamese tank and infantry units, not terrorists, broke down the gates outside the South Vietnamese government buildings.

Following the war, the U.S. military still maintained the strongest conventional force in the world, rivaled only by that of the Soviet Union. The United States also possessed a nuclear arsenal, again matched only by the Soviets, that was capable of destroying the world many times over. Yet despite this conventional and nuclear power, the U.S. had little or no ability to combat the lowly terrorist.

Throughout its history the United States has looked upon its military as a force dedicated exclusively to fighting opposing armies. Except for the occasional need for uniformed personnel to assist in time of natural disasters, Americans prefer to keep their armed forces off the streets. Using the military to maintain law and order in the civilian community goes against the fundamental ideas of freedom and democracy. Furthermore, to fight the beast of terrorism the Americans would have to act beastly themselves, and they were unwilling to assume such a role.

Prior to the 1970s the local or state police handled the occasional "mad bomber" or arsonist. In extreme emergencies, including cases of kidnapping, the Federal Bureau of Investigation (FBI) provided assistance or took over the cases. Outside the United States, individual Americans and businesses had to rely on the host nation for protection and law enforcement.

By the early 1970s only two countries possessed military units capable of countering terrorism: Great Britain and the state of Israel. The British Special Air Service Regiment (SAS) fought both communist guerrillas and terrorists in Malaya in the 1950s. Israelis experienced decades of fighting Arab terrorists, both before and after their creation of an independent state in 1948. In 1957 the Israelis formalized their counterterrorism efforts with the formation of Sayeret Mat'kal, also known as General Staff Recon or simply as "The Unit." A part of Sayeret Mat'kal, designated Unit 269, trained for special operations and counterterrorism outside the borders of Israel.

Despite terrorism in Malaya and Israel, the rest of the world believed that such activities could not happen within their own borders. They relied on their local police to handle incidents of kidnapping or bombing. It was not until the size of the threat overwhelmed the civilian capacity that officials, both in the United States and overseas, sought new methods to defend against terrorism. The lack of preparedness to combat dedicated terrorists came to the forefront on September 5, 1972, when eight Arabs invaded the Olympic Village in Munich and took Israeli athletes and coaches hostage. The worldwide cameras for the Olympics focused not on athletic competition but rather on hooded gunmen making demands for a free Palestine and for their own transportation out of the country.

Germany, neither able nor willing to comply with the demands, attempted a rescue with its Olympic security force. Snipers were designated to engage each of the terrorists as they attempted to board helicopters to effect their escape. At the critical moment several of the snipers either refused, or were too scared, to fire. Poor marksmanship by those who did shoot resulted in missed targets and a pitched battle. When the fight was finally over, eleven Israeli Olympians, one policeman, and five of the terrorists lay dead.

With much of the negotiations and the final battle taking place on worldwide television, many countries, including the United States, recognized the need to organize and train special units to combat this new level of terrorism, but Germany was one of the few to take any action.

The German government authorized the formation of Grenz-schutzgruppe 9 (GSG-9), a special counterterrorism unit, shortly after the failed rescue attempt. For a former Nazi country to create an elite combat unit, however, brought fierce protests from both internal and external factions. To appease these critics, the GSG-9 was subordinate to the Federal Border Police Force, which was responsible for security along the line of defenses that then separated the East and West German border, rather than to the regular army. Under the leadership of Colonel Ulrich Wegener the German commando unit officially became operational in April 1973.

Colonel Wegener and his GSG-9 commandos sought assistance in their organization and training from the British SAS as well as from the Israelis. On July 4, 1976, Wegener accompanied members of Israel's Unit 269 when they assaulted a hijacked Israeli airliner being held on the tarmac of the Entebbe, Uganda, airport. The precision attack rescued the passengers and killed the terrorists with only one dead Israeli.

The GSG-9 was likewise soon to be tested. On October 13, 1977, terrorists hijacked a Lufthansa airliner with eighty-six passengers and a crew of five and demanded the release of fellow Palestinians being held in German prisons. For the next four days the aircraft landed at a series of airfields, including Rome and Cyprus. At each, the terrorists threatened to blow up the plane and its passengers if they were not refueled. By October 17 the aircraft was on the ground at the Mogadishu, Somalia, airport, where the terrorists threatened to begin executing passengers if the Germans did not meet their demands.

Unbeknownst to the terrorists, units of GSG-9 had been following the hijacked plane in an aircraft of their own during the entire ordeal. Early on the morning of October 17 the German commandos scaled the sides of the plane with special noise-muffling, rubber-covered ladders. They blew open the access doors with explosives, threw "flash-bang" grenades in the aisles, ordered the passengers to duck, and killed three of the terrorists and wounded and captured the fourth. No passengers were wounded, and only one German commando was slightly injured.

The Israeli success at Entebbe and the German rescue at Mogadishu laid the groundwork for what was to become the American Delta Force. From inception to the present, all aspects of Delta Force have remained classified. For years the U.S. Department of Defense and the U.S. Army denied that Delta even existed. Although they no longer make these denials, the U.S. military refuses today to discuss any aspects of Delta Force history, organization, training, or operations.

As a result, for many years there was only one source of information about the early days of Delta. In 1983 Colonel Charlie A. Beckwith, U.S. Army, retired, considered to be the founder of Delta, published his account of the unit in a book titled *Delta Force: The U.S. Counter-Terrorist Unit and the Iran Hostage Rescue Mission*. While he used the book to settle many old scores with fellow officers and politicians, and despite the arrogance and oversized ego that come through on almost every page, the book, until recently, was the single source on the origins of Delta and provided the most extensive inside view of the unit's early years. That changed with the publication of *Inside Delta Force: The Story of America's Elite Counterterrorism Unit* (Delacorte Press), by Eric L. Haney, which came out in 2002. Haney gives a detailed firsthand account from a soldier's perspective in Delta Force and his book is a welcome addition to Beckwith's.

"Chargin' Charlie" Beckwith was the first to voice a need for a counterterrorism unit and dedicated much of his career to its authorization and formation. Although Delta, or something like it, would have surely appeared sooner or later, Beckwith's role was critical. For the first four years of its existence, Delta Force and "Chargin' Charlie" were very much one and the same.

Beckwith had ten years in uniform and had served with the Special Forces in Laos in 1960 when the Department of the Army selected him for an officer exchange program with the British SAS in 1962. Shortly after joining the SAS as a company commander, Beckwith realized that their abilities in executing special operations were missing in the U.S. Army. In his book he later recalled his reaction: "I thought, God, this is what we ought to do at home."

Beckwith deployed with the SAS to Malaya, where he confirmed his beliefs in the need for elite units other than Special Forces to combat guerrillas and terrorists. Beckwith later wrote, "I felt the U.S. Army needed a unit that could do what the SAS could do. It needed to be able to go out in small patrols and blow up bridges and dams and railroad lines, to take out an enemy commander, say, like Rommel, to collect information for air strikes or for attacks made by conventional forces. The American army not only needed a Special Forces capability, but an SAS one; not only a force of teachers, but a force of doers."

Beckwith returned to Fort Bragg, North Carolina, after his tour with the SAS with a written report recommending that the U.S. Army organize a unit along the lines of the SAS as soon as possible. By the fall of 1963 the report had made the rounds of Special Forces commanders and found few supporters. Beckwith continued to hone his report and added a proposed organization and equipment list. He forwarded copies to the combat development section at the Department of the Army and even went outside his chain of command by mailing a copy of the report to a senator from his home state of Georgia. All of these efforts accomplished little except to gain Beckwith a reputation as a loose cannon. Some of his fellow officers even referred to him as "Crazy Charlie" instead of "Chargin' Charlie."

Despite his reputation, Beckwith was selected to attend the Command and General Staff College at Fort Leavenworth, Kansas, in 1964. One of the school's requirements was a term paper. Beckwith updated his report and gave it a new title: "The Need to Organize in the United States Army—A Special Operations Force." The academics at Fort Leavenworth were no more impressed than the rest of the army with the idea and awarded Beckwith only an average grade.

Following graduation in 1965, Beckwith put aside his lobbying for a special operations force and volunteered for Vietnam with the 5th Special Forces Group. Upon his arrival he assumed command of the Delta Project, Detachment 52. Beckwith found the project's team members living well and doing little in Nha Trang. He quickly reduced his command from thirty to seven, keeping only those who preferred to fight in the jungle rather than sit on the resort beaches of the South China Sea. Beckwith added other volunteers and was soon conducting long-range patrols into enemy-held territory. He consolidated his teams to reinforce threatened Special Forces outposts when needed.

While Beckwith gained much experience and had the chance to try out many of his theories of counterguerrilla warfare, his Delta Project resembled the later Long Range Reconnaissance Patrol (LRRP) units more than the future Delta Force. Even the name of the Vietnam unit was unrelated—it came from a series of units within Special Forces known as the Greek projects, including Omega and Sigma.

Beckwith did, however, establish and refine many of the recruiting methods he would find useful in the Delta Force. While seeking men for his Vietnam unit, he issued a flyer that stated, "Wanted: Volunteers for Project Delta. Will guarantee you a medal, a body bag, or both." During his tour with Delta, Beckwith made both friends and enemies with officers who would be making decisions about the army's future organization.

A .51-caliber gunshot to the stomach ended Beckwith's tour, and he was evacuated to the States. After his recovery, he assumed command of the Florida Phase of the U.S. Army Ranger School at Eglin Air Force Base in northwest Florida, where he changed the training from a conventional warfare orientation to one tailored to the Vietnam conflict. Beckwith also worked on a proposal for the organization of a Ranger battalion along the lines of the SAS, but again he found little support.

In February 1968 Beckwith served a second tour in Vietnam as a lieutenant colonel in command of an infantry battalion in the 101st Airborne Division. He then joined the Pacific Command headquarters in Hawaii and, upon completion of the assignment, remained in Honolulu to complete his bachelor's degree. In 1973 he joined the Joint Casualty Resolution Center (JCRC) in Thailand to assist in recovering the remains of American servicemen missing in Vietnam. His boss at the JCRC was Brigadier General Robert Kingston, a fellow veteran of the SAS exchange program.

While in Thailand, Beckwith was passed over for promotion to full colonel. He returned to Fort Bragg with limited opportunities for future command and the lingering tag as a loose cannon. After a year's hard work, however, he was promoted and appointed the commandant of the Special Forces School. His fortunes became even better when Bob Kingston took command of the entire school and center.

Beckwith had pretty much given up on his idea of a special operations unit until late in 1975. Kingston, with no forewarning, approached Beckwith and ordered him to put together a concept for a unit based on the SAS. "Chargin' Charlie" quickly revised his old papers, and within weeks Kingston was discussing the idea with a friend, Lieutenant General Edward C. "Shy" Meyer, the army's operations officer. Many within and outside the military considered Meyer to be the most brilliant man in uniform, and his support of the concept would be critical to its success.

The post-Vietnam army, however, moved slowly. Money

and manpower were in short supply, and a new unit, which would be expensive and would draw the best leaders away from conventional units, was not something that would be quickly accepted. In August 1976 Kingston and Beckwith presented the special unit concept to a conference of senior leaders at Fort Benning, Georgia, chaired by General William DePuy, the army's training and doctrine commander. DePuy liked the idea and remarked that the army should have been listening to Beckwith's idea much earlier. DePuy's approval brought others on board, and by the end of the conference there was a general agreement that the army needed a capability similar to that of the SAS.

Nevertheless, the senior leadership in the Pentagon had to be convinced. DePuy, in response to the world political and military situation, required that the counterterrorism concept emphasize the unit's missions of freeing hostages in buildings or from hijacked aircraft, operating in periods of darkness or low visibility, and dressing in civilian clothing if necessary.

Planning continued into 1977 until DePuy finally was satisfied with the plan. At the end of one of the briefings, he asked, "By the way, what should we call the unit?"

Beckwith immediately responded, "Delta. Call it 1st Special Operational Detachment—Delta." He then explained that the Special Forces had A-Teams led by captains, B-Teams commanded by majors, and C-Teams commanded by lieutenant colonels. Beckwith then said, "Why not have a D detachment commanded by a full colonel?" Although the SAS was commanded by a lieutenant colonel, Colonel Beckwith not only wanted the unit authorized, but also wanted to be its first commander. DePuy concurred with the name and command rank.

The next step in gaining authorization for the Delta Detachment was through the Fort McPherson, Georgia, Forces Command (FORSCOM) headquarters that commanded all regular army units within the United States. Several senior officers at FORSCOM opposed the formation of Delta, saying it would merely duplicate the Ranger battalions. They also noted that there were only so many "special" soldiers to go around and that Delta would draw much-needed leaders away from the Rangers and the regular army.

Beckwith countered that while the Rangers were primarily young soldiers trained for commando-type raids, his Delta Force would be mature professionals. He added his most important selling point when he told them that Delta would be the army's only unit focused on counterterrorism. This latter point sold the concept to most of the FORSCOM staff. Although several officers remained protective of the Rangers, Beckwith convinced the FORSCOM commander, General Frederick Kroesen, to support the concept.

On June 2, 1977, DePuy, Kingston, and Beckwith briefed the Army Chief of Staff General Bernard W. Rogers. "Shy" Meyer sat in on the meeting and continued to be Delta's most enthusiastic senior supporter. While Rogers admitted a void in counterterrorism capability, he voiced concerns about the cost in men and money of such a unit. By the end of the meeting, Rogers agreed with the basic concept but directed that Meyer determine how the unit could be put together and, more important, how much it would cost.

After the meeting Meyer directed Beckwith to submit a budget and a Table of Organization and Equipment (TO&E) within ten days. Beckwith returned to Bragg thinking that Delta was about to become a reality.

He was wrong. Kingston, one of Beckwith's and Delta's biggest and most powerful supporters, was leaving Bragg for command in Korea. His replacement, Major General Jack Mackmull, did not share his predecessor's enthusiasm for Delta or Beckwith. Many on Mackmull's staff believed that the Special Forces could and should handle all of the proposed Delta missions.

Mackmull told Beckwith that he thought that Delta was "too expensive," but since he had little choice, he allowed the colonel to follow Rogers's order to deliver a budget and TO&E to Meyer. Beckwith dusted off his old plans, revised them, delivered the documents to Meyer, and returned to Bragg to wait—and wait. Weeks, then months passed with no response from the Pentagon. The reason was simple. The U.S. Army in the mid-1970s faced post-Vietnam reductions in budget and personnel. Some finances previously available for operations had been diverted to recruitment to make up for the elimination of the draft and the shift to an all-volunteer force. The army, like the civilian community it represented, was also experiencing difficulties in race relations and drug use.

Beckwith, impatient as ever, bypassed his boss at Fort Bragg, and in August wrote directly to General Meyer at the Pentagon. Meyer, the strongest Delta backer on the army staff, was finally able to push the concept through the Pentagon bureaucracy. In mid-September Meyer summoned Beckwith to the Pentagon and ordered him to begin plans for acquisition of spaces and money. Because the army was officially limited in both areas, Beckwith would have to take men and dollars away from other units and programs. No new assets would be made available.

Over the next month Beckwith spent most of his time in Washington working with Pentagon personnel and budget offices. Assisted by a small staff provided by Meyer, he wrote decision paper after decision paper and presented countless briefings.

Beckwith returned to Bragg to secure a location for the budding Delta Force. He considered several sites but quickly settled on the Fort Bragg stockade, which had recently been abandoned, its prisoners transferred elsewhere. The nine-acre prison compound, located in an isolated part of the post, came complete with concrete buildings and a double chain-link fence topped with barbed wire. Its maximum-security cells also provided excellent ammunition and weapons storage areas.

One of Beckwith's first improvements to the stockade was the addition of a large rose garden on both sides of the entrance to his new headquarters. Beckwith was partial to roses and thought that the flowers lent a bit of class to a unit that would be performing dark and bloody operations.

Progress slowly continued until the middle of October. Beckwith was back in the Pentagon working on funding when news of the GSG-9 rescue of its plane and passengers in Somalia on October 15, 1977, hit the news. General Rogers received a note from President Jimmy Carter asking if the United States had anything like the West German counterterrorism unit. After much discussion among the army staff, the only agreement they came to was that no one wanted to tell the president that the U.S. did not have such an organization.

While the United States did not have an active counterterrorism unit, it did, however, have the approved concept for Delta Force. Motivated by the GSG-9 rescue—and the president's note—Rogers became more enthusiastic in his support for Delta. On November 19, 1977, Delta received its official orders of activation, which opened the door for Beckwith to acquire both money and men. Beckwith was ecstatic, but he was also aware that it would take at least two years to create, equip, and train an efficient force.

In addition to the time required to prepare a unit like Delta Force, Beckwith faced other problems. General Mackmull, concerned that his Special Forces might also be called upon to counter terrorism threats and also looking to maintain as much power within his command as possible, directed Colonel Bob Mountel to form a similar unit.

Over the next few months Beckwith's Delta and Mountel's unit, which became known as Project Blue Light, competed for men and assets. Beckwith appealed to Rogers and Meyer for support and clarification of Delta's mission and priorities. On March 8, 1978, Beckwith briefed Rogers on the difficulties he was having with the Special Forces Command.

Three days later General Meyer flew to Fort Bragg and met with Mackmull, Beckwith, and other involved commanders. Meyer began the meeting by informing the attendees that he had the power to fire anyone who disagreed with the decisions he was about to present. He then drew an organization diagram on a large piece of paper that showed Mackmull's Special Forces subordinate to the Department of the Army and the Delta Force subordinate to the Special Forces command. Meyer then drew a curved line connecting Delta to the Department of the Army and explained that Beckwith could go directly to him and Rogers if he came to an impasse with Mackmull's command. While this meant that Special Forces was responsible for maintaining and caring for Delta, Beckwith was given the authorization to bypass Mackmull and go directly to the top. In essence it meant that Delta now worked for Rogers and Meyer.

Mackmull had no choice but to accept the decision and made the best peace possible with Beckwith. Blue Light* disappeared, and Special Forces volunteers became available for Delta. Beckwith had well earned his title *Father of Delta*, but Meyer earned a reputation as one of its founders as well. Beckwith and his Delta operators began to refer to Meyer as "Moses" for his efforts to lead the unit through difficulties to the Promised Land of official recognition.

* Because of the secrecy of both Delta and Blue Light, and the refusal of the army to acknowledge their existence or to discuss their operations, the two special units are often confused as one. Although their original proposed missions were much the same, Blue Light was never officially recognized, nor did it perform any operations during its brief existence.

CHAPTER 8

✳✳✳✳✳✳

U.S. Army Delta Force: Today

WITH the approval of the Department of the Army, Beckwith began to organize and train Delta, or "the Unit." Much of Beckwith's original organization, policies, and procedures remain today, but from its initial formation Delta has been constantly changing and adapting to better accomplish its missions and to meet and neutralize new threats.

Beckwith copied much of the SAS organization, including the use of the term *squadron*, rather than *company* or *battalion*, for base units. The composition and strength of Delta Force have remained closely guarded secrets, but it is clear that the unit has grown and changed over the years. Beckwith began with a single squadron of about one hundred men, most of whom specialized as shooters or demolition experts known as doorbusters. The squadron was further divided into three troops composed of four-man teams that contained specialists in a wide variety of military skills such as skydiving, scuba operations, and sniping. They also possessed special attributes such as lock picking and operating civilian transportation and construction vehicles.

Over the years Delta has grown to a force of at least eight hundred individuals. The bulk are organized into three assault squadrons, designated A, B, and C, each commanded by a lieutenant colonel. During the past two decades these squadrons have varied in number from 75 to 150, with the larger figure likely their strength at the current time. As with their original organization, each squadron is broken down into troops of about twenty men led by captains or majors.

134

Since Beckwith was promoted to full colonel prior to his assumption of command of Delta, his successors have also worn the silver eagle that designates that rank. The Delta commander is supported by a staff of lieutenant colonels who head sections for personnel, intelligence, operations, and logistics.

A signal squadron that provides internal and external communications supports the three operational squadrons. An additional support squadron takes care of administrative and logistic matters. The support squadron contains a medical detachment and a selection and training element for the acquisition and preparation of replacement operators. A research and development department within the support squadron acquires and tests new weapons, equipment, and any other materials that might be useful during operations. A final part of the support squadron is the technical and electronics section, which employs the most up-to-date audio, video, and computer surveillance devices. These surveillance devices prove especially useful in monitoring terrorists' conversations and activities during hostage rescue missions.

In 1989 Delta added an aviation squadron so that it would not have to depend on other units for transportation and combat air support. These planes are frequently painted to resemble civilian aircraft, complete with fake tail numbers, when required by Delta missions. Additional aviation assets are also available from other army and air force units.

A final element of the Delta Force is the "Funny Platoon." From its initial days of organization, Delta suffered from late or even inaccurate intelligence provided by the army, the Central Intelligence Agency, and other information-gathering sources. Accurate, real-time intelligence is the key to successful hostage rescue operations, and Delta decided not to trust this critical aspect to outsiders. Its intelligence unit, or Funny Platoon, trains operatives to use false documents, disguises, and cover stories to enter other countries to gather intelligence prior to the arrival of the operations squadrons. The platoon also maintains an intelligence center at its Fort

Bragg headquarters that shares information with the CIA, the Defense Intelligence Agency, and other organizations.

The Funny Platoon is the only Delta unit that has employed female operators. During the early 1980s the platoon recruited women soldiers to infiltrate foreign countries as part of teams operating under a husband-and-wife cover. Also, women could pose as flight attendants in airplane hostage rescues. Several women were accepted into the unit and passed a modified training program. Many of the male Delta operators objected to females in their elite unit, and internal friction soon ended the mixed-gender experiment.

In the early 1990s the Delta Force once again began recruiting women for its Funny Platoon. Several were accepted, but apparently none to date have been used in actual operations.

All of these elements of Delta have evolved over the years, with constant changes in its size and structure. One of the few things that has remained fairly stable is the selection and assessment of potential members. Beckwith copied the SAS model of quietly seeking volunteers and requiring that they meet rigid standards of experience, physical fitness, and mental toughness. Then, as now, the most effective recruiting is done by word of mouth. Delta operators work extensively with Special Forces and Rangers, and when they spot talent they identify possible candidates to their superiors.

While the majority of volunteers come from the Green Berets and the Ranger battalions, the personnel detachment of the Delta support squadron actively seeks qualified personnel throughout the active army as well as the reserves and National Guard. This includes visits to units and to officer and NCO schools.

Recently the recruiting effort has become more open. Announcements now appear in print in unit and post newspapers as well as on various official Web pages. A posting on the U.S. Army Personnel Command Web page in 1999 seeking officer volunteers stated that Delta had assignment opportunities. It explained, "Delta is organized for the conduct of missions requiring rapid response with surgical applications of a wide variety of unique skills, while maintaining the lowest possible profile of U.S. involvement." Similar announcements seeking noncommissioned officers were also posted.

Delta also recruits operators from the Navy SEALs and the USMC Force Reconnaissance companies. Some of these sailors and marines receive interservice transfers to the army, while others serve a tour with Delta and then return to their original branches.

Regardless of the source, Delta recruits and accepts only the most experienced volunteers. The average Delta operator has at least ten years in uniform. Most of the NCOs are staff sergeants or above, and most of the officers are captains and majors. Few use tobacco in any form, and those who drink alcohol do so moderately. Most are married, living on post at Fort Bragg or in nearby Fayetteville neighborhoods. Their wives are provided cover stories for their husband's unit and frequent absences and join their spouses in keeping a low profile.

Generally, except for their age and experience, members of the Delta Force mirror the profile of members of the army from which they are recruited. There is one area, however, in which they differ. Delta is overwhelmingly white. African Americans have composed more than 30 percent of the total U.S. Army troop strength over the past three decades, but their presence has not been equal in Delta. While there are no official figures of the number of blacks in the unit, indicators suggest that the number does not exceed 10 percent.

Several explanations for this disparity exist, but no official response has ever been presented. Speculations range from "really is no reason" to "mathematically, some units have to have more or fewer of any one race." Still others point out that blacks as a whole are reluctant to volunteer. The first two of these explanations are ambiguous at best, and the latter is proven invalid by the fact that everyone in the armed forces is a volunteer in today's nondraft military. Also, blacks made up an above-average number of the troops in the army's only airborne division, the 82nd.

A better explanation may lie in the sociology of blacks as a whole. Black soldiers usually come from gregarious homes and neighborhoods where there is extensive interaction among families. Delta and other special operations units value men who are comfortable working alone or in small groups.

However, the most likely explanation for the low number of blacks in Delta and other elite units is the remaining vestiges of racism from the days of the segregated army. While the army as a whole is the most equal opportunity employer in the United States today, and it deals quickly and forcefully with any signs of racism, things have not always been so. "Chargin' Charlie" Beckwith, born and reared in the South, kept blacks out of the unit. Although Beckwith is long gone from Delta and today's officers are certainly more tolerant, the influence of its founder may still play a role in the racial composition of the Delta Force.

Members of all races, white, black, or other, who pass the physical exams and fitness tests report to a four-week Selection and Assessment Course. Beckwith ran the initial courses in the Uwharrie National Forest near Troy in south-central North Carolina using the SAS Training Manual as his guide. Over the years the course length has varied by a few days, and officials have adapted and changed the SAS manual to meet Delta needs. The course has also been moved to a more secure location at Camp Dawson, a former National Guard post in the Appalachian Mountains in West Virginia. Other facilities are also available for the assessment phase at Nellis Air Force Base north of Las Vegas, Nevada.

The assessment phase focuses on testing both the physical and mental strengths—and weaknesses—of the volunteers. Swim tests and speed marches of eighteen miles are the first eliminators. Each individual is then dispatched with a fifty-five-pound rucksack, a map, and a compass on a land navigation course. The volunteers receive no goals or time limits; instructors tell them to "do their best." At various checkpoints they receive additional instructions. If they take too long between checkpoints or become lost, they are dropped from the course. All the while, limited food and little sleep test the mental as well as the physical abilities of each soldier.

During and after the physical tests, instructors question potential Delta operators about what they would do in certain situations. These questions vary from queries about standard tactics and maneuvers to more general queries such as, "If you had to eliminate either your mother or father, which would you kill and why?" Other questions range from "Do you have a drinking problem?" to "Who is the greatest military leader of all time?" Rather than looking for specific answers, the instructors design their questions to see how a potential operator thinks on his feet and responds to pressure.

Candidates write autobiographies addressing their perceived strongest and weakest attributes. They write reports on military theory and practice books, including their perceptions.

The Delta chain of command and medical personnel, who assemble a psychological profile of each volunteer, evaluate all verbal and written responses. A final exam consists of an interview with the Delta commander and his subordinate squadron leaders. Individuals who are extremely physically fit and show stability, self-confidence, and the ability to think quickly are those who successfully complete the course.

Their numbers are few. Each six-month selection cycle begins with the review of about two thousand records of possible selectees. These files dwindle to two hundred to four hundred individuals who qualify for further screening, only one hundred of whom reach the Selection and Assessment phase. Of that one hundred, only ten to twelve successfully complete the course and join their squadrons for further training. This selection rate of only one-half of 1 percent is exceptional on its own. That Delta considers only the best to begin with makes the superiority of the Delta Force all the more apparent. These are truly the elite among the elite of today's American blood warriors.

Once Delta accepts a soldier, his real training begins. The

Operators Training Course lasts six months and covers all aspects of counterterrorism and covert operations. The course begins with individual training that includes such gentlemanly activities as how to dress and act to fit in while wearing civilian attire. Students also receive classes in memory enhancement, stress management, and methods of relaxation. Less gentlemanly—and more blood warrior—training follows, with classes in demolitions, operation of all kinds of civilian and military vehicles, and escape and evasion. Extensive training in communications and field medicine are also part of the course.

Once students master these general skills, the Delta recruits move on to what makes the unit unique. For nine weeks the new operators practice "assault and rescue operations." They learn how to enter buildings and rooms by silently breaking and entering or by blowing down doors and walls with explosives. They practice climbing barriers, rappelling from helicopters, crawling through mud, drilling—whatever techniques it takes to gain access to an objective—until they master them all.

Once they gain access to a target, the Delta operators practice again and again the single technique that will mean success or failure in their mission. Delta operators shoot and shoot to kill. Each new operator fires thousands of rounds from a multitude of weapons with one objective in mind—kill the bad guys and do it quickly.

Beckwith made this shoot-to-kill policy clear to U.S. political leadership before the first major mission by the newly formed Delta Force. During the planning phase for the ill-fated hostage rescue attempt in Tehran in 1980, Beckwith briefed President Jimmy Carter and his staff, telling them up front that his operators would "take out" the Iranian guards early in the operation.

Deputy Secretary of State Warren Christopher raised his eyebrows and inquired just what the colonel meant by "take them out." Beckwith responded that it meant they would "double tap" each guard—"shoot each in the head, twice."

Christopher naively asked if perhaps the Delta operators could shoot the guards in the shoulder to wound rather than kill. Beckwith replied, "No, Mister Deputy Secretary. My men have been trained to shoot them twice, in the head, and that's what they'll do."

No other part of the Operator Training Course and subsequent training is as important as the "twice in the head and dead" policy. In hostage rescue there is no time for enemy prisoners. A living terrorist can only result in dead hostages or dead Delta operators.

During its early years Delta conducted the Operator Training Course at its stockade headquarters and at various ranges on the Fort Bragg complex. In 1987 Delta moved from the former army prison to a new seventy-five-million-dollar facility at Range 19 located at the intersections of Gruber, Lambert, and Manchester Roads at the edge of the main post. In addition to command and control facilities which house the most up-to-date communications equipment, the Range 19 complex contains multitraining facilities for new recruits as well as the old hands.

Range 19 has full-scale mock-ups of various types of aircraft for antihijacking training and a full city block of various sizes and types of buildings for urban warfare practice. One area within the urban complex is the "killing house," so called because operators practice clandestine and violent entry, two shots to the head of terrorists, and hostage rescue. Another room has a panel of various locks from around the world for the operators to practice their picking skills. A large swimming pool provides an area for water training as well as relaxation for those off duty. Weight rooms, racquetball and basketball courts, and climbing walls are available to maintain physical fitness. The compound is completely self-contained with its own mess hall, dormitories for operators prepping for missions, and a small club for relaxation.

Outside the building complex at Range 19 are areas for all types of weapons, demolitions, and special training. Ranges for demolitions, sniper fire, and moving targets provide practice with every type of explosive and weapon available in the world. In addition to U.S. machine guns, submachine guns, rifles, pistols, and shotguns, the Delta operators have access to foreign as well as experimental weapons.

Delta does such an excellent job in its selection and assessment phase that few Delta recruits fail to successfully complete the Operators Training Course. Upon completion of the six-month course, they join their squadron and team. While each is a fully qualified operator, a new member is a rookie until he has completed five years with the unit. After their acceptance most Delta operators, especially the enlisted men, spend the remainder of their career with the unit. Officers frequently depart for senior military schools necessary for promotion, or fill command slots in the Rangers or with regular units. Many return after completion of these tours for additional time with Delta.

Training never ceases either for the new or the experienced Delta operator. Each member of the unit visits the firing ranges weekly or more often. It is not unusual for each operator to fire as many as five hundred rounds per day. Operators also attend courses offered by other branches of the military as well as those of allies. If required training, such as lock picking and heavy construction equipment operation, is not available within the services, Delta soldiers don civilian clothing, create a cover story, and attend civilian courses.

There is no standard authorized list of equipment for the Delta Force. Whatever they need, they get. Weapons, communications, transportation, uniforms, and anything else considered mission-essential comes through official channels—or unofficial sources, if need be. The early operators under Beckwith had to dye military uniforms and various denim trousers and cotton shirts black for night operations. Today they have access to a multitude of uniforms to fit any and every mission.

To gain entry into foreign countries the Delta soldiers

often grow their hair longer than military length and wear civilian clothing. When in uniform they rarely wear any patches or other adornments that might identify them. A small American flag sewed on one sleeve ensures that their assortment of field uniforms meet the requirements of various international military conventions on the identification of combatants. For many years Delta remained so focused on its secrecy that it did not have a unit patch. In the mid-1980s it adopted a symbol made up of a kelly-green triangle inlaid with a white bayonet or dagger. A small second gold triangle is superimposed over the dagger. The top of the dagger parts into a downward lightning bolt.

With all the expenses in equipment and manpower, it is no surprise that the U.S. political and military leadership looked to get their money's worth from the Delta Force quickly. On November 4, 1979, members of the Iranian Revolutionary Guards seized the U.S. embassy in Tehran and took fifty-three American hostages. Delta immediately began planning for a rescue that many believed would rival Israel's success at Entebbe and Germany's at Mogadishu. Instead, Delta and the United States were about to experience one of history's greatest counterterrorism failures and vastly erode America's confidence in its government and military.

Delta was well trained for the mission, but inexperienced in practical application of its skills. Bureaucracy then saddled the unit with a complicated plan that even under the best of circumstances would have required a great deal of luck to succeed. Although Beckwith commanded his Delta troops and a detachment from the Ranger battalions, the operation lacked a definitive chain of command. Beckwith had to rely on separate air force leaders for the support aircraft and refueling tankers and on a marine corps officer for helicopters for the actual assault on Tehran.

On April 24, 1980, these divergent elements rendezvoused at a site in the Iranian countryside known as Desert One. The surprise element disappeared when several civilian vehicles drove through the site on a road not mentioned by U.S. intelligence. Then several of the helicopters had mechanical difficulties, leaving an inadequate lift capacity to deliver the Delta operators to the embassy or to rescue the hostages. Beckwith, on a satellite phone to the secretary of defense and President Carter, recommended that the rescue be aborted. In the midst of all the confusion, two of the aircraft collided on the ground, killing eight men. The next day worldwide television showed jubilant Iranians posing with the destroyed aircraft, abandoned equipment—and dead Americans.

Delta had failed in its first mission, but many important lessons came from the disaster in the desert. Bringing together special assets and elites who did not train together and share the same chain of command could only result in failure. The dust had barely settled on Desert One before U.S. leaders began plans for a Special Operations Command that, after much debate and interservice fighting, was formally activated on June 1, 1987.

Beckwith took much of the blame for the failure in the Iranian desert before he left Delta and retired from the army in 1981. Prior to the colonel's departure, however, General "Shy" Meyer, now the army's chief of staff, had Beckwith sit down and write a document titled "Tasks, Conditions and Standards for Delta." This bible of Delta organization and operations, known within the unit as the Black Book, provided the first recorded doctrine for Delta. Previously Beckwith and his staff had avoided written policies and documents. During training, recruits received handouts that they returned upon the completion of each exercise. Beckwith knew that written materials might easily be leaked to the media or, even worse, to potential adversaries. Meyer's objective in reversing this policy was to ensure that Beckwith's replacement and future commanders would not have to reinvent what had already been perfected.

After leaving Delta, Beckwith ran SAS of Texas, a security consulting firm based in Austin, Texas, until his death of natural causes in 1994. Beckwith's revelations in his 1983 book remain today the best, and in many areas the only, source of information on the early developments of the Delta Force. Other members, before and since, have maintained the secrecy that surrounds the unit. Until recently, the Department of Defense has denied the existence of the elite force and has struck any mention of Delta from official and unofficial documents. These denials have recently eased, but the military, while not denying the existence of Delta, refuses to discuss any aspect of its history, organization, or operations.

Even though Delta has been able to maintain a veil of secrecy over its official organization and operations, it has become one of the best known and most talked about of the blood-warrior elites. In 1985 Lee Marvin and Chuck Norris appeared in a feature film titled *Delta Force* about the rescue of an airliner hijacked by terrorists. Five years later Norris appeared in a sequel and has since made a career of portraying a Delta operative. Additional movies, TV shows, and novels have filled the screens and bookshelves about the ultrasecret unit. Computer games based on and named after the Delta Force are among the most popular electronic combat programs available to wannabe gamers of all ages. Manufacturers also have filled the toy stores with dolls and action figures modeled after Delta operators. A quick check on any of the major Internet search engines today reveals nearly three hundred thousand separate hits when looking for the term *Delta Force*.

Despite the compromise of much of its secrecy and its failure at Desert One, there remained a compelling reason to continue the unit's operations. Terrorist bombings, airplane hijackings, and kidnappings increased worldwide during the 1980s and into the 1990s. The U.S. political and military leadership remained unsure how to use the elite blood warriors, but they were well aware that a need existed for their unique skills.

A little more than two years after the disaster in the desert, the Delta Force participated in Operation Urgent Fury to stabilize the government of the Caribbean island of Grenada.

Delta Teams freed several hostages from the island's Richmond Hill Prison and participated in securing an airfield and several other key installations. Much of the Delta action in the liberation remains classified, but it is known that at least eleven operators were injured in a helicopter crash.

During and after Operation Urgent Fury the Delta Force also engaged another enemy—this one an internal foe from various army and government auditing agencies. The secret nature of Delta operations and their budget gave certain members of the unit a virtual license to steal, and, unfortunately, some took advantage of the opportunity. Although Delta had a legitimate need for a wide assortment of weapons and support gear, it was difficult to explain expenditures to the auditor for hot-air balloons and luxury automobiles. Even more difficult to justify was the transfer of tens of thousands of dollars of operational funds to private accounts or front companies. When the investigation finally concluded, several Delta operators transferred to other units, some were cashiered from the service, and at least two officers served short terms in military prison.

The vast majority of the Delta officers and operators during this time, however, continued to train hard and maintain the utmost degree of professionalism, loyalty, and honesty. In the latter part of the 1980s they provided security advice for several international sporting events and deployed—but took no direct action—during several airplane hijackings in Europe and the Mideast.

In 1989 Delta Teams rescued an American hostage from a Panama City, Panama, jail but failed in their attempt to capture that country's rogue leader Manuel Noriega during Operation Just Cause. Two years later Delta teams deployed behind enemy lines to locate Scud missile sites during Operation Desert Storm.

It is also likely that at least one Delta team was at Waco, Texas, in 1990 during the Justice Department siege of the Branch Davidian compound. By law neither Delta nor any other regular military unit can participate in police actions within the borders of the United States. Although the alternative press has made much of the presence of the Delta operators at Waco, there is no reasonable evidence that they did anything more than observe and possibly lend advice.

Delta Force participated in another ill-fated operation in 1993 when members assisted a Ranger unit in attempting to capture a Somalian warlord and his lieutenants in Mogadishu. Plagued with a poor plan, a lack of armored support, and thousands of armed Somalians, the Delta Teams and Rangers had to fight their way out of the city. In a running battle that lasted more than twelve hours, eighteen Delta operators and Rangers were killed and another seventy-six wounded.

During the fight the Somalian rebels shot down an American helicopter. Two Delta operators, Master Sergeant Gary I. Gordon of Lincoln, Maine, and Sergeant First Class Randall D. Shughart of Newville, Pennsylvania, volunteered to be inserted by another helicopter to secure the crash site and any survivors. Using their own weapons and those from the downed chopper, the two operators fought off repeated attacks by the rebel mob before eventually being overrun and killed. Both received the Medal of Honor for their actions and sacrifice.*

Since the Battle of Mogadishu, Delta operators have continued their intense training, which still includes daily visits to the various shooting ranges to practice the "two to the head" standard. For several years after their return from East Africa they primarily provided security advice for international sporting events and political summits. Individual operators also have served as bodyguards for American diplomats

---

* Details of the Battle of Mogadishu are covered in Mark Bowden's book *Black Hawk Down*, released in 1999, and the subsequent movie by the same name in 2001. Bowden also reveals some insights into Delta operations in his 2001 book *Killing Pablo*, about the demise of Colombian drug lord Pablo Escobar in 1993. Many operators, as well as others in the U.S. intelligence community, are not pleased with Bowden's revelations of classified information. Bowden's lack of personal military experience is also apparent in his writings and demeanor.

during overseas meetings. Delta Teams also served in Bosnia, Kosovo, and Serbia during the recent peacekeeping missions.

The need for an elite counterterrorism force once again came to the forefront with the attacks against the World Trade Center in New York and the Pentagon in northern Virginia on September 11, 2001. Delta Teams joined other special operations forces to fan out across Afghanistan to destroy the Taliban and bring the terrorist leader Osama bin Laden to justice. An article in the U.K. newspaper *The Times* on November 24, 2001, quoted U.S. officials as stating, "Delta Force have killed hundreds of Taliban and al-Qaeda fighters in Afghanistan." The article further explained, "Afghanistan has provided the right environment, especially because they can operate covertly and without the prying eyes of television cameras."

Delta has gained attention in American newspapers as well during the operations in Afghanistan. An article in the semiofficial, government-funded newspaper *Stars and Stripes* on October 17, 2001, described the unit as "Elite. Daring. Covert. Super secret." It called them the "most feared and least known" force in the military. The article stated, "You don't get much better than Delta Force," and concluded, "The less that's known about them—and how they do their jobs—the better."

The September 11 attack on the United States has brought the realization to the American public that terrorism is a real threat at home as well as abroad. No country today can match the economic and military power of the United States in its position as the single world power. Its enemies, however, are many, and terrorism remains their most effective weapon. While Delta does its best to maintain secrecy, the fact is well known that it is at the tip of the blood-warrior spear. Wherever terrorism occurs, Delta will respond.

CHAPTER 9

****

U.S. Navy SEALs: History

NATIONS are unable to project power very far beyond their own borders without a viable naval force. Security of sea-lanes is critical for the delivery of troops and the supplies to maintain operations. Ships also provide excellent platforms for gun- or missile-delivered munitions against enemy targets. Below the surface, submarines have proven their worth in disrupting enemy shipping and in providing a delivery system for conventional and nuclear weapons.

While critical to a country's security, naval operations have remained a fairly "clean" method of warfare throughout modern history. Shells, torpedoes, rockets, and missiles are certainly lethal, but they kill from afar. Gunners who fire them do not remotely meet the characteristics of blood warriors. Even in the early days of ship-to-ship boarding operations, the sailors manned their vessels while specially trained marines went over the side to fight with cutlass and pistol. Camouflage uniforms and face paint are standard with the real blood warriors, while white uniforms are the standard in most of the world's navies.

Despite their clean uniforms, officer wardrooms, and even ice cream bars for the crews, the U.S. Navy does have a small cell of blood warriors who know and understand the techniques of killing up close and personal. Members of the navy's Sea, Air, Land (SEAL) units are among the world's best-trained blood warriors.

Unlike the army's Rangers and Special Forces, which can trace their lineage back to pre–Revolutionary War, the navy's

SEALs are a relatively recent development in the ranks of blood warriors. The navy did not formally organize the SEALs until 1962, but their predecessors within their service had been around for fully two decades, dating back to the early days of World War II.

When they finally stopped the Nazi expansion in Africa and Europe and curbed the Japanese aggression in the Pacific, the Allies began preparations to retake captured territory. To push the war into the German heartland and onto the Japanese home islands, offensives in both theaters would depend upon amphibious operations to land soldiers and marines on enemy beaches. Planners knew these beaches would be heavily defended by troops supported by concrete, steel, and wire obstacles.

The navy's responsibility extended from deep water to the high-water mark of the tide on the beaches. Since it was here that most of the obstacles were located, the navy had to prepare to breach these barriers to safely land invasion forces. To accomplish these objectives they formed a variety of units, including Scouts and Raiders, naval combat demolition units, and underwater demolition teams. While none of these early organizations still exists today, all played an important role in what would evolve into the modern SEALs.

On August 15, 1942, naval officer Phil H. Bucklew assembled a joint force of navy and army volunteers at the Amphibious Training Base in Little Creek, Virginia, to train the first unit of amphibious Scouts and Raiders. Bucklew earned the title *Father of Naval Special Warfare* as he prepared the sailors and soldiers to identify and reconnoiter their objectives, maintain positions on the designated beaches prior to the main attack, and guide the assault waves to the landing sites.

These missions, although critical, ignored an important factor for any amphibious assault. Someone would have to clear the obstacles in the water around the beach for the invasion force. In September 1942 the navy formed a seventeen-man detachment of salvage personnel to train with demolitions at

Rangers from the 75th Ranger Regiment, headquartered at Fort Benning, Georgia, fast-rope from an MH-60 Black Hawk onto the roof of a training site. After exiting the Black Hawk, they slide down the rope and then clear the building of any hostile targets. (Nancy Fischer)

During a training exercise, a Ranger fires a .50-caliber machine gun mounted on top of a Ranger Special Operations Vehicle. (Nancy Fischer)

A Ranger, firing an M-4 carbine, is backed up by a soldier firing a Carl Gustov, a reloadable antitank weapon. (Nancy Fischer)

A Special Forces soldier exits a building after clearing it. (U.S. Army Special Operations Command)

A Special Forces soldier observes direct-action drills during a joint training exercise. (S.Sgt. Amanda C. Glenn)

75th Ranger Regiment soldiers take part in a fast-rope extraction from a 160th Special Operations Aviation Regiment (Airborne) MH-60 Black Hawk helicopter. (Spc. Jon Creese, USASOC PAO)

Rangers from the 75th Ranger Regiment ride on the pods of a 160th Special Operations Aviation Regiment (Airborne) MH-6 Little Bird. (Spc. Jon Creese, USASOC PAO)

(above and right)
Students of the U.S. Army John F. Kennedy Special Warfare Center and School participate in the school's Nasty Nick obstacle course. (Spc. Jon Creese, USASOC PAO)

U.S. Army Special Forces soldiers practice urban combat techniques. (U.S. Army)

Special Forces soldiers practice hand-to-hand combat. (U.S. Army)

A U.S. Army Ranger prepares a needle for an intravenous injection. (Spc. Jon Creese, USASOC PAO)

A Special Boat Unit delivers a SEAL team to the beach. (U.S. Navy)

A SEAL team approaches the beach aboard a rubber boat. (U.S. Navy)

SEALs use a submersible vehicle for underwater transportation. (U.S. Navy)

SEALs train in the mud as well as in the water and air. (U.S. Navy)

SEALs exiting an aircraft using high-altitude low-opening parachute techniques. (U.S. Navy)

Air Force combat controllers often accompany their fellow army and navy blood warriors into battle. (U.S. Air Force)

An Air Force Special Tactics pararescueman establishes perimeter security for a casualty evacuation point. (U.S. Air Force)

Little Creek. Neither the Scout/Raiders nor the demolition men had much time to train for their first mission, which was the planned invasion of North Africa. Fortunately for them—and the invasion force—the Axis likewise had little time to prepare beach defenses while they focused on fighting the British forces already in the theater.

Both teams did, however, accomplish their missions. The Scout/Raiders provided guides on the beach, while the demolition teams cut a cable and net barrier that crossed the Wadi Sebou River in Morocco. This demolition allowed the USS *Dallas* to traverse the river and deliver U.S. Army Rangers to Kenitra, where they secured the Port Lyautey airfield.

Naval planners realized that future invasion sites would not be so unprotected and formalized the concept of teams to clear beach obstacles. On May 7, 1943, the chief of naval operations, Ernest King, ordered Lieutenant Commander Draper L. Kauffman to establish a training center to prepare sailors to eliminate obstacles on enemy-held beaches prior to an invasion. On June 6, 1943, Kauffman began training the first members of the navy demolition teams at Fort Pierce on the east coast of Florida.

Kauffman, who would earn the title of *Father of Naval Combat Demolitions*, was well qualified for the task. After his graduation from the U.S. Naval Academy in 1933, Kauffman had worked for the United States Steamship Company until the Germans invaded France in 1940. Kauffman volunteered for the French army and served as an ambulance driver from March 1940 until he was captured by the Germans the following June. In July he escaped and made his way to England, where he joined the British navy.

Kauffman remained ashore in the United Kingdom performing as a junior officer in charge of mine and bomb disposal. By the time he resigned his commission in November 1941 and sailed to America, he had been twice decorated by both the British and French governments.

Back home in the States, Kauffman accepted an appointment as a lieutenant in the U.S. Navy Reserves and joined the

Naval Bureau of Ordnance. Within days the navy rushed Kauffman to Hawaii to defuse bombs that had not exploded in the Japanese attack on Pearl Harbor. His skillful defusing and then disassembling of a five-hundred-pound bomb earned him the Navy Cross as well as provided the navy valuable intelligence information on Japanese ordnance manufacturing techniques. For the next two years Kauffman assisted the navy and the army in establishing bomb disposal training programs.

Because Kauffman's school at Fort Pierce was not fully operational before the Allies invaded Sicily on July 10, 1943, naval commanders in the theater formed a detachment of twenty-one men known as Naval Combat Demolition Unit One (NCDU1) prior to the operation, but the team had little impact. Again the Allied invasion confronted little resistance on the beaches, and the new unit acted more as a guide than a clearer of obstacles.

Training continued at Fort Pierce with volunteers from the regular navy, navy Seabee battalions, and marine raider units. From its beginnings the Fort Pierce school emphasized physical strength and endurance. In addition to mastering hydrographic beach surveys, the combat swimmers learned to use a variety of explosives to clear lanes through water and beach obstacles. The school had not yet delivered its first teams to the war zones before the need for such units became obvious with the bloody invasion of Tarawa in November 1943.

On the morning of November 20 marines left their ships for Tarawa aboard amphibious tractors and landing craft. The first wave made it to the beach despite heavy fire from Japanese infantry protected by concrete and log bunkers. When the second wave attempted to come ashore, their landing craft high-centered on a coral reef a hundred yards from the beach. Japanese machine gunners and rifle marksmen zeroed in on the men wading to shore in the chest-deep water. The marines eventually took the island, but many of their 990 dead and 2,300 wounded were a direct result of the lack of knowledge about the beach obstacles and tides.

With more island invasions scheduled for the Pacific and D-Day in Europe approaching, the navy leadership ordered the Fort Pierce cadre to rush their newly trained NCDU teams, originally planned as six-man units but now increased to thirteen, to both theaters' fronts. The first units assisted the landings at Kwajalein in January 1944 and again at Eniwetok a month later.

Because the Japanese built most of their defenses inland and expended few resources on beach obstacles and barriers, the NCDU teams primarily charted underwater barriers and checked beaches for suitability of landings. They also marked lanes, recommended landing positions, and reported the location of beach defenses.

The German defense of Fortress Europe differed in that the Nazis planned to meet the invasion on the beach and to push it back into the sea. Hundreds of miles of steel, concrete, and wire obstacles, supported by mines in the water and on the beach, stretched along the entire French coastline. Interlocking machine-gun fire, mortars, and artillery covered the beach obstacles.

The Fort Pierce school deployed NCDU teams in April 1944 to assist in preparation for the amphibious attack at Normandy. Because of the extensive defenses and obstacles on the Normandy beaches, a twenty-six-man detachment of army combat engineers joined each thirteen-man NCDU team. On June 6, 1944, the NCDUs and the army engineers led the American infantry divisions onto the Normandy shore at Utah and Omaha Beaches.

Each team was responsible for clearing a fifty-yard-wide path through the defenses. At Omaha the demolition teams faced concentrated obstacles, mines, and heavy German machine-gun and small-arms fire. Despite the nearly overwhelming opposition, the teams fully cleared eight paths and partially opened two more. They paid a high price for their performance, however, as they suffered thirty-one dead and sixty wounded—a casualty rate of more than 50 percent.

The NCDUs at Utah Beach met less enemy fire and fewer obstacles. They cleared seven hundred yards of beachfront during the first two hours of the invasion and another nine hundred yards by early afternoon. Casualties at Utah were significantly lower than on Omaha, with six killed and eleven wounded. The teams were extremely proud of their performance on both beaches and were also quick to note that all of their casualties were sustained by enemy action. Not a single man was injured by the improper handling of explosives.

The NCDU survivors from Omaha Beach returned to Fort Pierce shortly after the invasion to pass along their experiences to those still in training. Teams from Utah Beach assisted in a minor amphibious landing in southern France in August 1944 before also returning to Florida.

Now that the Allies had a foothold on mainland Europe, there was no longer a need for amphibious assaults in that theater. The NCDUs turned their full attention onto the Pacific area of operations. Along with the normal evolution and education of the teams, two major changes took place. The large number of casualties suffered by the teams on the Normandy beaches showed that teams that went near shore by boat and then walked through the surf to their objectives were extremely vulnerable. Normandy was the last invasion for these "walking" teams. All future operations would begin with teams maintaining a low profile as they swam ashore.

The second change was in the combat swimmers' name. As the teams reoriented from the Atlantic to the Pacific and from "walkers" to "swimmers," the NCDUs became underwater demolition teams (UDTs). After the disaster at Tarawa the Pacific naval leaders established a UDT training center for 30 officers and 150 enlisted men at Waimanalo, Hawaii. This initial group provided two teams for the invasion of the Marshall Islands on January 31, 1944. When Commander Kauffman and his NCDUs departed Florida for the Pacific, they joined UDTs that were already operating in the theater.

In February 1944 the UDT center moved to Kihei, Maui, next to the Kamaole Amphibious Base. The NCDUs joined them there and assumed the name *UDTs*. During this period the operational swimmers of the Office of Strategic Services (OSS) also assisted the newly formed UDTs. The OSS swimmers began training in California at Camp Pendleton and Catalina Island in November 1943 before moving to the Bahama Islands the following March.

Although only half a dozen OSS swimmers ever actually participated in combat missions with the UDTs in the Pacific, they did make significant contributions in equipment. The OSS had perfected flexible swim fins, or flippers, that attached to a swimmer's feet, greatly adding to the propulsion of each leg kick. Fins allowed a swimmer to propel himself with leg action alone, leaving his hands free to carry and use navigation or sounding devices, demolitions, and weapons.

In addition, the OSS also introduced improved face masks, uniforms, and explosives. The OSS and UDTs also experimented with various underwater breathing devices. Although Frenchman Jacques Cousteau had invented the Aqua-Lung—which later became known as the Self-Contained Underwater Breathing Apparatus, or scuba—shortly before the war started, military authorities never considered the system sufficiently reliable for use in combat operations during World War II.

UDT missions, organization, and procedures changed constantly during the Pacific campaign as members adopted technology, tactics, and procedures. By late 1944 their mission had evolved to reconnaissance and clearance of areas from the six-and-a-half-fathom curve (a depth of twenty-one feet) to the high-water mark on a prospective landing beach.

The UDTs refined their preassault operations to the point that they closely resembled the operations of today's SEALs. Between twenty-four and forty-eight hours prior to the invasion, small, fast-moving boats delivered the UDTs to points about five hundred yards from the beach under the cover of darkness. The UDTs exited the boats in pairs several yards apart parallel to the shoreline and then swam toward the beach. Along the way they recorded soundings and other hydrographic data as well as any obstacles that might hinder landing craft. Once they reached the beach the teams reconnoitered possible avenues of approach, natural obstacles, and enemy defensive positions. They also gathered samples of soil from the beach to determine if it would support heavy amphibious vehicles.

After the UDTs completed their reconnaissance they crept back into the water, swam out to pickup points, and boarded high-speed boats to return to the main fleet to deliver their information. Their mission, however, was far from complete. Just prior to the actual invasion the UDTs reboarded their boats and headed back toward the beach. Again they swam the last quarter mile, but this time they each carried forty or more pounds of explosives and detonators. They fixed these to underwater and shore obstacles and "daisy-chained" them with detonator cord so they could be blown simultaneously. The swimmers also emplaced buoys and lights to guide the marines ashore. When their work was done the UDTs once again swam back to sea for pickup.

From their inception in early 1944 until the end of the war in the Pacific, the UDTs participated in every major amphibious assault, including Saipan, Guam, Tinian, Angaur, Ulithi, Leyte, Ligayen Gulf, Zambales, Iwo Jima, Okinawa, Labuan, and Brunei Bay. They saw their last combat of the war at Balikpapan on Borneo on July 4, 1945.

Far fewer combat swimmers were killed or wounded in the Pacific than were lost on the bloody beaches of Normandy. Three main factors contributed to their good fortunes—they swam instead of walked ashore, they faced few Japanese emplaced obstacles, and they planned precisely and trained diligently. Fewer than 1 percent of the combat swimmers became casualties, and some of those were the result of Japanese attacks against their ships prior to invasions.

By the end of the war there were thirty-four operational UDTs composed of thirty-five hundred men. Because of their work, the UDTs became known in the armed forces and to their civilian admirers as frogmen. Their patch featured a wiry frog wearing a Dixie cup sailor cap cocked on one side of its head. A cigar stub in the mouth and a "Popeye" snarl completed the face, while one hand held a lit stick of explosives.

This attitude noted in their patch carried over to their work as well. Signs that announced WELCOME, COURTESY OF THE UDT frequently greeted leading waves of marine and army units assaulting beaches across the Pacific.

In a manner similar to the rest of the armed forces, the underwater demolition teams rapidly demobilized at the end of World War II. By 1946 the navy had reduced the number of UDTs to four, with two stationed on each coast of the United States. Their wartime number of one hundred men per team slipped to seven officers and forty-five enlisted men per UDT.

Although their numbers were few, the UDTs used the postwar years to refine their procedures, weapons, and equipment. When North Korea invaded South Korea on June 20, 1950, the teams deployed to the war zone. They cleared mines from harbors used to land the United Nations forces that were pouring onto the peninsula. When they completed that duty, they joined marine reconnaissance units to form a unit called the Special Operations Group that conducted raids along the North Korean coast to destroy railroad tunnels and bridges.

These demolition operations had just begun when the UDTs were recalled to do what they did best. By the end of July the North Koreans had pushed the UN forces into a defensive perimeter around Pusan on the southern tip of South Korea. UN Commander General Douglas MacArthur proposed a bold amphibious counterattack at the port of Inchon just twenty-four miles southwest of Seoul. Critics expressed concerns about the plan not only because of the distance behind the lines but also because of the extensive mudflats and tides that varied more than thirty feet at the landing site.

MacArthur, who had used many amphibious assaults in the Pacific campaign during World War II, was confident in his plan. On the morning of September 15, 1950, UDTs 1 and 3 preceded the invasion scouting the mudflats, marking clear channels, and placing beacons to guide the lead boats.

Following the successful Inchon landings, the UDTs worked with minesweepers to clear Wonsan Harbor. When two minesweepers struck mines and sank on October 12, the UDTs rescued twenty-five sailors from drowning. A day later the UDTs conducted the first U.S. combat operation using scuba gear when they went underwater to determine damages on the USS *Pledge*.

By early 1951 the UDTs had cleared the harbors and other waterways of mines and other obstacles and resumed duties "beyond the high-tide mark." The teams conducted raids against North Korean coastal positions and resumed demolition missions against enemy bridges and rail tunnels. Some team members also assisted the CIA in delivering supplies to South Korean guerrillas operating on islands along the west coast of the peninsula. These units, known as Salamander Teams, also assisted in the infiltration of agents into North Korea.

During the summer of 1952, UDTs 3 and 5 participated in Operation Fishnet, which attacked the North Korean commercial fishing fleet. The frogmen destroyed a few nets and sank some sampans. More important than the direct action, the operation added to the North Korean food shortages by forcing many fishing vessels to remain in port.

More than three hundred frogmen served with the UDTs in Korea. Their operations in mapping beaches and removing obstacles were repeats of what they had done in World War II. In Korea, however, they added the skills of inland reconnaissance and raids that would become an important part of future SEAL operations.

During the post–Korean War years the UDTs continued to experiment with various equipment and weapons to increase their capabilities. With assistance from the army, they added parachute training so they could enter target zones by air as well as by water. Most of their actual missions during this Cold War period remain classified today, but the frogmen did deploy to such trouble spots as the Dominican Republic, Lebanon, and Africa to assist in peacekeeping missions and the extraction of American citizens.

During the 1950s the United States and the Soviet Union maintained extensive nuclear forces capable of mutual self-destruction in the event of total war. While the superpowers managed to keep their nuclear weapons in check, other countries and causes around the world fought limited conventional conflicts. Groups and factions unable to carry on conventional military operations turned to guerrilla warfare to accomplish their objectives.

Some groups used both conventional and guerrilla warfare. The Vietnamese communists, or Viet Minh, employed guerrilla warfare against the occupying Japanese in World War II and then elevated their actions to conventional tactics to defeat the French at Dien Bien Phu in 1954. Shortly after the peace agreement divided Vietnam, the northern communists began guerrilla operations to topple the democratic government in the south. Eventually the conflict drew America into the longest war in its history. It also provided the proving ground for the modern SEALs and established them among the best of the blood warriors.

UDT operations in Southeast Asia were limited during the first few years after the division of Vietnam. Members of UDT 12 surveyed sites for amphibious landings south of Haiphong, North Vietnam, in support of landing craft that helped, in accordance with the peace agreements, move those in the north who opted to relocate to the south. Their next action did not occur until June 1960, when Mike Detachment of UDT 12, based in Yokosuka, Japan, sailed to Saigon aboard the USS *Okanogan*. The ten-man detachment led by Lieutenant David Del Giudice guided a flotilla of ten landing craft up the Mekong River into Laos to be used for riverine operations. The team successfully delivered the landing craft on

July 4 and flew back to Saigon and then on to their base in Japan.

Southeast Asia was not the only area where guerrilla warfare was on the increase. Fidel Castro took over Cuba in 1959 and installed a communist government only ninety miles from the U.S. shore. Castro then soundly defeated a liberation attempt by other Cubans, supported by the American CIA, at the Bay of Pigs in April 1961. Other insurgencies were ongoing in Africa and Central America.

Naval leaders realized that while their submarines had a large role in nuclear deterrence and the surface fleet dominated the world's oceans, they had few assets to oppose guerrilla operations. They were also well aware that newly elected President John F. Kennedy enthusiastically supported the advancement of the U.S. Army Special Forces, which meant counterguerrilla operations would play an important role in future U.S. military policy, as well as in budget authorizations, and naval leaders wanted to secure their part.

In early 1961 the Navy Strategic Plans Division studied how to add a counterguerrilla capacity. With support of the Plans and Policy Office, the Strategic Plans Division submitted its proposal to the chief of naval operations (CNO). The proposal recommended the formation of Sea, Air, Land teams (SEALs) that would be responsible for reconnaissance and direct action raids on targets in close proximity to bodies of water. The proposal also called upon the SEALs to develop doctrine and to test new equipment.

The CNO approved the recommendation, requiring more specific planning and budget acquisition before the SEALs could become a reality. With the buildup in Southeast Asia in mind, the planners added the additional task of providing advisers to assist friendly countries to accomplish special maritime operations. The planners recognized that their most qualified sailors for the proposed missions were in the UDTs and recommended that some of the frogmen become the first SEALs in order to conserve personnel and budget resources.

When President Kennedy signed documents on January 1,

1962, authorizing the expansion and utilization of America's counterguerrilla and unconventional warfare capabilities, the navy was well prepared. On the day of the president's signature, the navy officially established SEAL Team One on the West Coast to support the Pacific Fleet and SEAL Team Two on the East Coast as a part of the Atlantic Fleet.

Sixty members of UDTs 11 and 12 formed SEAL Team One, with David Del Giudice, the officer who had led the flotilla up the Mekong to Laos, in command. Within weeks of their activation, SEAL Team One dispatched two officers to South Vietnam to determine how the team could best support the Vietnamese government. Meanwhile, back in the States, other members of the teams spread out across the country to attend navy, marine, and army schools to acquire additional skills for their new missions.

The formation of the SEALs reduced the number of UDTs, but the frogmen still had important duties to perform. Beginning on January 4, 1962, a detachment of West Coast UDTs operating off the USS *Cook* spent three weeks gathering hydrographic and beach information on the coast at Vung Tau, Qui Nhon, Cam Ranh Bay, Nha Trang, Quang Tri, and Da Nang. The reconnaissance of the Da Nang beach proved useful when regular marine regiments came ashore in 1965.

In March 1962 advisers from SEAL Teams One and Two began six-month tours to assist the South Vietnamese navy in preparing and conducting clandestine operations. The SEAL teams also provided mobile training teams composed of one officer and nine men to advise and assist the South Vietnamese navy in training frogmen and in forming commando platoons.

SEAL training in the States and the limited adviser role in Vietnam worked well from the start. Just days before his assassination on November 22, 1963, President Kennedy wrote the chief of naval operations, Admiral David L. McDonald, "When I was in Norfolk in 1962, I noticed particularly the members of the SEAL teams. I was impressed by them as individuals and with the capability they possess as a group. As missiles assume more and more of a nuclear deterrent role and as your limited war mission grows, the need for special forces in the navy and the Marine Corps will increase."

Over the next several years the UDTs continued to conduct beach surveys while the SEALs advised the South Vietnamese navy. SEALs and UDTs also participated in operations conducted by the Studies and Observation Group (SOG) after its formation on January 16, 1964. SEALs worked with SOG until the group's deactivation on April 30, 1972.

As the war in Vietnam escalated and the number of U.S. troops increased, the need for additional special units became apparent. In February 1966 the first SEAL units deployed to Vietnam with the specific mission of taking direct action against the enemy. They established their headquarters at Nha Be south of Saigon and began operations in the multiple waterways, swamps, and jungle of the Rung Rat Special Zone. Other SEALs from Teams One and Two began rotating to Vietnam on six-month tours.

Multiple platoons made up each of the two SEAL teams. Two officers—an officer-in-charge (OIC) and a second-in-charge (2IC)—and twelve enlisted men comprised each platoon. These platoons could operate as a unit or split in half with an officer in charge of each squad.

Additional platoons soon deployed to Vietnam, where they conducted raids, ambushes, prisoner snatches, and reconnaissance missions for the remainder of the war. Their number, however, always remained small. At no time during the Vietnam conflict were there more than eight SEAL platoons in-country. Even adding those SEALs detached to SOG and as advisers to the South Vietnamese brought their total number to no more than 150 men in the war zone at any one time.

Despite their small number, the SEALs accounted well for themselves. Officially they earned an enemy count of 580, but the fog of war and the fact that the SEALs often operated deep into enemy territory did not always allow time to count corpses. Their actual number of kills was probably double or triple the official number.

Because of their training, detailed planning, and execution, the casualty rate for SEALs was relatively low. Even though they performed some of the conflict's most dangerous missions, fewer than fifty SEALs were killed in the long war. This number includes several SEALs killed while serving with SOG or as advisers. In addition to Purple Hearts, the SEALs earned three Medals of Honor, two Navy Crosses, and forty-two Silver Stars for their valor in combat with the enemy.

The last SEAL platoon departed Vietnam on December 7, 1971. A few individual SEALs remained in-country as advisers until their withdrawal in March 1973. The SEALs gained extensive experience during their long service in Vietnam, and veterans of the war returned to the States to pass along their knowledge and to train new volunteers. As with the UDTs in World War II and Korea, the SEALs used the postwar period to develop and test new concepts and equipment.

The success of the Vietcong and the North Vietnamese in Southeast Asia showed the world that guerrilla warfare, supported by terrorism, would play an important role in future conflicts. Although the United States had not been victorious, it had gained valuable experience in unconventional warfare. SEALs in particular had shown the effectiveness of small teams that were capable of entering enemy territory via the sea, air, or land. With Vietnam behind them, the SEALs faced a future in which their skills, training, and dedication would continue to be in demand.

CHAPTER 10

✷✷✷✷✷✷✷✷

U.S. Navy SEALs: Today

*D*URING the years following the Vietnam War, the SEALs, like their fellow blood warriors in the Rangers and Special Forces, faced personnel and budget cutbacks in an environment where the American public displayed little respect for anyone in uniform. The SEALs did have one great advantage over the army's elites in that the navy had remained a volunteer force throughout the conflict in Southeast Asia. While the army, and even the marine corps, had had to rely on the draft to fill their ranks during the war, the navy had the luxury of screening volunteers and accepting only the most qualified. Young men of draft age flocked to the navy recruiting offices to avoid infantry duty as a soldier or a marine despite the longer commitment.

Of course, not all sailors were looking for easy duty. Many navy recruits sought out the difficult duties aboard submarines and surface vessels, while a select few volunteered for the UDTs and SEALs. Because of the large number in the general ranks, the frogmen and SEALs never had any difficulty, even in the postwar years, in filling their teams.

While the UDTs and SEALs had no problems in securing volunteers, they did find that many naval leaders questioned their existence. Most planners believed that advancements in technology and weapons had made "over-the-beach" amphibious landings a thing of the past. Helicopters could now deliver units inland and avoid beach defenses. Maintaining the expensive frogmen and SEALs seemed extravagant. Some traditional surface and submarine officers resented the UDTs and SEALs for their arrogance and believed them to be difficult to control in conventional situations.

The navy blood warriors had far more opponents than supporters during the decade after their departure from Vietnam. Most of this time the teams trained quietly as the veterans of the war passed along their skills and experiences to new recruits. As with the Rangers and Special Forces—and later the Delta Force—the SEALs found their destiny not in the past but rather in the current world unrest and the rise of terrorism.

During the same time that the army was forming its Delta Force, the SEALs were studying their capability to field a special counterterrorism unit. On the West Coast, SEAL Team One included counterterrorism training for all of its twelve platoons. SEAL Team Two took even greater measures by dedicating two platoons to specialize in counterterrorism operations.

These platoons, known as Mobility Six, or MOB 6, began developing doctrine and training for maritime situations involving terrorism. In the aftermath of the failed Iranian hostage rescue attempt at Desert One in April 1980, the navy's leaders decided it was time to form their own elite counterterrorism unit. In a manner similar to the army eliminating Project Blue Light and giving priority to Delta, the navy disbanded MOB 6 and authorized the formation of SEAL Team Six in October 1980. Many of the MOB 6 SEALs, including their commander, joined the new team.

The next major change occurred on May 1, 1983, when the navy eliminated UDTs. With their mission mostly duplicated by the SEALs and the World War II–type amphibious assault no longer considered practical, the veteran frogmen transferred to new SEAL teams or to swimmer delivery vehicle teams (SDVTs), which later became SEAL delivery vehicle teams (SDVTs).

About this same time the twelve-man platoons used in Vietnam changed to sixteen-man units. Their mission, however, continued to be to prepare to conduct a variety of special operations in all environments. These include clandestine ground operations, waterborne reconnaissance, and direct action assaults in a maritime, littoral, or riverine environment.

SEALs and support personnel who operate and maintain special delivery vehicles (SDVs) and dry deck shelters (DDSs) comprise the SDVTs. SDVs are submersible vessels used in direct action, reconnaissance, or the delivery of SEALs to their objective areas. The DDSs maintain, launch, and recover SDVs from host submarines. This team of submarines, DDSs, and SDVs provides the most clandestine maritime delivery system in the world. While naval special warfare did not begin experimentation with submersibles until the mid-1960s, its historical roots date back to Italian and British units that used early underwater delivery systems in World War II.

Special boat (SB) units joined the SEAL force about the same time as the SDVTs. The SB units trace their lineage back to the patrol boat torpedo squadrons of World War II, which evacuated General Douglas MacArthur prior to the fall of the Philippines in 1942 and harassed Japanese shipping throughout the Pacific. In the European Theater other PT boats delivered OSS agents to the French coast in April 1944 to organize resistance prior to the Normandy invasion.

Today's special boat units are responsible for operating and maintaining a diversity of special operations ships and craft, including rigid inflatable boats and coastal patrol ships. These vessels have the mission of conducting riverine and coastal interdiction and supporting navy and joint special operations.

SEALs, SDVs, and SBs initially formed two special warfare groups, with one supporting the Pacific fleet and the other assigned to the Atlantic. When the Department of Defense activated the U.S. Special Operations Command (USSOCOM) on June 1, 1987, the navy, as ordered in the authorization documents, created the Naval Special Warfare Command (NAVSPECWARCOM) as a subordinate organization. However, the new command contained only the Naval Special

Warfare Center at Coronado, California. Naval leaders did not assign the SEALs and their supporting units to the new command because they thought these units could better serve their Pacific and Atlantic Fleets than they could USSOCOM. The fact that the majority of the USSOCOM units, as well as its commander, were from the army may have also influenced their decision.

USSOCOM leaders lobbied Secretary of Defense Caspar Weinberger, advocating that the special operations community and the country would benefit from all the elite units being under one command. Weinberger agreed, and on October 1, 1988, the SEALs and supporting units became a part of NAVSPECWARCOM subordinate to USSOCOM.

Today Naval Special Warfare Command remains at Coronado, where it supervises all SEAL training as well as subordinate operational commands. Naval Special Warfare Group One, composed of SEAL Teams One, Three, and Five, shares the Coronado port. In addition Group One commands SEAL Delivery Team One, stationed at Pearl Harbor, and other support units in the Pacific.

Also subordinate to the Special Warfare Command is Naval Special Warfare Group Two assigned to Little Creek, Virginia. Group Two heads SEAL Teams Two, Four, and Eight, along with SDV Team Two, which is also at Little Creek. Supporting units are co-located throughout the Atlantic and Caribbean. Also directly subordinate to NAVSPECWARCOM are Special Boat Squadron One at Coronado and Special Boat Squadron Two at Little Creek.

Each of the SEAL teams in the new organization retains its former area of specialization. While the six teams are generally qualified for deployment to trouble spots anywhere in the world, each focuses its preparation—including language training—on specific regions. Team One has the responsibility for preparing for operations in Southeast Asia, Team Three for the Middle East, and Team Five for South Korea. The Atlantic teams also have areas of responsibility, with

Team Two focusing on northern Europe, Team Four on South America, and Team Eight on Africa.

During the past two decades the SEAL teams have conducted operations both within and outside their specialty areas. In 1985 SEAL Team Four participated in the liberation of the Caribbean island of Grenada, where it provided a beach reconnaissance for the marines landing at Pearls airfield. SEAL Team Two assisted in Operation Just Cause in Panama, helping to destroy several boats and an airplane to prevent the escape of Panamanian leader Manuel Noriega.

SEAL teams were in the Persian Gulf prior to the war to liberate Kuwait. From 1987 to 1989 teams rotated to the Gulf to prevent the laying of mines that would disrupt shipping. Part of the teams' duty was boarding and searching Iranian ships suspected of laying mines. SEAL Teams One, Three, and Five performed several missions once the Gulf War began in 1991. In addition to clearing mines in waterways adjacent to Kuwait and keeping the shipping lanes open in the Persian Gulf, SEAL teams also neutralized several Gulf oil platforms from which Iraqi soldiers were firing on U.S. aircraft. Other teams assisted in the rescue of downed Allied pilots both on land and at sea. SEALs provided reconnaissance for the advance into Kuwait City, later escorted the U.S. ambassador to the capital, and provided security for the American embassy.

SEALs remained in Kuwait after its liberation to help rebuild the Kuwaiti navy by training special boat and commando units. They continue to operate in the region today to help enforce the U.S. embargo of Iraq.

Platoons from the teams deployed to Bosnia in 1998 to assist in the search for war criminals. Although the recent offensive against the Taliban is in landlocked Afghanistan, SEALs are working with other USSOCOM special operators in the search for bin Laden and his henchmen.

SEAL Team Six participated in most of these operations as well as in others. Information about its actions is more restricted than that of the other teams, but it is known that members of Team Six rescued and evacuated Governor Sir Paul Scoon from the communist occupiers of Grenada. They took part in the unsuccessful hunt for Noriega early in the invasion of Panama and assisted officials in Colombia's search for drug lords as early as 1990.

In 1991 SEAL Team Six helped rescue Haitian President Jean-Bertrand Aristide after he was deposed in a coup. The same year they deployed to the Persian Gulf, where they attempted unsuccessfully to capture or kill Saddam Hussein. They also worked with the other teams in Bosnia and are currently playing a key role in the war against terrorism.

The NAVSPECWARCOM also contains the Naval Special Warfare Development Group, directly subordinate to the Naval Special Warfare Command. The "Dev Group" is not a new organization but rather an evolution of SEAL Team Six. Like Delta Force, much of the history, organization, and missions of SEAL Team Six have never been made public. Apparently even its name was the result of secrecy and deception. Although there were only two active SEAL units at the time of its activation in 1980, the navy designated the new counterterrorism unit SEAL Team Six in order to confuse the Soviets and other potential adversaries about their total number.

Much of what is known about the early days of SEAL Team Six and the formation of the Delta Force comes from similar sources. Where "Chargin' Charlie" Beckwith's book *Delta Force* is the primary source of information on the army's elite counterterrorism force, a book titled *Rogue Warrior* tells much of SEAL Team Six's story.

However, while Beckwith faded from public notice after his book, the author of *Rogue Warrior*, Richard Marcinko, has managed to remain in the spotlight. Marcinko, born in 1940 in Pennsylvania mining country, quit school and enlisted in the navy in 1957. Prior to the Vietnam War he joined the UDTs and earned a commission. He then served two tours as a SEAL in Vietnam, where he received a Silver Star and four Bronze Stars with combat V for valor. Marcinko remained with the SEALs after the war and advanced through the ranks to commander. By 1980 he was in charge of SEAL Team Two at Little Creek.

In the fall of 1980 the navy ordered Marcinko to form a special counterterrorism unit within the SEALs in the aftermath of the failed rescue attempt at Desert One in Iran and as a result of increased terrorism worldwide. Marcinko formed MOB 6 with volunteers from Team Two and from men he recruited from Team One. When MOB 6 became SEAL Team Six in October 1980, Marcinko remained its commander.

Marcinko began an accelerated training program within the unit as well as sending its members to train with the army, including Delta, and with allies. Within six months Team Six was fully operational. In addition to the team's focus on foreign targets, Marcinko formed what he called Red Cell and assumed the responsibility for testing the navy's counterterrorism measures at its ports and bases.

Red Cell operatives penetrated supposedly secure weapons sites and even took base commanders and their families "hostage." No one, no matter what rank, was immune from attack by Red Cell. At one point they even planned an operation against the president's Air Force One airplane.

Red Cell revealed many flaws in naval security, but Marcinko made a large number of enemies in the process. Where many in the army had considered Beckwith a loose cannon, more than a few in the navy believed Marcinko to be a whole fleet of unstable weapons. The SEAL commander took liberties in acquiring equipment and other resources for his operations. About the same time the army was investigating the Delta Force for alleged misappropriations, naval authorities began an inquiry into SEAL Team Six. Marcinko and his supporters claimed that the navy was just out to get the controversial SEAL commander, but ample evidence surfaced for the navy to sentence him to two years at the Petersburg Federal Prison and fine him ten thousand dollars.

Shortly after his release from prison, Marcinko teamed with best-selling author John Weisman to write *Rogue War-*

rior, which hit the stands in 1992. In addition to Marcinko's personal story, the book includes details on the formation and early operations of SEAL Team Six. The book, like Marcinko himself, is "over the top" in descriptions of combat, hardship, and bravery—particularly that of the author. Despite many scenes that read more like comic books than reality, *Rogue Warrior* became a best-seller, bringing to the SEALs more publicity than that of all their previous service in Vietnam and peacetime combined.

Marcinko and Weisman have since teamed up to produce a series of novels about special operations and counter-terrorism. Although pure fiction, the books use the same first-person, "in-your-face" manner as the original and even retain *Rogue Warrior* in most of the titles. In addition to his writing and appearances on various news shows as a counter-terrorism expert, Marcinko today runs a private security firm in Alexandria, Virginia.

Although revered in some SEAL circles as an almost mythical figure, Marcinko remains out of favor with the navy's leadership. The navy changed the name of SEAL Team Six to Marine Research Facility (MARESFAC), officially to provide increased security for SEAL operators. It is reasonable to assume, however, that many navy leaders wanted to remove any vestiges that remained of the Rogue Warrior Marcinko.

MARESFAC, pronounced *marizfack*, was not a popular name with the team, and its trim, extremely fit members did not remotely resemble tenants of a research facility. Shortly after the former SEAL Team Six became subordinate to the Naval Special Warfare Command in 1988, the navy redesignated it as the Naval Special Warfare Development Group (Dev Group). While the new name is as ambiguous as its former moniker, Dev Group remains today as the designation of the navy's counterterrorism unit. References to Dev Group as SEAL Team Six, especially by the media and fans of the military, continue to the present.

Dev Group currently occupies a headquarters and training

center southeast of Norfolk at Dam Neck, Virginia, and has the mission of overseeing developments in naval special warfare. Its primary job, however, remains to be prepared to launch anywhere in the world as a part of the U.S. Special Operations Command to counter terrorism or perform whatever other mission is necessary.

The exact numbers and composition of the Dev Group remain classified. From information that is available, it appears that the group is composed of about two hundred operators supported by an administrative staff of three hundred. Boat and other water transportation is provided by the special boat units. The Dev Group has a few organic helicopters, but its primary source of air transport is assets assigned within USSOCOM.

Within the Dev Group are six teams. The Red, Gold, and Blue Teams are assault or "shooter" units. They are supported by the Gray Team, which coordinates transportation; the Black Team, handling reconnaissance and surveillance; and the Green Team, which provides training. Cells within each team focus on the recovery of downed airmen, rescue of hostages, and protection of VIPs. Specialists in such skills as sniping and diving are assigned within each cell.

The Dev Group has complete training facilities at its Dam Neck headquarters including a "kill house" and mock urban center where members can practice their assault techniques. The facility has multiple indoor and outdoor ranges where group members can practice their marksmanship. Like the Delta operators, the Dev Group members fire their weapons at least weekly and often daily.

Members of the Dev Group are experienced, career sailors. They come from the ranks of the regular SEAL teams, and there is some transfer back and forth among the teams, the SBUs, and the Dev Group.

Sailors on active duty in the navy can volunteer to become SEALs by submitting applications through their chain of command. They must pass several physical exams, have above-average aptitude scores, and be a male U.S. citizen twenty-eight years old or younger. SEALs remain one of the few parts of the navy restricted to men.

Anyone interested in joining the navy can also volunteer to become a SEAL. While recruiters can guarantee a recruit the opportunity to join the navy's blood-warrior elite, the route to actually becoming a SEAL is long and difficult. Naval volunteers who meet the physical and mental entrance requirements must first select one of the twenty-three rates or specialties accepted by the SEALs out of the one hundred enlisted programs in more than sixty career fields offered by the navy. These rates include specialties in aviation, gunnery, communications, intelligence, and logistics.

Once a recruit completes his basic and source rate training, he reports to the SEALs. Recruiters emphasize to volunteers to carefully select their rate, because that is where they will serve out their enlistment if they do not successfully complete SEAL training.

Officers come from the fleet or directly from the Naval Academy, Naval ROTC, or officer candidate school. They follow similar entrance procedures and must meet the same physical and mental requirements to volunteer for SEAL training. Those accepted participate in training on an equal basis with the enlisted volunteers. The only difference between enlisted men and officers during training is that the enlisted men must score at least 70 percent on all tasks, while officers must attain 80 percent or better. There is no rank among SEAL candidates, and all receive the same treatment during training.

Officers and those sailors within the navy whose requests are approved join those volunteers who complete their rate training and report to the Basic Underwater Demolition/SEAL training course, or BUD/S, at the Naval Amphibious Base in Coronado, California. Over the years SEAL training has changed and evolved with changes in missions and equipment. Since the first forefathers of the SEALs began their training to join Commander Draper Kauffman's naval combat demolition units in Florida in 1943, the navy has emphasized physical conditioning and mental preparation so that the SEALs make proper decisions and accomplish the mission no matter the degree of fatigue or danger.

Kauffman's standards continued among the UDTs and SEALs. Shortly after their formal organization in 1962, the SEALs began their first BUD/S classes. The training is as tough as any in the American, or any other, armed forces. The only comparable military training is the army's Ranger School. SEALs must endure nearly everything in training that the Rangers do, and must be even more proficient in or under the water.

The BUD/S students begin their training with a two-week indoctrination course. This gives the students an under-standing of the required techniques and performance standards. The first thing they learn is the course's unofficial motto, "The Only Easy Day Was Yesterday." In addition to various pass/fail swim tests, each man must complete a two-mile ocean swim with fins in less than ninety-five minutes and a four-mile run in less than thirty-two minutes.

Those who successfully complete the indoctrination move on to the First or Basic Conditioning Phase. The First Phase emphasizes physical conditioning, with longer swims and runs combined with extensive calisthenics that increase in difficulty while decreasing in time allowed. Students also become familiar with SEAL equipment and practice teamwork with small-boat drills during this phase.

The first four weeks eliminate those not completely motivated and prepare those who remain for the most difficult phase of training. Since Kauffman's NCDU school during World War II, this special naval training has included one week that makes the others seem easy. Known as Motivation Week during Kauffman's tenure and as Hell Week today, the five and a half days push SEAL recruits to their limit and often beyond.

During Hell Week the recruits sleep only four hours—not each day but for the entire week. Only the strongest and most dedicated endure as they learn to recognize their own limits and to rely on teamwork as the key to survival. Those who successfully complete Hell Week spend the last three weeks of the First Phase continuing their physical training and learning how to conduct hydrographic surveys and charts.

Upon successful completion of the First Phase, the SEAL candidates move to the seven-week-long Second or Diving Phase. Between timed swims and runs, with maximum times lowered each week, the recruits learn combat scuba techniques. This capability of all SEALs to approach objectives from beneath the sea is unique among blood-warrior training programs.

The ten-week-long Phase Three has even longer swims and runs with continually reduced maximum times. During this phase the SEAL recruits study demolitions, weapons, reconnaissance, and offensive tactics. They also cover map reading, land navigation, and rappelling. The final four weeks of Phase Three are a field exercise on San Clemente Island, where the students practice what they have learned.

Upon completion of the Third Phase each SEAL class travels to Fort Benning, Georgia, where they attend the army's Basic Airborne Course. During their third week of training, they make five parachute jumps.

The long training phases take their toll on potential SEALs. Many drop out on their own, while others leave the course because they cannot meet the minimum requirements. Only about 25 to 30 percent of each class successfully completes all the requirements. This low number is even more astounding when you consider the rigorous assessment and entrance requirements.

Graduation from BUD/S, however, does not mean a sailor is now a SEAL. After graduation enlisted men and officers join SEAL teams, where they serve a six-month probationary period. SEAL team members themselves decide whether or not a man becomes a SEAL. Only after a recruit's fellow team members approve does he receive the coveted trident SEAL badge.

By their own nature and for mission security, most SEALs—with the exception of Commander Richard Marcinko—have never sought the spotlight. Marcinko's books, as well as a few personal narratives by Vietnam-era SEALs, brought these underwater warriors to the attention of the general public. Several films have also featured SEALs in training and operations.

Publicity has brought mixed results. On the positive side, more and more young men are enlisting and volunteering to attempt to earn their trident badge. On the negative, literally thousands of wannabes and charlatans have added *SEAL* to their résumés or made great claims about their time with the navy's elite. The fake SEALs have become so prevalent that one organization of SEAL/UDT veterans estimates that there are more than fifteen thousand men, and, incredibly, at least one woman, who claim to be SEALs. Interestingly, this number of fakes exceeds the number of actual SEAL and UDT veterans, who number only about thirteen thousand—including the twenty-two hundred active duty enlisted men and officers currently serving with teams.

Today's real SEALs attract the same dedicated, motivated sailors who first formed the UDTs in World War II and served in the first teams to deploy to Vietnam, Grenada, Panama, and the Gulf. A personality survey of more than one hundred SEALs in 1999 described the typical SEALs as men who "seek excitement and dangerous environments, but are otherwise stable, calm, and rarely reckless or impulsive."

The navy has released little information thus far about SEAL operations in the war against terrorism in Afghanistan and other countries. SEALs are no doubt among the first casualties of the conflict, however, as they continue to seek and find "exciting and dangerous environments."

CHAPTER 11

✳✳✳✳✳✳✳✳

U.S. Air Force Special Tactics

T_{HE} contribution of air power in past wars and in today's operations against terrorists is immense, but the image of the typical member of the U.S. Air Force is far from that of a blood warrior. Huge numbers of enlisted maintenance, ordnance, and supply men work hard to place a few officer pilots in the cockpits of a limited number of fighter aircraft. Bombers and transport planes, manned by officers and enlisted personnel, deliver explosives, men, and supplies to worldwide locations. Yet at the end of the day, flight crews return to bases fully equipped with dining facilities, recreation rooms, and air-conditioning, where they sleep between clean sheets.

Although there is certainly a chance of airplanes being shot down or crashing because of mechanical, weather, or other difficulties, the air force is a relatively safe service—especially when compared to the risks in the Rangers, Special Forces, and other ground blood-warrior units. Of the more than fifty-eight thousand Americans killed in the Vietnam War, fewer than two thousand wore the blue uniform of the U.S. Air Force.

More than 60 percent of the air force's casualties in Southeast Asia were officers, most of whom were pilots. Air force enlisted men are no less patriotic than their comrades in the other services, but they do not in all cases share the dangers of either their own officers or the other services. In 1983 in Washington State the senior noncommissioned officers of the army's Fort Lewis, the navy's Bremerton Naval Base, and the

air force's McChord Air Force Base met to discuss mutual issues. The senior NCO from each service presented brief remarks to begin the conference. When the turn came for the
senior air force sergeant to speak, he rose and said, "I've
never been able to understand the army and navy. You soldiers
accompany your officers on the front lines in the mud and
slime. You sailors go on ships and submarines with your officers for cruises at sea for as long as six months. At my air
force fighter wing, we ready the planes, help the pilots into
the cockpit, watch them take off, and then go to the club for a
beer."

The role of the air force, like that of the other services, is
constantly changing in response to technology and to potential threats. Its nuclear weapons delivery capability maintained the policy of mutual self-destruction that kept the Cold
War from ever becoming hot. In every conflict since its authorization, the U.S. Air Force has gained air superiority
through its fighter strength and raised havoc in enemy territory and on combatants through bombings. Air force trans-
ports have supported ground operations through the delivery
of paratroopers, munitions, and supplies to maintain far-
flung operations around the globe.

An integral part of these air force missions is the support
provided by that service's few blood warriors. Combat control teams (CCTs) prepare landing and drop zones and coordinate all types of air support and operations. Pararescue
teams (PJs) are prepared to recover and administer medical
assistance to downed airmen or other isolated individuals,
military and civilian, on land or at sea.

Within the U.S. Special Operations Command, the CCTs
and PJs combine into Special Tactics teams to operate with
army Rangers, Special Forces, and the Delta Force and with
the navy SEALs. The Special Tactics teams primarily support
the blood warriors, and much of the reason for their inclusion
with these military elites is proximity rather than direct action. However, the CCTs and PJs are among the military's

best trained and are more than qualified to shed a bit of enemy blood.

Prior to World War II the fledgling U.S. Army Air Corps limited its actions to air-to-air combat, aerial reconnaissance, and the occasional strafing or light bombing of ground forces. By the time the United States joined the Allies against the Axis in 1941, technology had advanced to the point that the air corps could maintain air superiority over friendly lines while also delivering tons of bombs deep into enemy territory. The air corps then received the new mission of delivering paratroopers to unsecured drop zones and aerial resupply to units operating behind enemy lines.

During its initial airborne operations the air corps dropped paratroopers all over the countryside, often as much as thirty miles from their intended drop zones. Pilots, who relied on crude instruments and on what they could see on the ground, needed assistance if the airborne soldiers were to parachute onto their assigned drop zones. To assist the transport pilots, the army developed Pathfinder teams whose mission was to precede the main assaults by parachuting into drop zones first. They then relayed weather and ground information to the main assault force and marked the drop zone with homing devices, lights, smoke pots, or colored panels to guide the pilots to their objectives.

In September 1943 the air corps relied on the Pathfinders, who performed their first combat mission by jumping into Italy several minutes ahead of the main force. The air corps again dropped Pathfinders during the Normandy invasion but wind, weather, and enemy activity prevented many from reaching the correct drop zones to mark them properly. Few paratroopers of the 82nd and 101st Divisions landed anywhere near their assigned areas, but the airborne infantrymen regrouped as quickly as possible and took much of the pressure off the beach landings. In fact, the Germans were so confused by the widespread rather than concentrated airborne drops that they thought they were being engaged by a much larger force.

The Pathfinders learned from their shortcoming at Normandy and were much better prepared by the time of Operation Market Garden in Holland. On September 17, 1944, the air corps put Pathfinder teams in twenty-five minutes prior to the arrival of the main force. Pilots then followed homing beacons and visual markers placed by the Pathfinders, who guided the entire force of paratroopers and gliders onto their designated drop zones.

When the United States established the air force as independent from the army on September 18, 1947, the new service took the Pathfinders, claiming that only qualified airmen should guide air force aircraft. The air force assigned the Pathfinders to aerial port squadrons, which were soon reassigned to the new Air Resupply and Communications Service and renamed combat control teams (CCTs).

The army continued to train Pathfinders on its own for a while after World War II but closed its school at Fort Benning in 1951 after the air force assumed all air combat control duties. However, advances in helicopters and experiments with the 11th Air Assault Division quickly revealed that there was still a need for Pathfinders in the army. The school reopened at Fort Benning in 1955 and continues to train soldiers today.

Army Pathfinders train in four-man teams to perform airborne, small-boat, vehicle, and foot insertions and to control air traffic, mark landing zones, compute delivery routes for aerial resupplies, and measure winds and weather conditions. The army's Pathfinders served in Vietnam and have led or accompanied most heliborne assaults in every conflict since. The majority of their service, however, is limited to the army. The primary control of air assets remains a responsibility of the air force CCTs.

From their activation in the early 1950s, the CCTs have been at the center of action, whether that action is in combat or natural disasters. CCTs deployed to Cuba, Lebanon, and the Congo during the 1950s to coordinate the movement of men and supplies into these trouble spots. During the attack and siege of Khe Sanh in Vietnam in 1968, members of CCTs coordinated the delivery of supplies and men from the middle of the base. When the Americans finally evacuated their embassy in Saigon in 1975, two combat controllers were among the last to be airlifted from the building's rooftop.

In the 1970s CCTs proved their worth in peace as well as war when they deployed to Central America to establish landing areas for relief supplies after a series of deadly earthquakes leveled parts of the region. Combat controllers also were with the Delta Force at Desert One in 1980 in the futile effort to rescue the hostages in Iran. In 1983 the CCTs were back in combat when twelve controllers accompanied the lead elements of the army's 75th Rangers, who jumped into Grenada to restore that island's government. In addition to their forty pounds of parachute gear, the CCTs carried ninety additional pounds of communications equipment. While the Rangers eliminated the Cuban resistance and moved barriers blocking the main airfield, the combat controllers quickly established a command and control radio net and ground-to-air communications to coordinate subsequent drops and air landings. The CCTs then acted as forward observers for air force and navy fighters and gunship support.

In 1989 CCTs again joined the Rangers as they secured two key airfields in Panama during Operation Just Cause. The combat controllers guided the main force to the tarmac and also directed the air support for the continued ground operations. CCTs were once again on the ground in Operation Desert Storm in 1991 as they coordinated air traffic and communications.

CCTs deployed to Somalia in 1992 in what began as a relief effort to bring provisions to that country's starving population. They controlled all the arrivals and departures of aircraft that delivered food, medicine, and other needed supplies. When the Rangers and Delta Force attempted in August 1993 to capture several warlord bandits who were stealing or otherwise keeping the supplies from the general population, the CCTs again were in the midst of the blood warriors. After hordes of bandits surrounded the Rangers and shot down two of their helicopters, a single combat controller went in with reinforcements to reestablish communications and direct air support to minimize casualties. Combat controllers were also among the first on the ground in 2001 in the war against terrorism in Afghanistan.

Like the combat controllers, the air force's pararescue teams also trace their origins to World War II. In August 1943 a disabled C-46 aircraft forced twenty-one men to bail out over uncharted mountains and jungle near the China-Burma border. The site was so remote that the only way to reach the survivors was by airdrop. Lieutenant Colonel Don Fleckinger and two medical corpsmen volunteered to parachute into the jungle to assist their fellow soldiers. The bravery of the colonel and two medics is all the more remarkable because none had any parachute jump experience or airborne training.

These first pararescue jumpers earned the nickname *PJs*, still in use today. Just jumping into the jungle did not end their mission, however. On the ground they assisted the injured and continued to do so for the next month as they marched to friendly lines. Among the men rescued from the Burmese jungle was a young man who became one of America's longest-lasting and best-known journalists. Eric Sevareid later wrote of the PJs who came to his assistance, declaring, "Gallant is a precious word; they deserve it."

When the air force became a separate service in 1947, it continued to develop and train pararescue units. By 1952 there were forty-five seven-man teams of PJs deployed globally as a part of the Air Resupply and Communications Service. PJs made several daring rescues during the Korean War, including the extraction of one downed pilot more than seventy-five miles behind enemy lines.

After the cease-fire in Korea, the PJs, like the rest of the armed services, downsized, but they quickly found a new role to keep them in the forefront. PJs added scuba capabilities to their numerous skills and during the early 1960s assisted NASA in the space program. When the early astronauts and their capsules returned to earth for ocean splashdowns, the PJs were the first to welcome them back and ensure their safe recovery.

Pararescue men joined the war in Vietnam in 1965 and over the next decade were directly responsible for the recovery of pilots from all the services on land and at sea. During the long Vietnam War only nineteen airmen earned the air force's second highest award for valor in combat. Ten of these Air Force Crosses went to PJs. In recognition of their long-term service and their early performance in Vietnam, the air force chief of staff approved the wearing of maroon berets by the pararescue men in 1966.

PJs have performed rescues in every conflict since Vietnam and continue to uphold their motto, "That Others May Live." PJs recovered and cared for many of the casualties during the brief but intense invasion of Panama during Operation Just Cause in 1989 and performed several daring rescues of pilots downed behind Iraqi lines during Desert Storm in 1992. A pararescue team also joined the combat controller on the ground in Somalia to assist the Rangers and Delta Force in the Battle of Mogadishu in 1993.

In addition to their courageous actions in war zones, the PJs have saved the lives of stranded mountain climbers, earthquake victims, and sailors aboard sinking ships. During the last decade several books and films have featured the pararescue airmen, bringing them more public attention than all previous operations. Sebastian Junger's book *The Perfect Storm*, published in 1997, and the subsequent major Hollywood film made *PJs* a household word across the United States.

Despite all this attention, today's PJs are a modest group who readily admit that they are much more motivated to save lives than to participate in armed combat against aggressors.

Their creed simply states, "It is my duty as a Pararescueman to save life and aid the injured. I will be prepared at all times to perform my assigned duties quickly and efficiently, placing those duties before my personal desires and comforts."

Although the PJs might easily be the gentlest of the blood warriors, they are more than worthy of inclusion in America's elite forces because of proximity and numbers. PJs work daily with the CCTs in peace and war. Only three hundred pararescue men are on active duty today. In every conflict involving the U.S. military since their first mission in Burma in World War II, the PJs have been in the midst of the heaviest action. While they are there "so others may live," they are qualified and more than able to defend themselves as well as those they are dedicated to rescue.

Master Sergeant Pat McKenna provided perhaps the best description of the PJs in an article in the air force's official magazine. In the February 2000 edition of *Airman*, McKenna wrote, "Unlike other special operators who search and destroy, PJs 'search and save.' Think of them as SEALs with stethoscopes. They're extreme emergency medical technicians, a kind of cross between Schweitzer and Schwarzenegger. In a pinch, a PJ is a pilot's best friend, and the bad guy's worst enemy, just as accurate with a 9 mm pistol as he is with a syringe. One minute, you might find these Rambos of resuscitation subduing an enemy patrol and the next, jump-starting a heart with a pair of defibrillator paddles."

Training to become a PJ or combat controller takes from twelve to fifteen months. Enlisted airmen who want to volunteer must first complete basic training and then score above average on mental and physical tests. They must be high school graduates and U.S. citizens who qualify for Secret security clearance. Slots within the PJs and CCTs are restricted to males only. Officers must meet the same qualifications, and once training begins no distinction from enlisted volunteers exists.

The CCTs and PJs share many things, including their training. During the 1980s and 1990s the combat controllers and pararescuemen trained together in ten-week indoctrination courses at Lackland Air Force Base, Texas. In 2001 the combat controllers reduced their stay at Lackland to two weeks and now conduct the majority of their indoctrination at Pope Air Force Base in North Carolina.

The indoctrination courses for both PJs and the CCTs are among the most demanding in the U.S. armed forces, comparable in many ways to those for SEALs and Rangers. Instructors at both schools explain simply that "If you train warriors, you get warriors." Candidates push themselves in long runs and swims that they must complete in progressively less time. Lack of sleep, combined with extreme physical and mental demands, eliminates those who cannot respond while fatigued, under pressure, or both.

For an airman to become a PJ or CCT he must master Pipeline Training. At certain points along the Pipeline, the PJs and CCTs train together at air force schools as well as courses provided by the army and navy to learn skills such as survival, parachuting, and diving. Separate courses teach specific skills. CCTs remain together to learn all the aspects of air traffic control at Keesler Air Force Base, Mississippi, during a fifteen-and-a-half-week course taught by the air force. PJs join army medics at the Special Operations Combat Medic Course at Fort Bragg, North Carolina, for twenty-two weeks.

By the time they complete their training CCTs and PJs are qualified to enter their target areas by foot, air, or water to accomplish their missions. Their training is not complete, however. Advanced skills training (ATC) continues for as long as a year so they can also learn free-fall parachuting and advanced diving. During this time they join their permanent teams, where training never ceases as the PJs and CCTs continually perfect learned skills and acquire new ones.

After the formation of the U.S. Special Operations Command (USSOCOM) in 1987, the air force supported the organization with its 23rd Air Force, which contained an assortment of units including PJs and CCTs. In 1990 the 23rd was renamed the U.S. Air Force Special Operations Command. Within that organization PJs and CCTs became a part of the 720th Special Tactics Group (STG).

The 720th STG is headquartered at Hurlburt Field, Florida. In addition to PJs and CCTs, the group contains combat weather units and administrative and support staff for a total of eight hundred personnel. Its motto combines that of the CCTs and PJs—"First There . . . That Others May Live."

The mission of the 720th STG is to organize, train, and equip Special Tactics forces worldwide in order to establish and control air-ground coordination in an objective area. In addition to providing long-range operational and logistical planning, the STG is responsible for deploying teams in support of USSOCOM missions. The 720th STG also has the responsibility of monitoring and supervising all military parachuting, diving, and other Special Tactics skills for the air force.

To accomplish its primary mission of providing support for USSOCOM operations, the 720th STG has four subordinate units in the United States and two overseas. These include Special Tactics squadrons at Pope Air Force Base, North Carolina; McChord Air Force Base, Washington; Hurlburt Field, Florida; and Fort Bragg, North Carolina. While the two overseas Special Tactics squadrons outside the U.S.— at Kadena Air Base, Japan, and RAF Mildenhall, United Kingdom—are commanded by overseas groups, the 720th retains a functional management responsibility.

The PJs and CCTs are extremely confident and proud men who by their participation and performance in campaigns large and small over the past two decades have earned the respect of the blood warriors they accompany. PJs and CCTs, although small in number, have shared dangers and hardships with the Rangers, Delta Force, Special Forces, and SEALs. Even though the air force is better known for its fighter pilots with their squadron scarves tucked into clean flight suits and for its bomber and transport pilots going to war in planes complete with coffeemakers, the PJs and CCTs are the only ones wearing blue uniforms who look their enemies directly in the eye. They are indeed blood warriors.

CHAPTER 12

✳✳✳✳✳✳✳✳

U.S. Special Operations Command (USSOCOM)

F_{ROM} the formation of the first blood-warrior units in pre-Revolutionary America until the decade following the Vietnam War in the twentieth century, each of the armed forces kept a close hold on its elite units. Interaction and cooperation among the army, navy, marine corps, and later the air force were minimal and only to the degree necessary; each service carefully guarded its assets and budget allotments.

For more than two hundred years blood warriors followed the orders of their commanders and rarely worked with—and even more rarely took orders from—leaders who did not wear the same service uniform as they. President Kennedy, who recognized the need for elite units capable of performing special deeds prior to the Vietnam War, played an important role in the advancement of Special Forces and SEALs. Then the war in Southeast Asia itself demonstrated the advantages that Rangers and USMC Force Recon could offer. While there were some efforts in Vietnam to combine the talents of these blood warriors within the Studies and Observation Group (SOG), the services remained parochial in their unwillingness to yield any control over what they considered their own assets.

The post-Vietnam era brought an end to direct combat, but as President Kennedy had noted in his 1963 State of the Union address, "The mere absence of war is not peace." Even before the United States ended its involvement in Southeast Asia, terrorism took center stage when Arab terrorists attacked

Israeli athletes and coaches at the 1972 Summer Olympic Games. Continued terrorist activities and subsequent counteractions by Israeli and German special operations units encouraged the United States to form its own elite counterterrorism Delta Force, organize peacetime Ranger battalions, and expand the Special Forces and SEALs. These actions, however, took place within each of the services, with virtually no coordination for joint deployment, command, or control.

By the 1980s the United States had multiple special operations and counterterrorism units in its arsenal but no plan or guidelines for using them. The magnitude of the organizational ineptness of the services came to the forefront during the disaster at Desert One where the Iranian hostage rescue attempt failed. On April 25, 1980, the highest-ranking officers of the army, navy, air force, and marine corps sent their best troops to the remote desert site without an overall commander of the mission, without a coordinated plan of attack, and without compatible communications equipment. Many of the participants had not even met, much less trained together, before their rendezvous in the desert. When the Iranians easily spotted the invading Americans and their primary rescue helicopters were disabled by maintenance difficulties, confusion reigned.

Colonel "Chargin' Charlie" Beckwith, as commander of the Delta Force, used a satellite communications relay to Secretary of Defense Harold Brown in Washington to recommend the cancellation of the mission. Brown informed President Jimmy Carter, "I think we have an abort situation."

Carter responded, "Let's go with his [the ground commander's] recommendation."

A few minutes later two aircraft collided as the ground assault forces and helicopter crews were still wildly boarding the planes. Eight men died in the ensuing inferno. As the survivors lifted off from the desert, they left behind American dead, burning aircraft, and intelligence documents. They also left on the dry desert sand the reputation of the American military as elites, and the confidence of the American public.

The disaster in the desert served as a wake-up call to the American political and military leadership. Something had to be done to improve the capabilities of special warfare operations. Elected officials talked about the problem but took little action. With Vietnam only a few years in the past, anything to do with the military usually had unfavorable repercussions with the voters back home. Also, the country was in an economic slump, with rising interest rates and unemployment—issues that made real and immediate differences at the polls.

Officials within the Department of Defense were also slow to react. Instead of taking direct action, they decided to "study the problem." The Defense Department appointed Admiral James L. Holloway, former chief of naval operations, to head an investigative panel. The Holloway Commission's report and recommendations resulted in the formation of a joint task force and an advisory panel at the Department of Defense level, but neither had power to make significant changes.

The only major action to result from the failure at Desert One took place within the army. General Edward C. "Shy" Meyer, who had been the army's operations officer during the formation of Delta Force and was now chief of staff, called for a restructuring of all special operations capabilities into a Department of Defense joint force. When the other services disapproved of his recommendation, Meyer formed his own unit within the army. Meyer authorized the 1st Special Operations Command in 1982 with the Rangers, Special Forces, Delta Force, and support units under its control.

In 1983 several influential members of the U.S. Congress began to study military reform. With the election of Ronald Reagan to the presidency, the political leadership looked to rebuild a military that had been deteriorating in size and morale since the Vietnam War. In June the Senate Armed Services Committee, under the chairmanship of Arizona Republican Senator Barry Goldwater, began a two-year-long study of the Defense Department and special operations. Two major incidents occurred during the study to emphasize the need for the ability to combat terrorism and to fight low-intensity conflicts.

On October 23, 1983, a lone terrorist with a truck bomb killed 237 U.S. Marines at their barracks in Beirut, Lebanon. On October 25 the U.S. and Caribbean allies invaded the island of Grenada to restore its government. Although unrelated, both incidents underscored a changing agenda for the military.

The Grenada invasion was successful; however; difficulties in command and control delayed the operation and increased the number of friendly casualties. Rangers, SEALs, Delta Force, and others performed well as individual units, but failures in teamwork and the lack of a unified command proved costly. The problem became obvious: Commanders who were not within the special operations community did not know how to properly use the blood warriors for maximum advantage.

In response to pressures from the public and Congress, the Department of Defense created the Joint Special Operations Agency on January 1, 1984. Although the agency's title reflected importance, it was merely an effort on the part of the Department of Defense to appease its critics. The Joint Special Operations Agency was toothless. It had neither operational nor command authority over any special operations force or other unit.

Despite the lack of real progress, several civilians within the Department of Defense—including Noel Koch, principal deputy assistant secretary of international security affairs, and his deputy, Lynn Rylander—continued to lobby for special operations reforms. They were not alone. Bipartisan Senate leaders led by Georgia Democrat Sam Nunn and Maine Republican William Cohen, both members of the Armed Services Committee, began efforts to reform the special operations forces. Virginia Democrat Dan Daniel, chairman of the Readiness Subcommittee of the House Armed Services Committee, joined them.

The general belief of the three was that the Department of

Defense was not properly preparing for future threats and that it was reallocating funds authorized by Congress for special operations to other programs. Overall they believed that special operations were not receiving the attention they deserved.

On October 16, 1985, the Senate Armed Services Committee published a 645-page study titled "Defense Organization: The Need for Change." In its Letter of Submittal the study's director, James R. Locher III, wrote, "The purpose of this study is to strengthen the Department of Defense. The capabilities of the U.S. military forces have been improved over the past five years. In many respects, American forces are better manned, equipped, and led than has been the case for a long time. The full potential of this revitalization cannot, however, be realized under current structural deficiencies. This study does not suggest that this revitalization of American military capabilities should be slowed or that defense spending reductions should be made. On the contrary, substantial force improvements will continue to be necessary for the foreseeable future. This study does, however, see the need for a parallel revitalization of antiquated organizational arrangements."

The study noted in great depth what it called the "imbalance between service and joint interests." In fairly direct language it stated that too often the army, navy, and air force placed the interest of their own service above that of the overall Department of Defense. The study concluded with a dozen specific recommendations for the integration, or jointness, of the services. Senior officers defined the recommendations a bit more simply. Instead of the green-suited soldiers, white-suited sailors, and blue-suited airmen always looking out first and foremost for their own service, they were now to act and think as "purple-suiters" who represented the entire defense establishment.

In response to the study, Congress passed the Goldwater-Nichols Department of Defense Reorganization Act of 1986. The act created the most significant defense reorganization since the National Security Act of 1947. It centralized operational authority through the chairman of the Joint Chiefs as opposed to the service chiefs. The chairman was designated as the principal military adviser to the Secretary of Defense, the National Security Council, and the president. Furthermore, the act added the position of vice chairman of the Joint Chiefs and streamlined the operational chain of command from the president to the Secretary of Defense to the unified commanders.

The Goldwater-Nichols Act made far-reaching changes in the way the Department of Defense conducted its operations. No longer did each service approach a mission on its own. Planning, preparation, and execution of operations were now organizationally, doctrinally, and technically fully joint, providing much more responsiveness and flexibility.

Although the Goldwater-Nichols Act did not directly authorize or even call for a separate joint command for special operations, it laid the groundwork for that eventuality. While Congress was still debating the basics of the act, reform bills were introduced in both houses for a joint military organization for special operations. Senators Cohen and Nunn cosponsored a Senate bill that called for a joint special operations command and an office in the Department of Defense to oversee funding and policy matters for special operations and low-intensity warfare. Representative Daniel on the House side went even further when he recommended that special operations become a national agency that would bypass the Joint Chiefs and report directly to the secretary of defense.

Congress held hearing on the bills throughout the summer of 1986. Needless to say, many senior leaders in the Pentagon opposed the elevation and possible separation of special operations. Admiral William J. Crowe Jr., chairman of the Joint Chiefs of Staff, led the opposition. Crowe agreed to the need for a special operations unit but wanted it to remain under his control and be commanded by a three-star rather than a four-star general—meaning that it would not be on an equal level with the other joint commands.

The strongest lobbying for the separate command came from retired officers who had "been there and done that" and had the liberty to speak their minds without endangering their careers. Retired Army Major General Richard Scholtes, who had commanded special operations forces in the Grenada invasion, gave the most compelling testimony both before the committees and behind closed doors with individual senators and representatives. Scholtes explained how conventional force commanders misused the special operations forces in Grenada by not allowing them to employ their unique skills. The general did not mince words in declaring that these failures directly contributed to the number of dead and wounded Americans.

Both the Senate and House passed reform bills and then met in conference committee to reconcile their differences. The resulting compromise bill provided for a unified special operations command headed by a four-star general, an assistant secretary of defense for special operations and low-intensity conflict, and a board within the National Security Council to coordinate low-intensity conflict. Equally important, or perhaps more so, the bill authorized a new Major Force Program (MFP-11) as a separate funding source for the new command. This so-called special operations checkbook was key to its separation and independence. The final bill, attached as a rider to the Defense Authorization Act of 1987, amended the Goldwater-Nichols Act and was signed into law in October 1986.

Neither the White House nor the Pentagon liked the Nunn-Cohen Amendment to the Goldwater-Nichols. Neither appreciated Congress reminding them of past failures and directing them as to how to handle future threats. Neither was in any rush to execute the specifics or the intent of the new law. One of the first issues was the appointment of the assistant secretary for special operations and low-intensity conflict. The Pentagon protested that all eleven of its assistant secretaryships, the number authorized by Congress, were filled. Congress responded by authorizing a twelfth assistant secretary.

Still the Pentagon did not fill the position. In December 1987, more than a year after its authorization, Congress passed Public Law 100-189 that directed Secretary of the Army John O. Marsh to perform both his and the assistant secretary's duties until a suitable candidate was nominated and approved. President Ronald Reagan, who did not appreciate Congress's directions on how to handle special operations, finally nominated an assistant secretary. Congress confirmed Charles Whitehouse, the former U.S. ambassador to Laos and Thailand during the latter years of the war in Southeast Asia, and he assumed the position of assistant secretary nearly eighteen months after the position had been authorized.

The actual establishment of the USSOCOM headquarters provided problems of its own. By law the Defense Department had to have the command in place no later than April 16, 1987, and time was growing short. Personnel had to be selected and transferred. Buildings, equipment, and furnishings had to be procured. Planners from the Joint Special Operations Agency initially sought a new location but then realized that the U.S. Readiness Command at MacDill Air Force Base, Florida—which had lost much of its mission in the aftermath of the Goldwater-Nichols Act—also presented the advantage of having as its commander General James J. Lindsay, who had joint, as well as some special operations, experience.

On January 8, 1987, the Joint Special Operations Agency presented two options to the Joint Chiefs, one for forming a new command and the other for using the Readiness Command assets. On January 23 the Joint Chiefs recommended to the secretary of defense that the latter option be adopted, using already established personnel slots and facilities. The secretary agreed, and on April 13 President Ronald Reagan approved the action.

The Department of Defense met its deadline and established the USSOCOM on April 16. It nominated General Lindsay as its commander, and the Senate accepted him without debate. The long road to establishing a command to centralize the blood-warrior elites had finally come to fruition.

Many of Lindsay's fellow generals thought he had made a poor career decision in accepting the command of a unit that the Pentagon bitterly opposed. Lindsay, a veteran of Vietnam with multiple medals for valor, welcomed the challenge. He, like most in the Pentagon, knew that Congress wanted a special operations command, and now it was time to make it work.

USSOCOM was officially activated on June 1, 1987. Guest speakers at the ceremony included Deputy Secretary of Defense William H. Taft IV and Admiral William J. Crowe Jr. Although the two had led the Pentagon opposition against the formation of the unit, they understood that it was now a reality that deserved unqualified support. In his speech Admiral Crowe called upon General Lindsay to quickly integrate the new command into the mainstream military: "First, break down the wall that has more or less come between special operations forces and the other parts of our military, the wall that some people will try to build higher. Second, educate the rest of the military—spread a recognition and understanding of what you do, why you do it, and how important it is that you do it. Last, integrate your efforts into the full spectrum of our military capabilities."

Lindsay immediately confronted these objectives. He organized and trained his staff as he established the necessary command and control relationships, defined worldwide requirements, and planned for the future of the command. Lindsay framed many of his early decisions so they could be modified, added to, or eliminated. USSOCOM, from its beginnings, remained flexible in adapting to new challenges and missions. To accomplish these tasks Lindsay organized his headquarters into subordinate staff sections using the traditional joint staff model, with sections for personnel, intelligence, operations, and logistics.

Not all the early decisions were complex or even mission-essential. Although Lindsay inherited a headquarters, facilities, and much of the personnel from his old Readiness Command, small details did matter. When USSOCOM began it did not even have a shoulder patch to identify its members. Lindsay initially selected a sea griffin holding a sword and lightning bolts on a black background with UNITED STATES SPECIAL OPERATIONS COMMAND scrolled across its top.

Shortly after the USSOCOM activation, Lindsay received an unofficial patch worn by the Office of Strategic Services during World War II. Lindsay liked the simple gold spear point on a black background and understood that the OSS was a lineal predecessor to modern special operations. He modified the spear point slightly, kept the original colors, added UNITED STATES SPECIAL OPERATIONS COMMAND around the outside, and declared the result the command's official patch.

Other problems were not so easy to solve. Although the law that established USSOCOM stated, "Unless otherwise directed by the Secretary of Defense, all active and reserve special operations forces of all armed forces stationed in the United States shall be assigned to the Special Operations Command," all three services resisted completely complying with the law. Each wanted to maintain direct control over as much of what it considered its own assets as possible.

Of the three, the army was best prepared and the most willing to join USSOCOM. The army's special operations forces had been working together since their formation by General Meyer in 1982 and had already participated in several combat operations, including the invasion of Grenada. Upon the activation of USSOCOM the army placed its Rangers, Special Forces, Delta Force, the 160th Special Operations Aviation Group, and the JFK Special Warfare Center and School under Lindsay's command. Initially the army, with approval of the Secretary of Defense, withheld psychological warfare and civil affairs units because it feared they would not receive proper attention and care in the new organization. Lindsay disagreed and on October 15, 1987, received permission to add PSYOPS and civil affairs to USSOCOM.

The air force complied with the law, placing its special operations forces under USSOCOM by assigning the 23rd Air Force to Lindsay's command. It left many non-special-operations units in the 23rd, however, and maintained part of the force under its Military Airlift Command (MAC). Again Lindsay lobbied the Pentagon and the air force, stating that he expected all three of the special operations branches to be major command equivalents and that the organization of the 23rd would create problems. It took some time, but once again Lindsay proved successful. On May 22, 1990, the air force removed all non-special-operations units from the 23rd and redesignated it as the Air Force Special Operations Command (AFSOC).

The navy did even less to meet the requirements of the law that authorized USSOCOM. While it did establish the Naval Special Warfare Command on April 16, 1987, this new unit contained only the training command of the Naval Special Warfare Center. Navy officials argued that although SEAL and special boat units were stationed within the United States, their missions called for them to support the Atlantic and Pacific Fleets. Transfer to the Special Warfare Command would detract from their relationship with these fleets and decrease their proficiency.

Lindsay again took a strong stance on his interpretation of the law and his belief about what was best for U.S. special operations. He reasoned that the naval special operations units' relationship with the Pacific and Atlantic Fleets was no different than that of U.S.-based army Special Forces with overseas commands. On October 23, 1987, the Secretary of Defense concurred with Lindsay and ordered the navy to act. The navy moved slowly but finally complied on October 1, 1988, when the Naval Special Warfare Command assumed control of SEAL and special boat units.

By the end of 1988 the U.S. Special Operations Command had finally assumed control over all the primary American blood warriors. Although the command had thousands of support and administrative personnel, it also had the Rangers,

Special Force, Delta Force, Special Tactics, and SEAL units. For the first time in modern American military history, its elite units shared one command and control headquarters.

Since its beginnings USSOCOM has been an ever-changing organization. While evolution is common in all military commands, USSOCOM has one great advantage in making rapid changes. The congressional legislation that established USSOCOM also provides it the unique power to control its own funding. Unlike the other major commands, which have to submit their budgets through their services and the Department of Defense, provisions of the original law created Major Force Program 11. MFP-11 permits USSOCOM to manage its own funding and to align its dollars with acquisition and training programs as it sees fit. This enables the command to operate its own research and development operations and to purchase "off the shelf" special items not available within normal supply channels.

The USSOCOM budget request for 2001 totaled approximately $3.8 billion. Of this amount, 41 percent pays the basic salaries of assigned personnel. Another 36 percent goes to operations and maintenance; 14 percent for procurement; 7 percent for research, development, training, and evaluation; and 2 percent for military construction.

The war against terror that began on September 11, 2001, certainly added additional funding to USSOCOM, but exact figures are not yet available. Expenditures for special weapons and equipment remain classified, but the war in Afghanistan has revealed some of the special requests made by USSOCOM. Early in their deployment to the war zone, army special operators discovered that their regulation Humvees were too large for the crude Afghan road network. The Humvees also stood out among the civilian vehicles. Without having to go outside their own command for financial approval, the Rangers, Special Forces, and other operators purchased the Toyota pickup trucks that are the most common vehicle in Afghanistan. Subsequently, they added all-terrain recreation vehicles to their transportation pools by direct purchase from the United States.

The war has also revealed insights into USSOCOM's development of weapons and equipment. In February 2002 the USSOCOM Advanced Technology Directorate announced that the army's Special Operations Command was compiling information from e-mails, letters, and after-action reports from the war zone and was interviewing returning operators to determine additional needs for equipment and capabilities.

Included on the list of recommended developments are lighter, longer-lasting batteries or power cells for radios and other equipment; improved communications so operators can more easily access satellites; better, smaller, lighter laser designators for guiding precision weapons dropped from aircraft; portable, collapsible, unmanned, expendable aerial vehicles for reconnaissance over rural and urban environments; and lightweight, portable countermortar radars to detect and locate indirect fires from any direction. While the normal military development and procurement process would take years, if not decades, to field this equipment, USSOCOM spokesmen state that the needed equipment is already being prepared and soon will be ready for issue to front-line operators.

Commanders of USSOCOM, like other military units, have also changed over the years. Three-year tours in command of USSOCOM have been the general rule. The most notable exception is General Henry H. Shelton, who assumed command on February 29, 1996. He left SOCOM on September 25, 1997, after only twenty-one months in command, to become the chairman of the Joint Chiefs of Staff a week later. Shelton, a veteran of numerous Special Forces and Rangers assignments, became the first chairman to be selected from the ranks of special operations. The nomination not only showed the confidence of the political leadership in Shelton, but also served as a strong indicator that special operations were key to future defense issues.

USSOCOM mission statements also evolved over the years as the command matured and situations changed around the world. Less than a year after assuming command, Shelton slightly refined the statement in December 1996 to declare the mission of USSOCOM to be to "Provide Special Operations Forces to the National Command Authorities, regional Combatant Commanders, and American Ambassadors and their country teams for successful conduct of worldwide special operations, civil affairs, and psychological operations during peace and war."

When General Peter J. Schoomaker assumed command of USSOCOM on November 5, 1997, he retained Shelton's mission statement. Schoomaker did, however, add a sentence that articulated his own vision for the future of USSOCOM: "Be the most capable and relevant Special Operations Forces in existence—living personal and professional standards of excellence to which all others aspire."

To better accomplish this vision Schoomaker did away with the traditional joint staff alignment and incorporated the similar or complementary functions into five "centers of excellence." These include command support, intelligence and intelligence operations, operations plans and policy, requirements and resources, and acquisitions and logistics.

Nine specific principal missions and seven collateral activities support the USSOCOM mission statement. These principal and collateral missions have remained fairly stable over the last decade. The most recent change occurred in 2000 when the collateral activity of "Peace Operations" was eliminated. It originally called for USSOCOM to "Assist in peacekeeping operations, peace enforcement operations, and other military operations in support of diplomatic efforts to establish and maintain peace."

Elimination of this task certainly seems appropriate. Making war, not peacekeeping, is USSOCOM's primary mission.

Along with the elimination of peacekeeping as a collateral activity, USSOCOM also noted its limitations in its 2000 Posture Statement published by the Office of the Assistant

Secretary of Defense for Special Operations and Low Intensity Conflict. "As with any highly specialized capability," the statement begins, "it is equally important to understand the limitations of SOF."

The statement explains, "SOF operators require extensive training, often years in duration. They cannot be replaced quickly and their capabilities cannot be expanded rapidly. Squandering scarce SOF resources on inappropriate missions or inordinately dangerous tasks runs the risk of depleting the SOF inventory early in the conflict. SOF are not a substitute for conventional forces; they provide different capabilities that expand the options of the employing commander. SOF should not be used for operations whenever conventional forces can accomplish the mission."

The statement continues to explain its elimination of peace-keeping from its mission list: "SOF are not the solution to peacetime operations. SOF have a role to play in peacetime operations, just as they have a role to play in war. Peacetime operations almost always require an integrated, interagency approach to solve the problems encountered. SOF alone cannot do this."

The statement of limitations concludes, "SOF logistics support is austere. A large number of SOF units generally cannot maintain themselves for extended periods of time without significant support from the conventional support structure."

The authorized personnel strength of USSOCOM for 2001 was 45,690. About two-thirds of this number is from the regular military, while the other third is from the reserve forces, who augment and reinforce the active forces in time of need. Officers make up 19 percent and enlisted personnel 75 percent of this total. Civilian employees make up the other 6 percent of the USSOCOM staff.

Today's USSOCOM headquarters remains at MacDill Air Force Base, Florida, with the staff organization of five functional centers it formed in 1988. All of the special operations forces subordinate to USSOCOM based in the United States are organized into four separate subcommands. The army, navy, and air force separately head three of these, while the fourth is a joint headquarters responsible for studying and planning.

The U.S. Army Special Operations Command (USASOC) is located at Fort Bragg, North Carolina, and consists of Special Forces, Rangers, Delta Force, special operations aviation, civil affairs, psychological operations, combat and service support units, and the John F. Kennedy Special Warfare Center and School. Each has an important role in the command's mission.

While the bulk of America's and USSOCOM's blood warriors are assigned to the army's Special Operations Command, units in addition to the Rangers, Special Forces, and Delta Force are critical to their survival and success. The 160th Special Operations Aviation Regiment (Night Stalkers) employs state-of-the-art helicopters to provide force insertion and extraction, aerial security, armed attack, electronic warfare, and command and control support. Its motto— "Night Stalkers Don't Quit"—exemplifies their dedication and performance.

One of the lessons learned from the disaster in Iran was the need for a specially trained and equipped helicopter unit dedicated to supporting special operations. Shortly after the failure at Desert One the army formed Task Force 158 from aviation units of the 101st Airborne Division (Airmobile) at Fort Campbell, Kentucky. A year later the army redesignated it Task Force 160. In 1989 it was renamed the 160th Special Operations Group and a year later elevated to its present designation, 160th Special Operations Aviation Regiment. Despite the name changes, the unit is still commonly referred to as Task Force 160.

Since the group's inception the Night Stalkers have recruited only the best and most experienced pilots. They specialize in the use of the latest high-technology aircraft and night-vision devices that allow them to operate in darkness and all kinds of weather. From the battlefields of Grenada, Panama, Desert Storm, Somalia, and in Afghanistan today, the Night Stalkers have proven an important part of the special operations team. Blood-warrior operators have learned that they can depend on these aviators to deliver them to the right location, provide aerial fire support, and extract them regardless of the situation.

More than fourteen hundred soldiers, including a few women, are assigned to the 160th. Two battalions are based at Fort Campbell, while a third shares Hunter Army Airfield near Fort Stewart, Georgia, with the 1st Ranger Battalion.

USASOC's operators have always said about the opposition: "Grab them by their balls and their hearts and minds will follow." While direct military action is without a doubt the most effective method to accomplish its missions, the command also has special units to assist the blood warriors. Civil affairs supports the field commanders in their relationship with local authorities and the civilian population of a target area. These specialists assist in the areas of public safety, finance, agriculture, and refugee relocation.

Psychological operations units also support the blood warriors with specialists who train in the culture and language of operational areas. Their motto, "Persuade, Change, Influence," sums up their mission to induce or reinforce attitudes and behaviors favorable to U.S. national goals.

Other units within USASOC provide chemical reconnaissance and assessment, logistic support, health care, and communications. Its final component, the John F. Kennedy Special Warfare and School, supervises training, leadership development, and doctrine.

Members of USASOC wear a red spearhead patch with a centered black-and-white dagger. A red-on-black airborne tab tops the patch.

The Naval Special Warfare Command (NAVSPECWAR-COM) maintains its focus on both the Pacific and Atlantic by assigning its special operations forces to special warfare groups and special boat squadrons on each coast. The overall command headquarters and Group One are stationed at Coronado, California, while Group Two makes its home at Little Creek, Virginia. Development Group, the former SEAL Team Six, prepares for missions in both theaters from its base at Dam Neck, Virginia.

Three SEAL teams make up the core of each special warfare group. SEAL delivery teams support each group with their delivery and support capabilities from a variety of watercraft, including submarines. Special boat squadrons support each group by operating and maintaining special operations ships and craft, such as rigid inflatable boats and coastal patrol vessels. These extremely mobile units can deploy worldwide on short notice to support SEAL units. They also provide the special operations command its only small-craft and riverine capabilities.

The Naval Special Warfare Command's patch is circular, with the gold SEAL eagle, anchor, pistol, and trident badge superimposed on a green-and-black world globe. A gold rope border encloses the command's name around the outside border.

Although the air force contributes only a few hundred combat controllers and pararescue men to the ranks of the blood warriors, it provides massive support with both fixed- and rotary-wing aircraft. In addition to its Special Tactics units, the Air Force Special Operations Command (AFSOC) provides transportation, including clandestine infiltration, exfiltration, resupply, and aerial refueling. It can directly support ground operations with precision air strikes, and indirectly support by providing aerial platforms for radio and television broadcasts for psychological operations. Air force special operations personnel also advise and assist foreign governments in matters concerning aviation internal defense.

The AFSOC directs its subordinate units from its headquarters at Hurlburt Field, Florida. From there it also operates the USAF Special Operations School, which instructs service members from all U.S. branches and allied countries in aviation foreign internal defense, crisis response management, joint psychological operations, joint planning, and revolutionary warfare.

A black shield with a winged dagger topped by a blue star is the center of the command's patch. A scroll on the bottom reading AIR FORCE SPECIAL OPERATIONS COMMAND completes the design.

The fourth USSOCOM subordinate unit is the Joint Special Operations Command (JSOC) at Fort Bragg, North Carolina. The Department of Defense formed this joint headquarters in 1980 as one of its early attempts to bring various aspects of the services under one command. Over the years it evolved into a research and planning center that today is responsible for studying special operations requirements and techniques; ensuring interoperability and equipment standardization; planning and conducting special operations exercises and training; and developing joint special operations tactics.

A circular globe with four crossed swords makes up the center of the Joint Special Operations Command patch. Its name within a gold border circles the design.

Since its activation in 1987 the U.S. Special Operations Command has participated in every major military operation, including the Persian Gulf in 1987–1989, Panama in 1989–1990, Kuwait and Iraq in 1990–1991, Somalia in 1992–1995, Haiti in 1994–1995, and Bosnia from 1995 to the present. Extensive use of special operations forces initiated the war against terror after the attacks on New York City and the Pentagon on September 11, 2001.

The numbers of special operations units deployed to Afghanistan and other areas around the world are classified. The most recent figures released by the Special Operations Command's Posture Statement for 2000 reveal that special operations forces were deployed to 152 countries and territories in 1999. Even this number is not completely accurate, because it does not include classified missions. According to the report, "In any given week, 5,000 SOF operators are deployed in approximately 60 countries worldwide."

The U.S. Special Operations Command continues to adapt to changing situations to best meet its objectives and to accomplish its missions. In the foreword to its 2000 Posture Statement, the command's leader explained, "In the next century, the spread of information, the development of and access to new technologies, and an increasing recognition of global problems will present vast opportunities for economic growth, regional integration, and global political cooperation. Yet for all of this promise, the world remains a complex, dynamic, and dangerous place. It will continue to be an uncertain security environment, one [for] which U.S. special operations forces are uniquely suited, offering the capabilities to avert emerging threats and providing unprecedented opportunities to address the challenges in ways that advance U.S. interests."

✳✳✳✳✳✳✳✳

U.S. Marine Corps Force Reconnaissance: History

*T*HE U.S. Marine Corps is the only service branch not represented in the Special Operations Command, but that does not mean it is without its blood warriors. Within the marine corps is a small group of highly trained, extremely competent elites organized into Force Reconnaissance companies.

Despite their qualifications and stellar combat record, the marines of Force Recon have remained little known outside the corps and special warfare community. Much of this lack of recognition comes from the nature and personality of Force Recon itself. Recon marines are extremely well prepared, fiercely aggressive, and supremely confident. At the same time, the success of their missions—and their personal survival—depend on secrecy, silence, and stealth. Habitual clandestine behavior carries over into an avoidance of news coverage and public recognition. Also, it is not to be overlooked that the men of Force Recon know they are among the best and seek no acknowledgment outside their own units.

More to the point, however, is the simple fact that Force Recon members are first and foremost marines and believe that any additional recognition of their superior status is superfluous. As early as 1962 lesson plans for Force Recon volunteers included the statement, "The Recon Marine is no more and no less than an infantryman with special skills. He is not a superman, nor is he really a particularly special kind of marine. He is simply and proudly a marine doing a job which has to be done. The reconnaissance unit is a support unit that works for other people. Its mission of reconnaissance is a means to an end, not an end in itself."

The marine corps also resists touting any of its members as being better trained or more qualified than the others. Its official policy says, "We will be ready whenever the nation says 'Send in the Marines.' " It further declares, "Our ability to win our nation's battles rests, as it always has, on the individual marine. Regardless of the relentless pace of technology, people, not machines, decide the course of battles. Our basic tenet of 'every Marine a rifleman' reflects this firm belief."

What this statement implies is that the entire marine corps is elite. A long combat history of marine infantrymen joining army infantrymen to win America's wars supports this belief. However, the entire corps does not qualify as blood warriors. As elites among elites, the few marines who have earned the title *Force Recon* are the only ones to join this list.

The history of the U.S. Marine Corps since its establishment in 1775 is a story of dedicated service and valorous combat, but it was not until the twentieth century that reconnaissance became an essential part of its accomplishments. Of the 180 amphibious landings by the marines prior to World War II, reconnaissance forces preceded only three— Sumatra in 1832, Drummonds Islands in 1841, and Mexico in 1870. The principal reason for this lack of reconnaissance was the lack of amphibious warfare in general. Naval and marine planners did not focus on the seizure, preparation, and defense of forward land bases until the Spanish-American War of 1898.

Despite interest and need, the first formal American doctrine for amphibious reconnaissance did not appear until 1906. Marine Major Dion Williams, veteran of the Battle of Manila Bay—where, as a company commander, he helped raise the first American flag on Spanish soil—outlined reconnaissance requirements and responsibilities for a Naval War College study. Williams included missions from the sea to the shore and from the beach on inland. He stressed the need for gathering information on hydrographics, harbors, beaches, and established defenses.

Williams recommended that only special men be selected for these difficult tasks. He listed such qualifications as technical knowledge, high energy, resourcefulness, and attention to detail as important. He also said that each man should be a master of surveying and map reading.

Williams updated his study in 1917. He incorporated the use of airplanes and submarines to supplement watercraft and emphasized the need to acquire long-term planning information as well as gathering intelligence for operations in progress. He also developed a comprehensive mission statement: "The object of naval reconnaissance of any given location is to acquire all of the information concerning sea, land, and material resources of that locality, with a view to its use by the navy in peace and war, and to record this information that it may be most readily available for the preparation of plans for the occupation of the locality as a temporary or permanent naval base; the preparation of plans for the sea and land defense of the locality when used as such a base; or the preparation of plans for the attack of the locality by sea and land should it be in the possession of an enemy."

Although Williams recorded doctrine and philosophy for marine reconnaissance, no application of his ideas took place immediately. The failure of the allied amphibious invasion of western Turkey at Gallipoli in 1915 convinced many planners that attacks from the sea could not be successful against strong land defenses. By the time the Americans entered World War I, the battle lines had stabilized into trench warfare far inland, where marines fought as regular infantry.

It was another marine who actually first applied Williams's concepts. Major Earl H. "Pete" Ellis—who had gained his commission in 1900 and, after service in the Philippines, Japan, and the Mariana Islands, earned the Navy Cross, the service's second highest award for valor, on the Western Front during World War I—tried to prepare the navy for the future.

Despite health problems, which included kidney disease and lingering psychological disorders from his combat experiences—both compounded by alcohol abuse—Ellis sought new adventures and challenges after the armistice of 1918. On September 4, 1920, he wrote to the commandant of the corps, "In order that the Marine Corps may have the necessary information on which to base its plans for future operations in South America and in the Pacific Ocean, I have to request that I be ordered to those areas for the purposes of making the necessary reconnaissance."

The commandant forwarded Ellis's letter to the director of naval intelligence, who approved the request. There is no evidence that Ellis investigated South America, but his accomplishments in the Pacific easily rank among the most significant in the history of reconnaissance and intelligence.

Before departing for the Pacific, Ellis prepared and submitted a thirty-thousand-word paper titled "Advance Base Operations in Micronesia" based on his observations of the region prior to the war. The Department of the Navy approved Ellis's recommendations and redesignated the study Operations Plan 712 on January 28, 1921.

Ellis's report is one of the most amazing and insightful studies in American military history. Less than two years after the Great War, Ellis predicted that the United States would be drawn into the Second World War a little more than two decades later. He wrote, "Japan is a world power, and her army and navy will doubtless be up to date as to training and material. Considering our consistent policy of non-aggression, she will probably initiate the war."

Ellis continued with a detailed analysis of Japan's military capabilities and a discussion of the sea, air, land, climate, and native populations of the Pacific region. He concluded the paper with a strategy that the United States could use to retake key islands so as to establish forward bases for an eventual invasion of the Japanese homeland. He included requirements for airplanes capable of delivering torpedoes against watercraft and the development of large, automatic guns for shipboard offense and defense.

During the following years the navy made slight modifications to Operations Plan 712 and renamed it War Plan Orange. After the Japanese attacked Pearl Harbor in 1941, many of the American efforts against Japan—including mobilization requirements, timetables, and the island-hopping strategy—closely followed Ellis's outline of events.

Upon completion of his report Ellis sailed throughout the Pacific to validate his findings. Few of his observations, however, made their way back to the Department of the Navy. On May 21, 1923, the Japanese governor of the South Sea islands reported to the American authorities in Yokosuka, Japan, that Ellis was dead. When the Japanese provided no official cause of his demise, some fellow marines theorized that the Japanese had murdered him because he had discovered some aspect of their war plans. Others speculated that he had become so despondent because of his war experiences that he committed suicide, or that he had died from his medical ailments. A somewhat dubious account from a German merchant, Mr. O. Herrman, also made the rounds. Herrman, who briefly traveled with Ellis, stated that the major had become seriously ill after consuming a meal of canned eels and beer.

Japanese involvement became more viable when the naval attaché at Yokosuka dispatched Chief Pharmacist Lawrence Zembsch to recover Ellis's remains. When Zembsch returned to Japan from the South Sea islands on August 14, 1923, he was, according to the attaché, ". . . incoherent, his walk was unsteady and he was in a highly nervous condition. He would burst into tears, apparently without reason, talked of taking his own life, etc."

Zembsch also cringed in fear when approached by any Japanese—even those who had been close friends before his mission. It is likely that the Japanese officials in the South Sea islands drugged and tortured Zembsch. Naval officials deferred further debriefing until Zembsch could regain his health. That never occurred; both Zembsch and his wife died in a fire following an earthquake on September 1.

The cause of Ellis's death remains as mysterious as his visions and recommendations for the preparation and execution of the war against Japan remain extraordinary. Most Americans, however, languished in the belief that World War I was truly "the war to end all wars," supporting defense budget cuts and military manpower reductions. Those who remained in uniform did their best to prepare for future conflicts. Planners within the marine corps developed doctrines for amphibious warfare, emphasizing the need for advanced reconnaissance operations.

In 1938 the navy published FTP-167, titled "Landing Operations Doctrine." Important parts of the document included details on the role of immediate and long-range reconnaissance activities and the admission that ground observations were superior to those made from ships, submarines, or aircraft.

The navy tested its new amphibious and reconnaissance doctrine from January 13 to March 15 during Fleet Exercise 4 (FLEX 4) conducted on and near the Caribbean islands of Culebra, Vieques, and Puerto Rico. Reconnaissance objectives included locating and determining suitability of landing beaches, analyzing the extent and position of beach defenses, and pinpointing the location of reserve forces.

To accomplish these objectives, the exercise commander, Rear Admiral A. W. Johnson, formed reconnaissance teams from the 5th Marine Regiment and from attached U.S. Army units. Results were mixed, but considering their lack of training the recon teams did well. Although they failed to accomplish all their missions and had difficulty in relaying the information, they proved that they could contribute to the success of future amphibious operations. One of their most notable accomplishments was overseeing the first landing in marine corps history of a reconnaissance patrol from a submarine.

Fleet exercises over the next two years confirmed the need

for reconnaissance and refined doctrine for its use in amphibious operations. Major General W. P. Upshur, the chief umpire of the 1940 exercise, summarized, "I do not see how it is possible to issue final, definite orders before we have any knowledge of the location, disposition, and movements of the hostile force."

One of Upshur's subordinates, Brigadier General H. W. Smith, was even more succinct: "Without this phase both the admiral and the land forces would be fighting blind."

The corps recognized the need for reconnaissance units and had the doctrine in place for their use, but the continued austerity of the defense budget did not allow their formation. This quickly changed when the Japanese attacked Pearl Harbor on December 7, 1941.

Less than a month later corps leaders assembled two officers and twenty enlisted marines from the First Marine Division at Quantico, Virginia. Designated the Observer Group, this unit was the first in marine corps history to be officially organized and trained exclusively for amphibious reconnaissance.

The Observer Group initially concentrated its training on preparation for the invasion of North Africa. Captain James Logan Jones, the group's first commander, was particularly suited for this mission, because he had traveled extensively prior to the war in that region as a sales representative for the International Harvester Company.

Jones trained his men while marine staff officers developed doctrine for their use. When the War and Navy departments decided in September 1942 that the army would be responsible for the Atlantic and the navy and marine corps for the Pacific, Jones and his command moved to San Diego, California, where they joined the Amphibious Corps, Pacific Fleet.

The recon unit trained at Camp Pendleton, developing and testing new policies and procedures. Jones, as well as his superiors, understood that one of the keys to the unit's success was the proper selection and training of its personnel, as evidenced by Amphibious Corps, Pacific Fleet, Intelligence

Order 4-42 titled "Reconnaissance Patrols Landing on Hostile Shores," published on October 29, 1942. It stated, "The elements and principles of scouting and patrolling, as well as combat intelligence, must be so instilled in them as to be instinctive. The aggressive type of action involved combined with the strain of maintaining secrecy will necessitate, in almost all cases, exceptionally high physical condition and agility. Since the accuracy of the information to be obtained is of an importance which may determine the success or failure of a landing, it is advisable, when possible, to strengthen the patrols by officers who have received the same training."

The order, essentially a standard operating procedures manual for recon operations, also contained information on weapons, equipment, and patrolling procedures. It was so complete that it remained in effect with only minor changes for the remainder of the war. In 1948 the order was reissued virtually unchanged as MCS 3-1, "Combat Intelligence," as a guide to postwar reconnaissance.

The Observer Group so impressed officials at Camp Pendleton that they increased its size to six officers and ninety-two enlisted men and redesignated it as the Amphibious Reconnaissance Company on January 7, 1943. The company sailed to Hawaii on September 10, where members prepared for their first combat mission. While the company's junior officers supervised training, Jones accompanied the submarine *Nautilus* on its sixth war patrol. From the sub's periscope Jones conducted a photographic reconnaissance of the Japanese islands of Tarawa, Makin, and Apamama.

After his return to Hawaii a month later, Jones had a short time to further prepare his company before he and his men boarded the *Nautilus* and crowded inside the forward and aft torpedo rooms. On November 8 the submarine and its recon passengers departed Pearl Harbor for Apamama Atoll, located seventy-six miles south of Tarawa. Jones's mission was to determine the size and displacement of the island's Japanese defenders. A follow-on force would then assault the beach and secure the atoll as a forward support base for future island-hopping campaigns.

Despite being bombed by Japanese planes and attacked by shore batteries from other islands while running on the surface toward Apamama, the submarine reached the atoll with no damage. Shortly after midnight on November 21 the recon company paddled ashore in rubber boats, landed unopposed, and quickly determined that all but thirty of the Japanese defenders had recently evacuated.

Jones's mission was to recon and report, but when he determined that his opponents were so few he decided to attack. In his after-action report he later wrote, ". . . there wasn't room for the Japs and us too."

After a brief skirmish on November 25 in which the recon marines suffered their first fatality, the remaining Japanese committed suicide rather than surrender. With the loss of only one marine, Apamama Atoll became the first island in history to be captured by troops landing from a submarine.

On January 23, 1944, the Amphibious Recon Company again sailed from Pearl Harbor, this time aboard the destroyer USS *Kane*, to determine Japanese numbers on Majuro. A week later the unit rowed ashore to become the first Americans to set foot on territory held by the Japanese before their attack on Hawaii. Once again they found the atoll lightly defended and secured it without assistance from the main attack element.

Eniwetok was the next objective for the recon marines. After relaying intelligence to their superiors about the island's defenses, the recon men remained ashore to assist the 22nd Marine Regiment Combat Team. In the battle that followed, the recon company accounted for fifteen dead enemy soldiers with no friendly casualties.

The navy honored the Amphibious Reconnaissance Company when it returned to Pearl Harbor. Jones received the Legion of Merit and General Holland M. Smith, commander of the V Amphibious Corps, gave the company a special citation that recognized its "skill, courage, and determination." Smith concluded, "The high state of efficiency, intrepidity, and resourcefulness displayed by the men of the Amphibious Reconnaissance Company will serve as an inspiration to all ranks of the Corps."

On April 14, 1944, the V Amphibious Corps increased the company's authorized strength to 20 officers and 270 enlisted marines and redesignated it the Amphibious Reconnaissance Battalion. Jones, now a major, advanced several of his platoon leader lieutenants to captains in command of companies. He then selected experienced lieutenants from the regular marine regiments and secured direct commissions for NCOs from the company to lead the platoons.

The first use of the recon battalion came in the battle for Tinian in the Mariana Islands. A pre-invasion reconnaissance on the night of July 9–10, 1944, revealed the beach chosen for the assault to be well defended and reinforced with heavy fortifications and obstacles. However, the reconnaissance also discovered alternate beaches relatively free of defenses that changed the entire invasion plan.

After the invasion of Tinian the landing operations officer credited the recon marines for the success of the assault, stating, "In the absence of the detailed information which these reconnaissance units gave us on the extremely narrow and restricted beaches it would not have been sound to embark on this risky operation."

On August 26, 1944, once again back in Hawaii, the battalion underwent another name change to become the Amphibious Reconnaissance Battalion, Fleet Marine Force. The battalion continued to play a role in the island-hopping campaign toward Japan as it participated in the invasion of Iwo Jima in February 1945, Okinawa in March, and Ike Shima in April. In each invasion the recon men provided important intelligence that conserved manpower and munitions for the marines and sailors whom they served.

The end of the war brought about by the atomic bombings of Hiroshima and Nagasaki concluded the combat operations of the recon battalion. Marine leaders, knowing that the corps would be reduced to prewar numbers, disbanded the battalion at its Pearl Harbor base on September 24, 1945. Some of the recon marines accepted discharges and returned to civilian life, but many remained in uniform and transferred to the regular regiments. Their experience and expertise would prove useful when the corps once again recognized the need for reconnaissance units.

In the austerity of the post–World War II military, the marine corps continued to study reconnaissance doctrine and to refine equipment requirements. Several small units from regiments and divisions experimented with submarine delivery systems in the late 1940s, and recon teams joined the navy's underwater demolition teams to conduct raids during the Korean War.

A provisional recon company supported the First Marine Division in Korea. This unit drew the best of the corps, including many displaced persons and immigrants who had fled their homelands in the aftermath of World War II and the communist takeover of Eastern Europe.

The recon unit attracted a mixed group of colorful characters best described in an article written by Peter Kalischer in the October 25, 1952, issue of *Colliers* magazine. Kalischer called the recon company the "Foreign Legion of the Marine Corps." He included examples such as Private First Class Albert Type, a bridge-blowing member of the Polish underground who was captured by the Gestapo in 1943, tortured, and then sent as a slave laborer to the coal mines before being liberated by the Americans; Corporal Edward S. Chin Jr., an American-born Chinese who was almost drafted into the Red Army while attending school in Canton; PFC Miguel Alvarez, a refugee from Franco's Spain; PFC Michael Averko Olaff von Hiderbrand, a former member of German army intelligence proficient in nine languages and once a member of the Hitler Youth; PFC Vytautus Juskus, a Lithuanian refugee; Corporal Saznek Betrosian, an Armenian who had lived all but six of his twenty-two years in Iran and Russia; Corporal

George Feodorovich Homiakoff, a Shanghai-born white Russian; PFC French Roff, an Eyptian; PFC John Diener, a former German army tank crewman who at age fifteen had fought on the Russian front; Corporal Visvaldis Mangulis, an immigrant from Latvia; and PFC Steven J. Szkupinski, a former member of both the French Foreign Legion and the British army who could ask, "Which way to the border?" in eleven different languages.

Early in the Korean War the marine corps organized recon units on both the Atlantic and Pacific coasts to test new ideas and to provide replacements for the company in the war zone. On December 1, 1950, the corps activated the Second Amphibious Reconnaissance Battalion at Camp Lejeune, North Carolina. The activation of the smaller First Amphibious Reconnaissance Platoon followed on March 12, 1951.

After the cease-fire in Korea on July 17, 1953, the recon units went through a series of changes in their numbers and missions. The recon marines had proven their value in combat, but the corps was uncertain how to use them. Leaders understood that the over-the-beach amphibious assault was a thing of the past and that modern technology, including the helicopter, which had emerged as an important means of transportation in Korea, would dominate future battlefields.

With this in mind the commandant of the marine corps directed the activation of Marine Corps Test Unit Number 1 on July 1, 1954, with the mission of developing vertical-deployment and assault-by-helicopter doctrine. Shortly after the unit's formation its leaders saw the need for reconnaissance for proposed landing sites and operational areas before insertion of heliborne units.

On May 12, 1955, the test unit authorized the formation of a reconnaissance platoon. In addition to their entering reconnaissance areas by foot, boat, and helicopter, the recon officers saw that some reconnaissance zones could best be entered by parachute. During the spring of 1956 the platoon attended the army's paratrooper school at Fort Benning, Georgia, with some marines staying on to receive training as jumpmasters and Pathfinders. When they completed their training, the marine corps had the first parachute-qualified unit in its history.

Marine leaders declared the test unit a success on June 30, 1957, and transferred its members to other units to assume leadership positions there and to teach the new concepts of helicopter warfare. The test unit recon platoon merged with the First Amphibious Reconnaissance Company of the Fleet Marine Force to form the First Force Recon Company. A year later, a cadre from First Force transferred to the Second Amphibious Reconnaissance Company of the Atlantic Fleet Marine Force to assist in the transformation to the Second Force Reconnaissance Company.

From their formation in the late 1950s until escalation of American participation in the Vietnam War in 1965, the two Force Recon companies remained the only units in the Department of Defense specifically organized and trained to perform long-range reconnaissance. After their activation the Force Recon companies participated in every major marine and naval exercise around the world. They quickly developed a reputation as an elite within an elite as much for their intense physical fitness as for their field expertise and unfailing discipline. While the American public equated *marine* with the best of the fighting men, the marines themselves admitted that the recon men were a breed apart within the corps's own ranks.

During the early years of U.S. involvement in Vietnam, the U.S. Congress pressured the Department of Defense to limit the number of servicemen assigned there. To circumvent these restrictions, the military deployed men and units to Southeast Asia on "temporary duty" so that they would not count against the total number officially in-country. Although several recon marines served in Vietnam as advisers on official tours, the first Force Recon unit arrived on temporary duty.

Sub Unit Number 1 of the First Force Reconnaissance Company, composed of one officer and thirteen enlisted marines, arrived in Vietnam on July 6, 1964, for a thirty-day tour. From its base on Okinawa, Sub Unit 1 returned to Vietnam for several additional temporary tours over the next year.

By the time the marine corps began to deploy regular units to Vietnam in the mid-1960s, it had expanded its reconnaissance units. In addition to a recon company assigned to the Marine Force Command, each of the two subordinate divisions had an organic reconnaissance battalion.

Battalion and Force Recon units differed both in mission and method of operation. According to their mission statement, Force Recon was responsible for reconnaissance up to three hundred miles inland from the shore. Members were to gather information that Marine Force headquarters could use in long-range planning, including discovering rear-area assembly locations, determining enemy capabilities and morale, and analyzing the type and condition of enemy equipment and weapons.

Battalion Recon, on the other hand, was organized so that each of its three companies could support one of its division's three regiments. These companies could further be broken into platoons to be attached to the battalions subordinate to each regiment. Teams from Battalion Recon conducted patrols to gather information that could influence immediate rather than long-range operations. Because of their likelihood of directly engaging the enemy, Battalion Recon teams operated close to regular marine units so that they could be quickly reinforced.

During the Vietnam War many marines alternated tours between Force and Battalion Recon units. However, the smaller Force Recon companies accepted only the very best of their Battalion Recon comrades.

The First Force Recon Company arrived in Da Nang on August 7, 1965. Although it rarely had its full complement of assigned marines, the official table of organization for the company called for 12 officers and 145 enlisted men. The company headquarters contained five officers and twenty-six enlisted marines, while a single officer led a supply platoon of thirty-five marines. Six recon platoons, each composed of one officer and fourteen recon marines, made up the company's actual field operators.

Despite their training and abilities, the marine reconnaissance units did not fare well during their first months in Vietnam. They shared the frustrations of other units in having to determine how to fight a different kind of war against a dedicated and determined enemy. It also took a while for the senior marine commanders to understand the best methods for deploying their recon assets and how to use the information they produced.

As the war progressed, the First Force Recon Company learned to outguerrilla the guerrilla by using many of the enemy's own tactics—working in small groups, using the jungle and terrain to remain hidden, and striking only when it had the advantage. Replacements for wounded recon marines and for those who completed their tours came from the Second Force Recon Company that remained at Camp Lejeune. Many of the recon men rotated back and forth between the two companies for the remainder of the war. The corps formed another company when the need for additional reconnaissance assets in the war zone became apparent. Lead elements of the Third Force Reconnaissance Company arrived in Vietnam on October 2, 1967, and by the end of the month the entire company was conducting patrols against the enemy.

On January 31, 1967, the Corps formed the Fifth Force Reconnaissance Company at Camp Pendleton to provide another unit to train replacements and serve as a rotation base for veterans. One platoon accompanied the 27th Marine Regiment when it deployed to Vietnam in response to the Tet Offensive of February 1968.

Recon marines from all the companies quickly learned in Vietnam that stateside training and perceptions of the enemy back home were way off target. One recon marine near the end of his tour early in the war noted these deficiencies. According to Corporal John T. Morrissey, "I know most of the marines back in the States believe this war is nothing much at all. Well, you actually have to come over yourself and experience it. The marines back in the States, a lot of them believe that the enemy is just 'gooks' and that they're stupid. The VC [Vietcong] aren't good soldiers, but the NVA [North Vietnamese army regulars] are—they're professionals. The enemy is far from being the 'stupid Oriental' as many believe them to be. They've been fighting ever since before World War II—that's a long time. He knows lots of stuff. He can go on and on. Back in the States it's recon, recon, recon, all the way, gung ho, and all that kind of stuff. Running, running, running; pushups, pushups, pushups; deep knee bends, etc. That stuff is all well and good back in the States where it's mostly 'hot dog,' but over here, it's not going to do you that much good. The type of conditioning that you should be getting is to put on a 70- or 80-pound pack on your back and go humping five days, six days, maybe more, out in the brush climbing high mountains, down into ravines, crawling on your hands and knees through the brush."

The blood warriors of Force Recon adapted their training and tactics to meet and defeat their communist opponents. They soon discovered that, in addition to providing valuable intelligence through their reconnaissance, they could significantly contribute to the enemy body count through direct combat action.

Although the official doctrine for Force Recon outlined in Fleet Marine Force Manual 2-2, titled "Amphibious Reconnaissance" and published in 1963, dictated a supportive rather than a combative role for the recon companies, the recon men were more than willing to take on any mission assigned. They were soon operating in small groups deep in enemy territory, where they called in artillery and air support on large enemy concentrations and directly engaged small units with their organic weapons.

In August 1966 Force Recon began specific combat missions known as Stingray patrols. By the time the United States withdrew from Vietnam, the Force Recon companies had conducted 8,317 Stingray missions. These patrols accounted for 15,680 sightings of an estimated total of 138,252 enemy soldiers. The recon teams had called in 6,463 artillery-fire missions and 1,328 air strikes, resulting in 9,566 confirmed kills and 85 prisoners captured.

In addition to their superior performance on the battlefield, Force Recon made the first three combat parachute jumps in marine history. On June 14, 1966, Captain Jerome Paull led twelve marines from the Fourth Platoon of First Force on a parachute insertion near Hill 555 west of Chu Lai to establish an observation post in support of an offensive named Operation Kansas. The Force Recon patrol members jumped at night, assembled, and established their post on Hill 555, from where they relayed information to the operation commander on enemy activity in the area.

After the main force safely entered the area by helicopter, the Force Recon patrol returned to its base. The commander of the First Marine Division praised the patrol's success in a message that stated, "I report with pride that every Recon type, past, present, and future can stand tall in the shadow of the daring exploit of Paull and 12 First Force Recon marines, who made the first successful jump 37 miles deep into Viet Cong territory. I am honored they served with us."

On September 5, 1967, a team led by Gunnery Sergeant Walter Webb from the company's Fifth Platoon jumped into the Happy Valley region southwest of Da Nang. Unexpected high winds separated many of the marines during the drop, preventing the team from assembling to accomplish their mission.

The failure of this mission underscored the fact that helicopters could more safely deliver teams to their recon zones, thus ending marine parachute missions in Vietnam except for one final drop. A third jump took place on November 17, 1969, for the purpose of reestablishing the feasibility of parachute insertion as much as to perform reconnaissance. A six-man patrol led by First Lieutenant Wayne Rollings jumped on a shrub-covered drop zone along the beach of the South China Sea near the village of Nui Tran. The team jumped an hour before dawn and then assembled on the beach; from there they moved out on a successful four-day reconnaissance.

When the United States began to withdraw its forces and turn the war over to the South Vietnamese in late 1969, the Force Recon companies either returned to the States or were deactivated in the postwar troop reductions. Fifth Force Reconnaissance Company deactivated on October 15, 1969, followed by the Third Company the next August.

The First Force Reconnaissance Company arrived back at Camp Pendleton on September 11, 1971. In the postwar cutbacks the company was never at more than half strength. With no active aggressor in the Pacific and the Warsaw Pact still a threat along the Iron Curtain in Europe, the Second Company at Camp Lejeune received the most assets and priority because of its proximity to Europe.

As cutbacks continued the First Company became smaller and smaller. On September 30, 1974, fewer than half a dozen marines were still assigned to the company when it held its official deactivation ceremony and cased its colors. An era in blood-warrior history marked by dedication, bravery, tenacity, and sacrifice had come to an inauspicious conclusion.

To one side of the area where the ceremony was held was a trash bin. On its top was a discarded sign that had once been proudly displayed on the wall of the company's operations section. The faded letters declared, IF EVERYONE COULD BE FORCE RECON, IT WOULDN'T BE FORCE RECON.

CHAPTER 14

✳✳✳✳✳✳✳✳

U.S. Marine Corps Force Reconnaissance: Today

*F*_{OR} more than a decade after the Vietnam War, the Second Company stood alone to uphold the expertise and traditions of Force Recon. It drew many of its members from the ranks of Force Recon veterans of the war in Southeast Asia as well as from smaller conflicts that followed.

Marine leaders struggled to maintain as large and as effective a fighting force as possible in times of diminishing manpower and other resources. The failure to keep Vietnam free in the 1970s, the U.S. intervention campaigns—including Grenada and Panama—in the 1980s, and finally the fall of the Soviet Union in the 1990s greatly influenced their efforts.

At the beginning of the twenty-first century the corps numbers only 172,000 marines, organized into three Marine Expeditionary Forces (MEFs). Each MEF consists of a marine division, air wing, and service support group. Within the MEFs are Marine Expeditionary Units (MEUs) composed of twenty-one hundred men and all the support assets needed to sustain them for thirty days. These MEUs are usually forward-deployed aboard naval vessels and capable of immediate entry into hostile territory. The level of their readiness showed in late 2001 when an MEU was the first conventional unit to arrive in Afghanistan to support the war against terrorism.

Marine Force and Battalion Reconnaissance units also went through many changes during the three decades after the Vietnam War. The need for a recon capacity within the MEF area of responsibility remained constant. As a result each of the marine divisions maintained its recon battalion, with the mission of providing tactical reconnaissance. Although its physical and mental requirements are somewhat higher than those of regular regiments, Battalion Reconnaissance does accept marines serving their first enlistment. It does not require its members to be airborne-qualified and limits their missions to reconnaissance and surveillance. The lack of a direct action mission on the part of the recon battalions enhances their capability to perform its more limited reconnaissance mission.

While marine leaders agreed on the need for Battalion Reconnaissance, the debate raged about Force Recon. Supporters noted the emphasis on special operations after the failure at Desert One in 1982 and the increased threat in the Mideast and Central America. Detractors pointed out that Force Recon drained needed junior leaders from the infantry regiments by accepting only marines who had reenlisted for a second tour.

Despite the naysayers, the marine corps began plans in 1986 to reactivate the First Company. On May 27, 1987, the colors of the First Force Reconnaissance Company were unfurled at Camp Pendleton with many of its veterans in attendance.

The activation of First Force, however, did not end the debate over manpower assets. Over the next decade several tests and changes attempted to make the Force companies a part of Battalion Reconnaissance. None of these experiments has proven satisfactory, and additional reorganizations continue. In early 2002 only the First Force Reconnaissance Company at Camp Pendleton retains its independence. The Second Company is a part of the Second Reconnaissance Battalion at Camp Lejeune, and the Fifth Company is subordinate to the reconnaissance battalion on the Pacific island of Okinawa.

To provide a means of expansion and buildup in time of emergency, the marine reserve has activated two additional companies. The Third Force Recon Company is based at Mobile, Alabama, and the Fourth Company at Honolulu, Hawaii.

A detachment of the Fourth Company is stationed at Reno, Nevada.

While all of these units qualify to some degree as blood warriors, only the First Force Reconnaissance Company currently meets all the requirements for inclusion in this exclusive group. It also bears the distinction of being the only unit of blood warriors not subordinate to the U.S. Special Operations Command. While First Force and the forward-deployed Marine Expeditionary Units are "Special Operations Capable" and do, in fact, on occasion support USSOCOM operations, they are not subordinate to the command as are the Rangers, Special Forces, Delta Force, Special Tactics teams, and SEALs.

The marine corps, willing and prepared to support American military operations, has remained independent from USSOCOM. Marine leaders, with justification from their experiences in Vietnam and Desert Storm, fear that USSOCOM will deny them the use of their special assets in time of crisis. The marines appreciate having their own aviation and reconnaissance assets under their control and do not like the idea of them being consolidated under USSOCOM command. They strongly believe that marines are trained and best used to support other marines.

That is not to say that the marine corps and USSOCOM do not continue to work together. In 1993 the commander of USSOCOM and the commandant of the marine corps signed a Memorandum of Agreement that provides for a board of officers who act as a forum to coordinate common mission areas and similar procurement initiatives. This agreement has been renewed with the changes of commanders over the past decade.

The degree of cooperation between the corps and USSOCOM has varied with the personalities of their commanders and the world situation. Mostly the relationship has been cordial but without a direct command line. Basically, the policy has been that if USSOCOM needs marine assets, it politely asks for them. The corps either provides the requested units or politely declines.

During the counterterrorism operations in Afghanistan, USSOCOM needed the naval fleet as forward staging areas. An integral part of this fleet was the Marine Expeditionary Unit that eventually deployed into Afghanistan. While USSOCOM welcomed and required the use of the ships, it did not necessarily want the MEU involved in-country. On the other hand, the marine corps took the position that USSOCOM cannot use the fleet as a staging area without also using the MEUs.

At present it appears that USSOCOM needs the marines more than the marines need USSOCOM. Some sort of formal relationship between USSOCOM and the marine corps is likely forthcoming—and the reconnaissance community will benefit from the relationship in renewed interest, additional manpower, and budget resources.

In the meantime the First Force Reconnaissance Company continues to set the example for current and future Marine Force Recon units. Although First Force is a company with the assigned personnel strength of 162 typical of company-sized units, its organization is battalion based. A lieutenant colonel leads First Force, a major acts as executive officer, a sergeant major serves as the senior noncommissioned officer, and captains command the platoons. The company headquarters has a staff similar to that of a battalion, with sections for personnel, intelligence, operations, and logistics.

Six platoons, each composed of three recon teams, make up the company. The accelerated experience and rank structure continues within the six-man teams, with a staff sergeant in charge of five sergeants—an assistant team leader, a radio operator, and three scouts. The company totals 11 officers, 140 enlisted marines, and 11 navy enlisted medical corpsmen and dive personnel.

First Force Reconnaissance Company is currently subordinate to the I Marine Expeditionary Force at Camp Pendleton, California. The mission of First Force is to conduct amphibious reconnaissance, ground recon and surveillance, battlefield shaping (directing naval gunfire, air strikes, and artillery to channel the enemy), and limited-scale raids for the I MEF, other marine task forces, or joint task forces.

Subtasks include implanting and/or recovering ground sensors and emplacing guiding markers for helicopters, landing craft, and parachutists. Members also acquire targets, engage them with artillery, air, and other fire support, and then conduct poststrike, or bomb damage, assessment. In addition the company regularly provides personal security for high-ranking military and civilian personnel. These varied tasks are known as the "green" side of their mission within the company.

The last subtask of First Force separates it from Battalion Recon and solidifies its members among the ranks of the blood warriors. As a part of its mission to conduct limited-scale raids, First Force marines are prepared to "destroy critical enemy targets, capture selected enemy personnel, and recover sensitive items and personnel." This "black" side of the Force Recon mission differs little from that of the Rangers, Delta Force, and SEALs.

To accomplish these missions First Force trains in a wide range of insertion and extraction methods. In addition to their ability to walk to their target areas, the Force Recon marines use all types of wheeled and tracked vehicles for overland transportation as well as motorized-improved fast-attack vehicles (FAVs). Their stable of FAVs, which resemble civilian dune buggies, provide the recon marines a rugged, fast, low-profile vehicle particularly useful in desert environments. Annually, usually in December, First Force trains with the FAVs at the Twentynine Palms marine base in southeastern California.

The recon men are also experienced in the use of all types of water transportation, including surface Zodiac boats, submarines, amphibious craft, and open- and closed-circuit subsurface scuba gear. From the air they can reach their targets by fast-roping, rappelling, helicopter landing, static line parachuting, or high-altitude low-opening (HALO) operations.

The soul of Force Recon, like all the blood-warrior units, is the men who fill its ranks. Admission into Force Recon involves a lengthy and demanding selection process. Anyone within the corps may volunteer, but candidates must meet several qualifications before being considered. Volunteers must have already proven themselves as "good marines"— meaning that they have done well over a period of three to five years—and have likely reached the rank of sergeant, and reenlisted or are prepared to do so. They must have above-average intelligence scores, strong swimming and accurate shooting skills, and excellent physical stamina. Force, like the other blood-warrior units, accepts only males.

Volunteers generally come from the infantry battalions, but there are positions within the company for logistic and transportation specialists as well. Since all marines attend boot camp and infantry training, even these specialists possess the basic skills of marksmanship, land navigation, and patrolling.

Volunteers face one large obstacle even before attempting to gain acceptance into Force. Commanders are reluctant to release anyone to other units, especially the superior marines attracted to Force. Like the other services, the marines contain factions of those who dislike the concentration of the best men and the most budget assets into elite units. Force leaders counter that limited five-year tours with the company make a better-trained and -prepared marine who returns to his original unit. This does little to mollify the concerns of regular commanders, who need good leaders in the present rather than the future.

One day a month, usually on the last Thursday, First Force conducts its indoctrination test. There is no automatic acceptance into the company. Even marines reporting from other reconnaissance units must face and pass the company's selection process.

Over the years Force Recon has established standards for

selection, none of which includes harassing or demeaning volunteers. Selection begins with the Standard Physical Fitness Test. Enlisted men must achieve a score of 92 percent of the maximum, while officers must score 95 percent. A timed obstacle course and calisthenics exercise follows the PT test.

Next the volunteers enter a swimming pool for a series of swim tests. Those who pass the PT and swim exercises don fifty-pound packs, pick up their rifles, and move out over mountains and down the beach on a ten-mile forced march.

Marines who pass the physical tests then go through a psychological screening. Those found acceptable interview with senior company leaders. The company commander meets with officers, while the company sergeant major and several other senior NCOs interview enlisted volunteers.

It is rare for as many as half of the volunteers to pass the indoctrination process and be accepted into the company. Occasionally none of the candidates pass the rigorous physical and mental exams. Those who do not pass are welcome to return for future trials. It is not unusual for a marine to attempt the process three or even four times before gaining acceptance. Whatever the pros and cons of the indoctrination system, it works well. It is rare for a marine who passes the indoctrination to fail to complete the training and schools that makes him a full-fledged member of Force.

Upon acceptance into the company the new recon marines are organized into a platoon and begin a five-phase training cycle. Phase I, Individual Training, begins with the eight-week Basic Reconnaissance Course at Coronado, California, or Little Creek, Virginia, where the marines learn the techniques and skills of reconnaissance. The recon marines train during this period as a platoon using the unit's standard operating procedure manual, with members of the company operations section overseeing the training to ensure completeness and standardization. Upon completion of Basic Recon, the marines attend the army's paratrooper school at Fort Benning and the Combat Dive Course at Panama City, Florida.

Navy corpsmen accepted into Force to fill slots for medical support follow a similar training program. Although they attend field medical and other corpsman schools, Force medics are first and foremost combatants. When assigned to platoons they usually carry squad automatic weapons (SAWs) and are "shooters" first and "healers" second. A common saying among Force corpsmen is, "Fire superiority is the best type of combat medicine."

The Operations Cell also supervises Phase II, Unit Training, which lasts six months. In this phase the marines learn to use the individual skills acquired in Phase I to become effective teams that focus on amphibious operations and deep reconnaissance. This teamwork training takes place in all kinds of weather and terrain, including the rain forest and snowy mountains of Washington State, the swamps of Louisiana, and the deserts of Arizona and Nevada.

In addition to teamwork, the platoon members practice nautical navigation and hydrographic surveying; communications procedures; indirect fire control of artillery, naval gunfire, and air support; and first aid and trauma treatment. They also attend a three-week weapons and tactics course at Camp Pendleton, where each marine fires from five thousand to eight thousand rounds with his individual weapons. Next comes live-fire/immediate-action training to rehearse team patrol standard operating procedures. Weapons training concludes with a weeklong session at Fort Irwin, California, where marines receive instruction from the army on weapons used by allies and potential enemies.

By the time the recon marines complete Phase II, they have been in training for twelve months. During Phase III they join a Marine Expeditionary Unit (MEU) to train for forward deployment. During MEU training, individual recon marines also attend courses in demolitions and explosives. Some train in military free-fall parachuting or learn jumpmaster or Pathfinder skills. At least one in each platoon attends sniper school, and a few go to the army's Ranger School.

After eighteen months of continuous training with Force,

the platoon is prepared for deployment in Phase IV with a Marine Expeditionary Unit to the western Pacific, the Mediterranean Sea, or the Persian Gulf. During its deployment the platoon continues training or conducts actual missions against hostile force if required. One of these deployed platoons provided some of the first marines in Afghanistan in the war against terror that began in 2001. Other platoons rotating into the war zone have maintained a Force presence in Afghanistan since that time.

Upon completion of the six-month deployment, the platoon returns to Camp Pendleton for Phase V, Postdeployment. During this phase the recon marines take leave before assuming new positions within the company or as leaders or trainers of newly formed platoons. Officers are restricted to three years with Force, while enlisted marines are limited to five years. This generally allows an officer one deployment while enlisted men deploy twice before returning to the regular regiments. Although this policy allows Force veterans to share their expertise with regular infantrymen, it also means that the company must constantly recruit and train new members.

Force Recon marines definitely share the elite status of their fellow blood warriors in the Rangers, Special Forces, and SEALs. The current world situation and emphasis on counterterrorism may cause other Force Recon companies to emerge and may subordinate them all to the U.S. Special Operations Command. Whatever occurs, the recon marines will be on the forward edge of the battlefield.

CHAPTER 15

✳✳✳✳✳✳✳✳

Snipers: History

*W*HILE today's American military elites are concentrated in the Rangers, Special Forces, Delta, SEALs, Special Tactics, and Force Recon, there are many soldiers and marines in the regular infantry ranks who share the unique skills of blood warriors. These are the graduates of the army's and marine corps's sniper schools.

All infantrymen share the hardships and dangers of direct combat, but a few of these men, in the regular units as well as the elites, train to engage individual targets with special weapons and equipment. These blood warriors live by the code of "one shot, one kill" as they look through their telescopes at targets, pull the trigger, and often regain their sight picture in time to see the bullet strike.

Marksmanship has always been an important skill for any infantryman, and in the midst of combat accurate fire superiority is usually the key to success. Snipers, however, can turn the tide of a fight by eliminating leaders, machine-gun crews, and other critical personnel. A sniper striking from a "hide" position can also significantly impact enemy morale. Knowing that if he is visible, he is vulnerable, vastly reduces an opponent's mobility, and more important, his confidence. Soldiers, terrorists, and criminals lose their advantage when they become a target for "death from afar."

The idea of specially trained marksmen is not new, but their capabilities and acceptance are. Weapons capable of accurate, long-range killing have been available only for the past two centuries. Many countries, particularly the United

States, have been reluctant to train marksmen who strike from a hidden position because such tactics appear more appropriate for assassins than combat soldiers. Americans have traditionally not accepted these "one-shot killers" and have authorized them only in the midst of war. For its first two hundred years of independence the United States categorized sniping as an "ungentlemanly" form of warfare during peacetime and neither trained nor equipped special marksmen.

It was not until the Vietnam War and the rise of terrorism in the years that followed necessitated such skills that the authorization for schools, equipment, and slots for snipers within infantry and elite units finally emerged. The evolution of this process, like elite units themselves, has been dependent on the advances of the tools and methods of warfare itself.

By definition a sniper is an individual who uses a special weapon system, usually from a concealed position at a great distance, to shoot an individual. While a weapon's capability may exceed the ability of the shooter, no shooter can exceed the capability of his weapon. Logically, this means that the history of sniping parallels the development of weaponry.

Warfare, of course, is as old as mankind itself. The needs for food, territory, and propagation that led to fighting among clans and tribes have always been a part of human experience, regardless of culture and intelligence. Early man fought with clubs and rocks before he advanced to the use of spears. Warriors who could throw rocks or spears some distance and hit their targets certainly gained the respect of their allies and enemies as well as ensuring their own survival. However, the development of the sling and the bow and arrow did not greatly increase the killing ability of the individual. Although these weapons increased the lethality beyond a man's arm's distance, their lack of accuracy called for them to be used in mass rather than single aimed shots.

Thousands of years passed before weapons advanced to the point that with practice an individual could gain an advantage beyond personal strength. Improved bows and arrows and the introduction of the crossbow increased range, but mass rather than individual accuracy continued to characterize warfare.

The real future of individual marksmanship began with advances in the production of gunpowder. By the late twelfth century, inventors in China, England, and Germany had successfully experimented with the chemical mixture of potassium nitrate (saltpeter), wood charcoal, and sulfur to create a crude form of gunpowder. While the Chinese remained satisfied with using the explosive powder for ceremonial fireworks, the English and the Europeans began experimenting with using the blast energy to fire projectiles from iron tubes.

As early as 1247 the Spanish used gunpowder to fire cannon in defense of the city of Seville. The English were also successful in their use of gunpowder during this period and began to refer to the weapons as *guns*, a term apparently derived from the Teutonic words *gunhide* and *gundeine*, both meaning "war." By the mid–fourteenth century references to *gonne*, *gounne*, and *gunne* began to appear in English documents. An expenditure report for the court of Edward III in 1345 lists payment for the repair and transport of "13 guns and pellets."

Early guns required a "touch hold" at their rear, where the powder was ignited with a burning coal. Over the next two hundred years innovators added wooden stocks to control the metal barrels and protect the firer from the heat. Advances in powder production produced tiny pellets or "corns" that provided a quicker, more uniform explosion. Pans that allowed ignition by burning ropes called matches replaced touch holes.

By the latter part of the fifteenth century the Spanish and other armies began to issue crude muskets to some of their soldiers. At the Battle of Cerignola in Italy in 1503, Spanish General Fernandez Gonzalo de Cordoba armed several hundred men with .75-caliber muskets and interspersed them in his army of six thousand pikemen. When a French army of ten thousand soldiers carrying swords and pikes assaulted the

Spanish positions, rank after rank fell to the gunfire. The surviving French finally withdrew; no battlefield would ever be the same.

Over the next century armies throughout Europe and around the world began to adopt firearms as their principal infantry weapon. These smoothbore muskets were inaccurate and they, like the bow and arrow and crossbow, continued to be used in volley rather than aimed individual fire. Because the lack of reliability in adverse weather and the reloading time required left the infantryman vulnerable, bayonets were added to convert each musket into a short pike when needed.

Accuracy improved when manufacturers added grooves to the barrel's interior that made the bullet spin rapidly in flight, which stabilized its path. This "rifling" lent its name to more accurate weapons, but the expense of rifles and their increased loading time initially kept them out of the hands of common soldiers.

Many of the earliest European explorers of the New World carried firearms. Hernán Cortés defeated the Aztecs in Mexico in 1519 and Francisco Pizarro conquered South America in 1533 largely because of the advantage provided by their firearms. English and French colonists in North America also relied on muskets in their encounters with Natives.

Advances in firearms continued, with Europeans making the most significant innovations. In the middle of the seventeenth century gun makers perfected the flintlock, consisting of a spring-loaded hammer that held a flint. When released by the trigger, the hammer-held flint struck a steel edge to produce a spark that ignited the primer powder in a pan. By the end of the 1600s England, France, and other European countries had entire regiments armed with flintlock muskets.

Flintlocks eliminated the need for burning matches, but their open powder pans remained vulnerable to damp weather, which caused misfires. Covered pans helped somewhat, and paper cartridges reduced loading time.

These advances quickly made their way to the American colonies. Pennsylvania and New England gun makers added improvements by increasing barrel length and reducing bullet size. Their long guns with rifled barrels were the most accurate of the period and became the favorite of hunters and frontiersmen. These rifles could not be mass-produced, however, and their cost prevented their acquisition by the colonial militias or the English army.

By the time of the American Revolution, the Long Land Service Musket, better known as the Brown Bess, had become the standard English infantry weapon. It had a forty-six-inch-long barrel and weighed ten pounds. Infantrymen reloaded these .75-caliber muskets with .71-caliber balls. Although this accomplished the purpose of making reloading faster, it eliminated any degree of accuracy, because the smaller projectile literally rattled out of the smoothbore barrel.

The French fielded similar weapons of a slightly smaller .69 caliber known as Charlevilles. The Brown Bess and the Charleville were the primary infantry weapons employed in the American Revolution—both extremely inaccurate. Major George Hanger, a British ordnance expert, wrote about this after the war, stating, "A soldier's musket will strike a figure of a man at 80 yards; it may even at a hundred, but a soldier must be very unfortunate indeed who shall be wounded by a common musket at 150 yards, providing his antagonist aims at him; and as to firing at a man at 200 yards, with a common musket, you may just as well fire at the moon."

Not all the Americans, however, armed themselves with "common muskets." On June 12, 1775, the Continental Congress authorized officials in Pennsylvania to form six companies of soldiers equipped with long rifles. A few days later, Congress expanded this order to nine companies, and by the end of the month special marksmen were mustered into the new units.

The rifle companies underwent several changes in name and commanders over the next year. In July 1776 they became the 1st Pennsylvania Continental Regiment and joined the Rifle Corps led by Colonel Daniel Morgan. In the 1st Pennsylvania stood Private Timothy Murphy, who would become America's first expert combat marksman and a hero of the Revolution.

In the fall of 1777 the British began an offensive down the Hudson River Valley from Canada to divide the colonies in two. Morgan's riflemen stopped the advance at Freeman's farm in New York on September 19, 1777. The British commander, General John Burgoyne, dispatched General Simon Frazer to Bemis Heights over the Hudson River to scout the American position for a renewed attack. Frazer stopped about three hundred yards from the American positions, assuming he was out of their range. He was wrong. Private Murphy and another marksman each fired one shot at the general but missed. Murphy then climbed into a tree for a second shot, which knocked the British general out of his saddle with a mortal wound.

When he learned of Frazer's death, Burgoyne retreated to Saratoga, where the Americans quickly surrounded him and forced the British to surrender on October 17. Murphy's well-aimed shot not only led to victory at Saratoga, but also significantly influenced the outcome of the entire Revolution. The American victory convinced the French that the rebels might very well defeat the British. They soon recognized the independence of the United States and joined them as an ally in their fight for independence.

General Burgoyne also understood the influence of marksmanship in his defeat. He remarked, "Morgan's men were the most famous Corps of the Continental Army. All of them crack shots."

Some British officers made efforts on their own to field specially equipped and trained riflemen. Major Patrick Ferguson of the 70th Foot Regiment developed a precision rifle and led a unit of a hundred trained men to engage the rebels with accurate shots. Able to shoot at distances of more than two hundred yards, the British marksmen with their "Ferguson rifles" were successful, but many British officers detested this "unsportsman-like" method of killing the enemy.

Even Ferguson had doubts about engaging targets from

afar with no warning. His reluctance greatly influenced the survival of the American leader. Early on a foggy morning in October 1777, Ferguson and a guide ventured forward of the British lines at Germantown outside Philadelphia in the hope of finding an unsuspecting target. Shortly after Ferguson assumed his hide position, General George Washington and a few of his staff approached on a reconnaissance mission of their own. Ferguson's guide recognized the American commander and identified him for the British marksman. Before Ferguson could fire, however, Washington and his party turned back toward their own lines.

Ferguson did not shoot. He explained in a letter to a relative, "It is not pleasing to fire at the back of an unoffending individual who was acquitting himself very coolly of his duty, so I let him alone."

During the American Revolution, the expense of precision weapons kept them out of the hands of common soldiers. Wars of the early nineteenth century continued to be fought by massed infantry armed with smoothbore muskets. Advances in arms and ammunition, however, added to the accuracy of rifles and the lethality of the individual infantryman.

The Scottish Reverend Alexander Forsyth patented a percussion firing system in 1807 that used the strike of a gun's cock upon a plunger to explode a bit of detonating powder. This precision cap system and its accompanying lock made the system waterproof and reliable in all types of weather.

In 1848 French Captain Claude E. Minié created a conical-headed, iron-cupped-base bullet that quickly replaced the round balls used in guns for more than five hundred years. Grooves at the base of the "minié ball" expanded when fired to create a tight fit into the rifling, which added to accuracy while also scraping out powder residue as it exited the barrel.

By the time the American Civil War began in 1861, the percussion system, minié ball, and improved powder combined to produce the most accurate rifles in the history of warfare. Both sides fielded marksmen with the mission of engaging the enemy with single, well-aimed shots.

In August 1861 a New York City engineer named Hiram Berdan received permission to form a regiment of "sharpshooters." Berdan claimed in a recruiting poster that the regiment was "destined to be the most important and popular in the service." He also warned, "No person will be enlisted who cannot when firing at a distance of 200 yards, at a rest, put ten consecutive shots in a target, the average distance not to exceed five inches from the center of the bull's eye to the center of the ball."

Berdan selected the name *sharpshooter* not for the Sharps Model 1859 they carried but rather from the term already common for military marksmen in Europe. The first written reference to sharpshooters appeared in an 1802 English dictionary description of Austrian infantry. By the time of the Napoleonic Wars a decade later, the term was common in armies of both sides.

Berdan's Sharpshooters participated in most of the Civil War's major battles, including the Peninsula, Antietam, Chancellorsville, and Gettysburg, with companies of the regiment attached to Union divisions. Several accounts credit the Sharpshooters with more enemy kills than any other regiment in the northern army and with killing at least six Rebel generals.

The Confederate States also fielded marksmen, with units designating individuals to remain hidden prior to and during battles to engage artillery crews and senior officers. Confederate agents in England purchased at least eighteen Whitworth rifles in 1863 and shipped them through the blockade to the southern states. The .45-caliber Whitworths came with fourteen-and-a-half-inch-long telescopic sights* mounted on the left side of the stock. Rebel marksmen were soon killing their targets at distances of up to a thousand yards.

---

* Although the first telescopic scopes appeared in England and Germany as early as 1640, they were not durable enough for sustained combat use until the American Civil War.

Despite their small numbers, the Whitworth-armed Confederates made their mark. On September 19, 1863, a Whitworth marksman mortally wounded Union General William H. Lyle of Ohio. Another Whitworth sharpshooter spotted U.S. General John Sedgwick on May 9, 1864, during the Battle of Spotsylvania, Virginia. Several regular Confederate riflemen began firing at Sedgwick across an open field at a range of more than eight hundred yards. Most of Sedgwick's subordinates took cover, but the general criticized their caution, saying, "They couldn't hit an elephant at this distance." A second later a Whitworth bullet struck him in the head, knocking him dead from his horse.

By the end of the Civil War, soldiers on both sides had learned that a visible soldier was a vulnerable soldier. Additional developments in the United States and Europe continued to verify this knowledge.

Breech-loading rifles introduced in the later stages of the Civil War were perfected. Marksmen could now not only load faster, but also do so from the prone position rather than having to stand or rise to one knee as they had to do with muzzleloaders. Other inventors perfected the self-contained, center-fired metal cartridges, first introduced by New York inventor Walter Hunt in 1848. These cartridges decreased loading time and added to the barrel gas seal, resulting in greater bullet velocity. Alfred Nobel's invention of "smokeless" powder in Sweden in the 1880s eliminated much of the cloud of white smoke that revealed a hidden marksman's position.

It was also during the latter part of the nineteenth century that special marksmen began to be called snipers in armies throughout the world. The term apparently originated with the British in India, where off-duty officers hunted a slender-billed bird related to woodcocks known as the snipe. These birds, fleet of foot and wing, were difficult to hit, leading to those proficient at hitting the elusive targets becoming known as snipers. The British began calling all well-aimed shots, either friendly or enemy, snipes, and those who fired the rounds snipers.

The earliest existing written reference to snipers is in a letter home from a British officer in India in 1773. Another letter from India in 1782 stated, "The individual will be popped at or sniped as they call it from time to time." Three decades later, another British officer wrote from India, "Several Sepoys were killed and wounded by the enemy's snipers who generally stalk the sentries from behind stones." By the time the British were engaged in the Boer War in South Africa at the end of the century, *sniper* had become the preferred term for long-range marksman throughout the Empire.

When the First World War broke out in Europe in the early part of the twentieth century, the term *sniper* was common to English speakers and existed in various forms in other languages. After only a few months of mobile warfare, the conflict bogged down into the trenches, where the sniper proved particularly useful in both killing enemy leaders and adversely affecting the morale of soldiers, who were constantly vulnerable to a single well-aimed shot.

In 1915 the German logistic system scoured hunting clubs and factories for scopes and rifles and shipped twenty thousand sniper weapons to the front. The British countered with snipers of their own and began refining procedures for teams composed of a shooter and an observer.

When the United States entered the war in 1917, it did so with no trained snipers and no doctrine for their development. It did, however, already have a superior rifle in production and approved standards for telescopic sights on the books. The U.S. military had adopted the .30-caliber bolt-action M1903 Springfield in 1906. It proved so accurate and durable that it remained the primary American sniper rifle for the next three decades.

Two years before the adoption of the '03 Springfield, the army began negotiations with the Warner and Swasey Company of Cleveland, Ohio, for the production of telescopic sights suitable for military use. A brief entry in paragraph

269 of the army's "Small Arms Firing Regulation" for 1904 recorded the use of the Warner-Swasey scopes—the first official acceptance of telescopic sights in the U.S. military.

Even though they had the proper equipment and there was certainly a need for special marksmen, the Americans did not formally train snipers. Units at, or headed to, the front selected soldiers who had hunting experience or who were otherwise familiar with shooting and secured them scope-equipped Springfields. These men trained on their own before entering the trenches, where enemy soldiers replaced the paper targets.

There is no record of how many American snipers served in World War I, nor is there any account of their individual accomplishments. Despite the lethality of modern weapons— artillery, poisonous gas, and machine guns—that could and did kill an entire generation of combatants, no one wanted to discuss the very personal method of killing from a hidden position while staring at the prey through a telescopic sight.

Few developments in sniper weapons and training took place during the two decades of peace that followed the armistice that ended World War I. Once the Second World War began, however, the need for special marksmen again became apparent. By the time the German offensive stalled outside Stalingrad in 1942, both the Nazis and the Soviets included snipers as an integral part of their infantry. Soviet commanders found snipers so effective that they began training additional marksmen inside the surrounded city at the Stalingrad Lazur Chemical Plant. Infantrymen fired at painted targets on the plant's interior walls before rejoining the front lines as snipers.

After their victory at Stalingrad, Soviet leader Joseph Stalin recognized the contributions of the snipers. On May 1, 1942, he issued an order that advised, "Line troops must learn the rifle thoroughly, must become masters of their weapons, must kill the enemy without fail, as do our glorious snipers, the exterminators of the German invaders."

The Germans also understood the value of snipers and the

requirements of this special duty. A German officer praised snipers in the May 9, 1944, issue of a Hamburg newspaper, writing that their performance was "very satisfactory." He further provided a description of these marksmen that was true for the rest of the war—as well as today: "Not everyone becomes or is able to become a sniper. Not everyone meets the necessary requirements. Natural proclivity, passion for the chase, fanatical love of firearms—these assure the results of the trained sniper."

The British entered World War II with no trained snipers, remaining reluctant to use marksmen they considered "assassins" rather than infantrymen. Commanders believed that there was little need for the marksmen in the mobile warfare of the period. The number of casualties they suffered from German sharpshooters in North Africa soon changed their minds and had them opening a sniper school in northern Wales in September 1943. British units at the front also began their own sniper training at makeshift ranges just behind the front lines.

The United States likewise entered World War II with no snipers or policy for their development. Despite the obvious need for the marksmen, the U.S. Army did not establish a central program or policy at any time during the war, because senior leaders remained reluctant to formalize recognition of the "one-shot killers." The army left issues of sniper training and deployment up to individual leaders. Some division, regiment, and battalion commanders did not use snipers at all, while others actively recruited and armed soldiers who had hunting or competitive shooting experience. Training was often no more than zeroing the rifle before rejoining the ranks on the front lines.

The War Department did provide some limited guidance. Editions of Field Manual 21-75, "Infantry Scouting, Patrolling, and Sniping," included a chapter on basic sniping principles and established the minimum standard for snipers to be the ability to strike a body target at four hundred yards and a head target at two hundred yards. Even though the army updated the manual regularly during the war, the guidance for snipers never exceeded twelve pages in length.

While the army limited guidance for snipers, it did produce adequate weapons and equipment. Scopes for the standard M1 Garand made the basic infantry weapon into an adequate sniper rifle. Also, '03 Springfields were still widely available for snipers who preferred the bolt-action rifle over the gas-operated M1.

The marine corps, like the army, had no formal sniper program in place prior to World War II, but it had studied the concept and its leaders were much more willing to accept the idea of specially equipped and trained individual marksmen. Two years before the United States entered the war, Captain George O. Van Orden and Chief Marine Gunner Calvin A. Lloyd, while members of the Rifle Range Detachment at Quantico, Virginia, began a study of snipers. Early in 1941 the two men published their findings in a seventy-two-page, single-spaced report titled "Equipment of the American Sniper." The marine corps reproduced the study and forwarded a thousand copies to units around the world.

Van Orden and Lloyd's report, although brief, is the best source of documentation of sniper use prior to World War II and the best predictor of the need and use of future U.S. sniper developments. The two marines outlined the need for the special marksmen and listed the equipment requirements. At the conclusion of Chapter 2 the report emphasized, "The sniper has not survived merely because of the romantic, adventurous glamour which surrounds his campaign of individual extermination—the private war he wages. He is present on the battlefields because there is a real and vital need for him. It is safe to say that the American sniper could be regarded as the greatest all-around rifleman the world has ever known, and his equipment should include the best aids to his dangerous calling that the inventory genius of the United States can produce."

Marine leaders accepted the report's claim of a "real and vital need" for snipers and took measured steps to make them a reality. Van Orden and Lloyd recommended that the .30-caliber Winchester Model 70 equipped with an eight-power telescope manufactured by the John Unertl Optical Company be procured as the basic marine sniper weapon system. On May 29, 1942, the marine corps received 373 Model 70s from the Winchester Company, shipping many to units in the Pacific. The corps did not, however, formally adopt the Model 70 as its official sniper weapon, citing the logistic difficulties in supplying and maintaining an additional rifle type.

While Van Orden and Lloyd did not completely get their way in weapon selection, they did see the beginning of formal sniper training. Sniper schools opened at New River near Camp Lejeune, North Carolina, in December 1942 and at Green's Farm north of San Diego the following month. The marines used champion competition marksmen to command the schools and to act as instructors. Both schools issued M1s as the basic sniper weapon but also provided training with the '03 Springfields and the Winchester Model 70s.

During the five-week course the marine snipers learned scouting and patrolling techniques as well as marksmanship. Upon completion of the training the new snipers joined marine companies in the Pacific.

Marine-school-trained snipers and the less formally prepared army marksmen performed well in World War II, but neither service provided for snipers or sniper training in their postwar organizations. Leaders believed that the more mechanized and automated battlefield of the future would eliminate the need for snipers. While it was not officially mentioned, many officers continued to look upon sniping as unethical and unsporting. For several years after World War II the only support for American snipers came in the occasional article in professional journals. Competitive shooting matches also encouraged advancements in rifles and scopes.

At the outbreak of the Korean conflict in 1950, the army and marines were no more prepared to field snipers than they had been in 1941. Although there was an adequate supply of sniper weapons left over from World War II, there was no formal sniper school in either the army or the marine corps. Some units in Korea organized their own sniper training, while others procured a few weapons and issued them to their best marksmen. The use and number of these sharpshooters depended upon the desires of individual commanders rather than any servicewide policies. When the cease-fire finally took place in Korea in 1953, the soldiers and marines who had acted as snipers reverted to their positions of ordinary infantrymen, and returned their scoped rifles to unit arms rooms and regional arsenals.

The U.S. Air Force dropped hundreds of thousands of tons of bombs and incendiaries from twenty thousand feet on unsuspecting military formations and civilian centers. Army and marine artillery batteries fired huge-caliber explosive rounds with no warning at targets miles away. Machine gunners raked enemy lines with thousands of rounds. Anonymous killing at a distance was acceptable to the American leadership and public—unless it was by an individual marksman in a hidden position sighting his enemy through a telescopic sight and squeezing the trigger to fire a single deadly bullet.

The idea that the military would train and equip young men to kill at a distance with no warning was a concept that countered the values and scruples of many Americans. While they might, at best, be acceptable during war, there was no place for such one-shot killers in time of peace.

During the late 1950s and early 1960s, the American military continued to officially ignore the issue of snipers. A few junior officers wrote articles for professional journals touting the need for expert marksmen, but high-ranking decision makers took no action. Manufacturers continued to refine and improve rifles and scopes, but their market was civilian hunters rather than shooters in uniform.

Weapons designed for and adopted by the military focused on firepower rather than individual accuracy. The 7.62-millimeter M14 rifle that replaced the M1 as the standard infantry weapon in 1957 was durable and accurate, but it came with a twenty-round magazine. Many had selectors that allowed the firer to change from single shots to full automatic with the flip of a switch. The designers of the M14 did take into consideration that snipers might use the weapon and included a groove and screw recess on the left side of the receiver for a telescope mount. However, neither the army nor the marine corps initially adopted a telescope mount for the M14, making it impossible to use the weapon as a sniper rifle.

In the mid-1960s the United States replaced the M14 with the lighter, shorter-barreled, smaller-caliber M16. Each 5.56-millimeter M16 came equipped with a selector switch that permitted firing a single shot or a burst of automatic rounds. Each soldier could now carry twice the amount of ammunition and deliver tremendous amounts of automatic firepower—even if it was not necessarily accurate. As in the days of smoothbore muskets, the military once again focused on massed rather than accurate fire.

During this period the only soldiers and marines emphasizing single well-aimed shots were members of the service competition shooting teams. While military marksmen did well in national and international shooting contests, many questioned the value and cost of such teams. Some of the shooters, extremely comfortable in the relatively easy assignment of competition shooting, realized that their days were numbered if they did not come up with practical applications of their expertise. To save their jobs, as well as to emphasize skills many thought important to the battlefield, competition shooting leaders thus proposed that they train snipers while preparing for shooting contests.

Lieutenant Jim Land, officer-in-charge of the Marine Shooting Team in Hawaii, led the early efforts to establish a formal sniper course in the corps. Land prepared a paper for his superiors titled "The Neglected Art of Sniping," which related the success of special marksmen in previous conflicts. He concluded, "There is an extremely accurate, helicopter-transportable, self-supporting weapon available to the Marine

Infantry Commander. This weapon, which is easily adapted to either the attack or defense, is the M1C sniper rifle with the M82 telescopic sight in the hands of properly trained sniper."

In late 1960 the First Marine Brigade headquarters directed Land to begin sniper training for infantrymen assigned to Hawaii. Land and his rifle and pistol team organized a two-week course that focused on marksmanship and fieldcraft at the Puuloa Rifle Range near Barber's Point Naval Air Station. For the next several years the Hawaii sniper school was the only active one in the entire U.S. armed forces.

Because no other marine units organized sniper training, the Third Marine Division deployed to Southeast Asia in March 1965 with no qualified snipers. In Vietnam the marines quickly determined that they had to make many adaptations to successfully fight their Vietcong and North Vietnamese opponents. Although they had adequate artillery and air support to engage massed enemy formations, commanders realized that there was a need for specially equipped marksmen who could engage individual targets beyond the 460-yard maximum effective range of their M14s.

Colonel Frank E. Garretson, commander of the 9th Marine Regiment, recommended that snipers be reintroduced into the ranks. His division commander, Major General Lewis W. Walt, agreed and directed operations officer Colonel Don P. Wyckoff to "make it happen."

Wyckoff turned to Major Robert A. Russell with the simple order, "Start a sniper school. Let me know when you're ready to go."

Russell was the ideal marine for the task. A veteran of three wars, he had spent many of his twenty-two years in the corps on firing ranges as a member of competition shooting teams. Russell immediately assembled former shooting teammates and marksmanship instructors already in-country. He also requested Model 70 Winchesters and eight-power Unertl scopes from the States along with information on previous sniper training.

Russell began his first sniper class in September 1965 near Chu Lai with future instructors as students. When satisfied with their progress, he took them on actual operations to practice their skills against the enemy in the mountains and plains around Hue and Phu Bai. Over a period of six weeks the sniper instructors had several successful engagements with enemy personnel that included Staff Sergeant Donald G. Barker being credited with the first marine sniper kill of the Vietnam War.

Satisfied that his training program produced successful snipers, Russell moved his team to Da Nang in November. While they built shooting ranges at Hoa-Cam near Hill 327 a few miles south of the city, the division headquarters solicited volunteers from the regiments. Within a few weeks Russell was returning trained and equipped snipers to their units.

Russell kept few records and submitted fewer written reports during this period when combat preempted administrative procedures. One of the only official mentions of early sniper development in the war appears in the Marine Corps History and Museum Division's *U.S. Marines in Vietnam: The Landing and the Buildup, 1965*. One of the only three paragraphs on the subject explains, "The marines experimented with specially trained and equipped sniper teams. Fifty of the best marksmen were selected from each of the regiments. These troops were divided into four-man teams and equipped with Winchester Model 70 rifles and telescopic sights. During November and December, 20–30 teams operated in the marine TAORs [tactical areas of responsibility] daily. On 23 November a sniper team at Phu Bai killed two VC and wounded another at distance of more than 1,000 meters."

When the First Marine Division arrived in Vietnam in August 1965 its leaders, too, quickly saw a need for long-range marksmen. Initially they let each company designate a few of its best shooters as snipers but established no centralized training. When Major General Herman Nickerson assumed command of the division in the fall of 1966, he decided to formalize and expand the role of the unit's long-range marksmen.

Nickerson had stopped in Okinawa in August for briefing on his way to Vietnam. There he had a chance meeting with Jim Land, who he was aware had established sniper training on Hawaii. Nickerson proposed that Land join him in Vietnam to organize and train the First Division's snipers.

Land arrived in Vietnam in October with a list of every former shooting instructor and competition shooter currently in-country not already being used by Russell's school. He quickly assembled his team, field-tested them in a manner similar to Russell's, and a month later began training snipers at the Hoa-Cam Firing Range, which he shared with the Third Division.

The two marine sniper schools continued to train marksmen for the remainder of the war. In the fall of 1966 the corps established an additional sniper school at Camp Pendleton, California, to train marksmen heading to the war zone. A letter from the corps commandant authorized a sniper platoon for each regiment and reconnaissance battalion. According to the letter, snipers were to locate and destroy enemy personnel by precision fire, destroy or neutralize enemy personnel who opposed the approach of friendly personnel to an objective area, and deny enemy movement in the area of operations.

U.S. Army infantry units arrived in Vietnam shortly after the marines. The soldiers, however, were much slower to field snipers. A few units acquired M1s and M14s with scopes and issued them to their best marksmen. Other individuals had friends or family send them commercial scopes that they could fit to their M16s.

Officially, however, the army not only took no steps to field snipers in Vietnam during its first two years of operations but also actually took several steps backward. Field Manual 21-75, "Combat Training of the Individual Soldier and Patrolling," had included a brief chapter on sniper operations, and subsequent editions of the FM had updated the information. The 1962 edition of the manual had a mere eight pages on snipers and made it clear that sniping was an "extra duty" of the individual infantryman rather than a full-time vocation.

Editions of FM 23-5, "U.S. Rifle Caliber .30, M1," had extensive information on the employment and care of the M1 sniper models. The manual for the M1 in 1958 had more than forty pages on snipers and sniping, but subsequent FMs on the M14 and M16 included nothing on the subject. Various other FMs and training documents made vague references to snipers and agreed that there should be one assigned to each infantry squad. None of these documents, however, provided any authorization for sniper personnel, training, or equipment.

The U.S. Army had much to learn about counterguerrilla warfare, and sniping remained in the background. Despite the lack of focus and priority during this period, once it accepted that there was indeed a need for special marksmen, the army approached the issue in a remarkably precise and organized manner.

On February 23, 1967, the headquarters, U.S. Army, Vietnam (USARV), issued a Letter of Instruction to a subordinate study group, the Army Concept Team in Vietnam (ACTIV), ordering them to "determine the organizational, doctrinal, and matériel requirements for sniper operations by U.S. Army units in the Republic of Vietnam."

ACTIV members began procuring sniper equipment as well as gathering what little information was available on the subject. They also sought advice from the U.S. Marksmanship Training Unit (MTU) at Fort Benning. The MTU, like the prewar marine marksmanship units, contained the army's top competition shooters. While they had extensive time on firing ranges putting holes in paper targets and little practical experience in sniping, they were the army's best source of marksmanship trainers.

During June and July the ACTIV trained soldiers from most of the U.S. units in Vietnam. The ACTIV issued various weapons, including Winchester Model 70s, M14s, and M16s, as a part of its tests to determine the best rifle for the task.

From July through October 1967 the new snipers put their training to use in actual field operations. Upon completion of the test, the ACTIV received written reports from the shooters and their commanders. The leader of the ACTIV, Lieutenant Colonel David S. Moore, compiled the results and on February 23, 1968, exactly a year after the USARV letter had directed the study, issued the findings in a classified report, "Sniper Operations and Equipment."

Moore reported that the test included 7,512 man-days of sniper operations that resulted in 124 engagements and produced forty-six dead enemy soldiers and another nine wounded. He included information on the effects of terrain and vegetation on sniper success and noted that most of the kills were made at ranges of two hundred to nine hundred yards. The report also assessed that the M14 sniper system had proven to be the most available and durable.

The report concluded, "An adequate U.S. Army sniper-training program does not exist," and "there is a lack of definitive doctrine on employing snipers." Moore then recommended that the army develop sniper doctrine and training programs and that units be authorized sniper positions and equipment.

The ACTIV's test was remarkable in that it took place in actual combat. Its results are also notable in that its report cited the army's deficiencies in long-range shooters and spelled out how to solve the problem. The staff at USARV endorsed the report and forwarded it to senior headquarters, U.S. Army Pacific Command, in Hawaii. Copies, according to its distribution lists, went to other army commands and the other services, but events in the war zone delayed further action.

While the ACTIV report made its way through channels, the Tet Offensive broke out across all of Vietnam. For the next several months American and South Vietnamese units focused on retaking cities and villages occupied by the communists. Although the allies won the battle and inflicted tremendous casualties on the Vietcong and North Vietnamese, they, too, suffered losses—one of which was Moore's recommendations for a sniper program.

During and after Tet, many of the proponents of snipers became casualties themselves or completed their tours and returned to the States. By the time the dust settled and the gun smoke cleared from the Tet Offensive, the senior officer champions of snipers were no longer in-country. The report itself languished in various in-boxes at headquarters before being filed away with no action taken.

Just when it seemed that the army's sniper program in Vietnam would revert to the pre-ACTIV state, Major General Julian J. Ewell arrived to assume command of the 9th Infantry Division. Ewell later wrote, "In the spring and summer of 1968 we were looking for ways to bring the enemy to battle on our terms and were willing to try anything within the limits of common sense and sound military judgment. To do this we adapted known tactical innovations to the unique [Mekong] delta environment, resulting in tactical innovations which proved highly successful."

Ewell believed that his area of operations in the relatively open delta region south of Saigon would be ideal for sniper operations. On his way to Vietnam to assume command he stopped at Fort Benning and discussed sniper issues with the Marksmanship Training Unit (MTU). Ewell also convinced the Department of the Army to order the MTU to prepare a sniper program of instruction and to begin procuring weapons and equipment. In October 1969 the army published the MTU's findings as Training Circular (TC) 23-14, "Sniper Training and Employment."

Before the circular became official, draft copies were already available in Vietnam. In June 1968 Ewell arranged for Major Willis L. Powell and eight NCOs from the MTU to transfer from Fort Benning to the 9th Infantry Division. Upon their arrival, Ewell put the veteran competition shooters to work fielding qualified snipers.

Powell prepared a firing range and training center south of Saigon at Dong Tam, where he conducted a two-and-a-half-week course. In November his first graduates were in the field and on the nineteenth recorded the division's first sniper kill. Over the next months Powell trained additional 9th Division snipers as well as soldiers from units throughout South Vietnam.

Snipers soon gained enemy body counts all across the war zone. "Operational Report of the 9th Infantry Division for Period Ending 30 April 1969" (dated May 15, 1969) provides a concise summary of sniper training to that time. According to the then classified report, "A total of five classes were conducted and a sixth class began 27 April 1969. The outstanding results obtained by the 9th Infantry Division snipers have generated interest in the sniper training throughout USARV. As a result, the school has conducted training for snipers and cadre from six U.S. divisions and one separate brigade. These cadre will form the nucleus for sniper-training schools to those units."

Additional training teams from the MTU at Fort Benning deployed to Vietnam over the next year as the army increased its numbers of snipers across the war zone. The program was just hitting its peak when the United States began withdrawing troops and turning the war over to the South Vietnamese. When its major units returned home in August 1969 the 9th Division's sniper school transferred to the 25th Infantry Division at Cu Chi. The last MTU team arrived in Vietnam in early 1971 to train snipers of the 23rd (Americal) Infantry Division. In the summer of 1972 the final U.S. ground units, along with their snipers, withdrew from the war zone.

Neither the army nor the marine corps made any formal evaluation of its snipers in Vietnam. When America's longest war finally concluded, the military was suffering its all-time lowest level of respect from the civilian population it served.

Few in the military or the political structure wanted to look backward at what became known as "America's most unpopular war."

Information available indicates that snipers were the war's most economical killers. Analysis of ammunition expended reveals that American troops, equipped with their automatic M16s, fired about two hundred thousand bullets for every enemy death. Army and marine snipers, on the other hand, averaged one kill for every 1.3 to 1.7 rounds expended. Only about 1,250 soldiers and marines served as snipers in Vietnam, but they accounted for a body count of thirteen thousand, or 2 percent of the total enemy deaths.

CHAPTER 16

✳✳✳✳✳✳✳✳

Snipers: Today

S_{NIPERS} proved their worth during the long Vietnam War, but neither the army nor the marine corps included the one-shot killers in its postwar organization. The postwar budget austerity and the general animosity of the American public for all things military once again denied snipers a place in the peacetime armed forces.

That is not to say, however, that support for snipers did not remain. The marine corps took the most active role in the post-Vietnam years. During the withdrawal from Vietnam, the commandant of the corps, General Leonard F. Chapman, directed that snipers be phased out by 1972, but he also ordered several studies on future sniper organization and training.

Over the next five years marine planners developed and refined sniper doctrine. On April 7, 1976, the marine corps issued Fleet Marine Force Manual (FMFM) 1–3B, "Sniping," which replaced the 1969 edition used in Vietnam. The new manual detailed procedures for selecting, training, and employing snipers. With minor changes and updates, the manual remains today as the primary marine sniper document.

During this period marine ordnance experts tested several weapons to determine the best sniper system. In 1976 they recommended that the corps adopt the M40, a bolt-action rifle based on the Remington Model 700 used in the latter stages of the Vietnam War.

With its doctrine in place and a weapon system fielded, the marine corps opened the USMC Scout/Sniper School at

Quantico, Virginia, on June 1, 1977. For the first time in U.S. military history, snipers were officially a part of its peacetime organization.

The army was not as aggressive as the marines in planning for the training, arming, and fielding of snipers. During the 1970s the army focused on contingencies for armored and mechanized warfare against the Soviets in Europe. Army planners saw no need for individual marksmen in the tank battles that they envisioned would dominate the next war. There were, of course, also the lingering prejudices against snipers. With many civilians still referring to Vietnam veterans and the military in general as "baby killers," few planners were anxious to champion the idea of training snipers in time of peace.

During this period, however, several individual commanders maintained special marksmen in their units. This was particularly prevalent in light infantry and special warfare commands, where foot soldiers, not tanks, remained the primary weapons.

The John F. Kennedy Special Warfare School at Fort Bragg initiated sniper training in 1983, but internal conflicts within the command over where the marksmen fit into their organization ended the classes after only a few months. Two years later the school renewed the training as a part of its Special Operations Interdiction Course. About this same time the 82nd Airborne Division, also at Fort Bragg, and the 2nd Infantry Division in Korea opened their own sniper training courses.

By the late 1980s the American public was recovering from its negative view of the military and realizing that a strong defense was necessary to combat terrorism and direct threats. Bolstered by the renewed appreciation of the armed forces and the obvious need for long-range marksmen, the army finally approved the first servicewide sniper training in its peacetime history. In July 1987 the U.S. Army Sniper School opened its doors and rifle ranges at Fort Benning.

The service was ready. Sniper training began with the M21,

a modified, accurized M14 that had proven successful in Vietnam. Before the school opened, ordnance experts had been working on a new sniper rifle system. In 1988 the M24, which used the Remington 700 receiver group with a Kevlar-graphite synthetic stock, an aluminum bedding block, an adjustable butt plate, and a ten-power Leupold M3 Ultra scope, replaced the M21 system.

Army doctrine writers issued a revised version of TC 23-14, "Sniper Training and Employment," on June 14, 1989. Subsequent publications added selection qualifications for sniper school.

On August 17, 1994, the Department of the Army published a field manual to replace previous sniper publications and provide detailed instructions and authorizations for the long-range shooters. FM 23-10, "Sniping," also outlined the profile and mission of the army's modern sniper: "The sniper has special abilities, training, and equipment. His job is to deliver discriminatory, highly accurate rifle fire against enemy targets, which cannot be engaged successfully by riflemen because of range, size, location, fleeting nature, or visibility. Sniping requires the development of basic infantry skills to a high degree of perfection. A sniper's training incorporates a wide variety of subjects designed to increase his value as a force multiplier and to ensure his survival on the battlefield. The art of sniping requires learning and repetitiously practicing these skills until mastered. A sniper must be highly trained in long-range marksmanship and fieldcraft skills to ensure maximum effective engagements with minimum risks."

Field Manual 23-10 also provided the first official authorization for snipers other than as an additional duty of regular infantrymen. Sniping would now be a full-time job. According to the FM, "In light infantry divisions, the sniper element is composed of six battalion personnel, organized into three 2-man teams. The commander designates missions and priorities of targets for the team and may attach or place the team under the operational control of a company or platoon.

In the mechanized infantry battalions, the sniper element is composed of two riflemen (one team) located in a rifle squad. In some special units (Rangers, Special Forces, etc.), snipers may be organized according to the needs of the tactical situation."

Snipers today serve in all the blood-warrior units as well as the regular infantry. The marine corps's FM 1-3B and the army's FM 23-10 continue to provide the doctrine for sniper organization, equipment, and training.

Today's marine and army sniper schools differ in length and primary sniper weapons, but they share the same goal of producing marksmen who can kill at a distance with a single, well-aimed shot. The two schools share information on techniques and weapons and occasionally train members of each other's service.

The marine corps currently has approximately 340 authorized positions for snipers. Competition for these slots and selection for sniper school is fierce. Every two months the headquarters, USMC, issues a quota message announcing the number of training slots in the next sniper class. Each message states that students must meet the minimum requirements: an infantryman in the rank of lance corporal through captain, 20/20 vision or correctable to that standard, high physical training test score, a qualified swimmer, clean judiciary file, and qualified as an expert rifleman within the past twelve months. Each announcement concludes with the declaration, "Bottom line: Send the best, most experienced infantrymen you can."

There are more opportunities for selection for sniper school in the Battalion and Force Recon units because of their numbers of authorized snipers. Others come from the marine infantry battalions. The recon units and the infantry battalions heed the school's recommendation to "send the best." Both the recon and the infantry units conduct lengthy indoctrination and pretraining programs before they assign a volunteer to one of the coveted sniper school slots. The dropout and failure rate in the indoctrination courses is high, and only those most highly qualified and motivated are selected.

The eleven-week USMC Scout/Sniper School at Quantico, Virginia, is nearly twice the length of the army's course. The marine school's name itself explains the reason for the longer training period. Where the army school trains shooters, the marines train their snipers to be scouts as well. Nearly half of the marine course focuses on teaching land navigation, communications, patrolling, and calling in and adjusting artillery and air support.

Marine officers attend the course, but they are not designated as snipers upon graduation. Instead they use their new skills as sniper deployment officers and as commanders of scout/sniper platoons.

The U.S. Army Sniper School, conducted by C Company, 2nd Battalion, 29th Infantry Brigade, at Fort Benning, is a little less than five weeks in length. Sniper students at Fort Benning shoot the same number of rounds as do their marine counterparts but do not receive additional training in scouting.

Selection for training at the army's sniper school to fill its five hundred authorized slots in the special operations and infantry units is also extremely competitive. Like the marines, volunteers must meet exceptional standards in experience, physical fitness, and vision. Since the army established its sniper school in 1987, it has progressed to conducting six classes per year with thirty-two students in each class. After the current developments in the war against terrorism, the school has made plans to increase its number of classes to eight in fiscal year 2003. With 32 men in each class, this means that the army will be able to field 256 new snipers each year in the future.

Not all of those trained in sniper school are soldiers. Members of other services fill some of the course's slots in response to the school's assigned mission: "To train selected joint forces to engage point targets with long range sniper fire and be proficient in critical fieldcraft skills; provide joint forces with doctrine and subject matter expertise in sniper employment."

During the conflict in Vietnam and in the postwar years, neither the marine corps nor the army was forthcoming about its sniper schools. The passage of years and the rise of terrorism have made the need for the long-range marksmen more apparent. Tactical units of local and state police using snipers have made the military special marksmen more acceptable to the American public. As a result, in recent years both the marine and army sniper schools have allowed civilian newspersons to observe and report on their activities.

This acceptance is rather remarkable because all training by both schools focuses on teaching an individual to acquire a target from a hidden position or "hide," aim a specially designed and equipped weapon system, pull the trigger, and kill a human being. It is certainly a special skill that requires a unique person with detailed training.

Excluding the six weeks of scouting skills instruction, the marine corps school is extremely similar to the army's course. The basic skill of any sniper is, of course, the ability to hit his target with a single well-aimed shot. However, much more goes into accomplishing this task than just accurate shooting, and both the marine and army snipers spend many hours practicing these other skills.

The most important factor in a successful shot is range estimation. Sniper students learn how to use the dot reticles within their telescopes and binoculars to accurately determine the distance to a target. They also learn various mathematical formulas for determining range as well as the time-proven method of visual estimation.

Range estimation, however, is useless if the sniper cannot detect his target. Sniper students spend long hours learning to acquire targets by observing movement, sound, smell, camouflage, and disturbance of natural plant and wild life. They learn that to see a target they must consider shape, shadow, spacing, color, movement, and contrast to background. The simplest rule they follow in target detection is to determine not what belongs downrange but what is out of place in the environment.

While a sniper must be able to see, or stalk, his target and determine its range from his location, he must also learn to employ cover and concealment so that no one detects him before he engages his target and while he departs from his shooting position after a kill. Snipers learn how to select and approach their "hide" positions and to camouflage themselves and their equipment so as not be observed by enemy infantry or snipers. Patience is their most difficult lesson; they practice remaining in their hides for hours with minimum movement.

The U.S. Army Sniper School training schedule is almost boring in its repetition of range estimation, target acquisition, stalking techniques, and field firing. Not all of the training occurs on ranges that simulate forests or plains. Army snipers use a facility made up of houses, multistory buildings, and automobiles that resembles a city; it is called the Buchanan Complex and they use it to practice establishing hides and to engage targets in an urban environment. Students must regularly pass written and practical examinations on these subjects to continue in the course. Snipers also learn that their personal skills are useless if they do not properly take care of their weapons, equipment, and ghillie suits. Each day's training concludes with at least an hour of maintenance.

Sniper students practice range estimation, target acquisition, and stalking throughout the course, but they do so as a part of learning how to shoot and shoot accurately. They begin by firing at targets in the open at known distances during daylight hours and move on to camouflaged targets at unknown ranges during both day and night hours. They then advance to engaging moving targets.

In addition to practicing with the 7.62-millimeter rifles, students also become proficient with 12.7-millimeter (.50-caliber) sniper weapons. These powerful rifles allow snipers to shoot at longer ranges as well as through walls and other barriers. The marines and the army have experimented with several

.50-caliber sniper systems, but the most common is the Barrett Model 82, manufactured in Murfreesboro, Tennessee.

Although there is a long history of American snipers killing targets at distances of up to two thousand yards, the army and marine snipers spend most of their time shooting at ranges of three hundred to nine hundred yards. Experience has proven that these are the usual distances for target acquisition and yield the most accurate engagements. That is not to say, however, that the snipers do not practice shots at extended ranges. It is not unusual to hear a sniper say that if he can see a target, he can hit it—and that even if the enemy detects that he is a target and runs, it is futile for him, as he will only die tired.

Sixteen-hour training days are normal for sniper students. The few open days allow students to practice skills not yet mastered. Instructors are available for these extra training sessions. While the instructors are demanding, they also work personally with the students. Cadre-to-student ratio is one to four. In addition to intense instruction and close supervision, each instructor also serves as a mentor for his four snipers. The training schedule includes time for individual mentorship. An important part of these sessions, in addition to acquiring sniper skills, is to ensure that the graduates will ultimately be able to pull the trigger. Looking a man in the eyes through a telescope before killing him is different from spraying automatic rifle fire downrange—and the sniper must be mentally prepared to kill, and to kill again.

Both the marine and army sniper courses conclude with extended field-training exercises of forty-eight to seventy-two hours where the students put all they have learned into action. Upon successful completion, they graduate, receive the sniper military occupation skill code, and return to their units. Classes near the end of the course provide the students with practical exercises they can take back to their units to sustain their skills.

The military skill identifier *sniper* does not gain precision shooters extra pay or guarantee promotion. These men, like their fellow blood warriors, are first and foremost infantrymen. They are perhaps, however, the greatest all-around riflemen in the world today; and every terrorist and enemy of the United States knows that he is a target for the finest precision marksmen in uniform.

CHAPTER 17

✶✶✶✶✶✶✶

Airborne

O_{NE} of the basic skills of all the blood-warrior units is the ability to enter their areas of operations by parachute. The 75th Ranger Regiment, which includes the word *airborne* on its unit scroll, are Airborne Rangers to many. Airborne tabs top shoulder patches of the Special Forces and the U.S. Army Special Operations Command. SEALs, Air Force Special Tactics, and Force Recon all attend the army's Basic Airborne Course at Fort Benning, Georgia.

Other soldiers volunteer for parachute training so they can join the army's 82nd Airborne Division and the 173rd Airborne Brigade. Everyone assigned to these units is parachute-qualified regardless of his or her position or duty. Commanding generals and privates jump from the same aircraft with the same equipment. Artillerymen, engineers, supply clerks, cooks, and military police join infantrymen in the clouds with their parachutes. Women also attend Jump School and then join their male counterparts in airborne positions in combat support and combat service support units.

The parachute, however, is merely a means of transportation. Parachutes do not kill the enemy; paratroopers do. Graduation from Jump School does not make a soldier a blood warrior, but it does symbolize that he is willing to go an extra distance to accomplish his mission. Jumping out of a perfectly good airplane requires training and discipline, as well as more than a bit of courage. More important, it inducts the soldier into the group of those who consider themselves elite, and act accordingly, on the battlefield.

The importance of paratroopers is not what they do in the air but rather what they accomplish once they reach the ground. General Maxwell D. Taylor, who commanded the 101st Airborne Division during the invasion of Normandy, best explained the purpose and mystique of the paratroopers: "The ultimate pay-off of airborne operations is the battle on the ground where our successes in Europe were the result of the rugged fighting qualities of the airborne soldier. He was young, bold, rowdy, and sometimes offensively swaggering. Yet when the cards were down, he was the most soul-satisfying comrade a man could want on the battlefield."

Taylor also frequently told the story of asking new soldiers in his division if they enjoyed jumping out of airplanes. Most gave a resounding, "Yes, sir. Airborne, sir." One soldier, however, responded, "No, sir." When Taylor asked why then he had joined the 101st, the soldier responded, "Sir, I like to be with people who do like to jump."

The history of paratroopers, of course, does not begin until the invention of airplanes, but the concept predates flight by several centuries. Leonardo da Vinci, the Italian painter, inventor, and philosopher, made a sketch of a parachute-like device composed of canvas, rope, and wood in 1485 that could be used to escape tall buildings. In 1785 Pierre Blanchard of France successfully parachuted his dog to the ground from a gas balloon at an altitude of several hundred feet. Over the next century several daredevils parachuted from balloons to entertain crowds at fairs and other events.

About this time English author Samuel Johnson reflected on the possibility of military application of parachutes. In 1759 he wrote, "What would be the security of the good, if the bad could at pleasure invade them from the sky? Against an army sailing through the clouds neither walls, nor mountains, nor seas, could afford any security."

Benjamin Franklin, while acting as the American representative in Paris in 1784, observed French balloonists and parachutists. He later wrote, "Where is the Prince who can afford so to cover his country with troops for its defense, as that 10,000 men descending from the clouds, might not, in many places, do an infinite deal of mischief before a force could be brought together to repel them?"

The first practical proposal to use airborne troops did not occur, however, until near the end of World War I. In October 1918 the innovative aviator Colonel Billy Mitchell proposed to the American Expeditionary Force commander, General John "Black Jack" Pershing, that part of the U.S. 1st Infantry Division be dropped behind the lines from British Handley-Page bombers to attack the German-occupied town of Metz. Surviving records are unclear as to whether Pershing vetoed or postponed the idea because the armistice ended the war three weeks later.

Mitchell did not give up on his idea for airborne assaults. Shortly after the war concluded he staged a demonstration at Kelly Field in San Antonio, Texas, by successfully dropping six soldiers by parachutes from a Martin bomber. American military leaders were not impressed by the airdrop, but observers from the Soviet Union and Germany appreciated the possibilities.

Soviet paratroopers participated in military exercises at Veronezh, Russia, in 1930. German parachutists were also soon in the air, and by the outbreak of World War II in 1939, both the Soviet Union and Nazi Germany had parachute divisions trained to spearhead assaults.

In April 1940 the first actual combat parachute operations took place when German paratroopers jumped into Denmark and Norway. In both attacks the airborne troops jumped near airfields, surprised the defenders, and then secured the runways for additional troops to air land.

The successful German airborne assaults finally convinced the American military leaders of the need for their own airborne capability. In late April 1940 the War Department directed the army's Infantry Board at Fort Benning to form, equip, and train a platoon of airborne infantry. The Infantry School commandant selected First Lieutenant William T. Ryder as the test platoon's leader and First Lieutenant James A. Bassett as his assistant. The two lieutenants then conducted rugged physical fitness tests to select forty-eight enlisted men from more than two hundred volunteers from the 29th Infantry Regiment.

The test platoon moved into tents near Lawson Field at the southeast edge of Fort Benning. There they used an abandoned hangar for training and for a parachute-packing area. Lieutenant Colonel William C. Lee, an Infantry School staff officer, assisted the platoon and recommended they move temporarily to Hightstown, New Jersey, where they could train on 250-foot towers that had been used during the 1939 New York World's Fair to simulate parachute drops.* The platoon used the towers for eighteen days, which enabled them to test their parachutes and gain confidence.

On August 16, 1940, after forty-five days of training, Lieutenant Ryder made the platoon's first parachute jump from an airplane, a Douglas B-18, in flight. Private William N. "Red" King, who won a lottery within the platoon, joined Ryder as the first enlisted man to exit the aircraft. On August 29 the entire platoon made the first mass parachute jump in U.S. history.

After their successful mass drop, the test platoon disbanded and joined the newly formed 501st Parachute Infantry Battalion as cadre to train new paratroopers. Major William M. Miley, who commanded this first American airborne battalion, was instrumental in working with the Civilian Conservation Corps to clear wooded areas around Fort Benning to form additional drop zones.

It was also during this time that the traditional paratrooper cry, "Geronimo," originated. The new paratroopers often argued about the fear of jumping and just how much control they had when they exited an airplane. Private Aubrey Eberhart proclaimed that he was in such complete control that he

---

* The army later moved the towers to Fort Benning, where they are still used to train paratroopers.

would shout "Geronimo" on his next jump as proof. Other members of the 501st adopted the cry, and later units also shouted the word when they leapt from the doors of airplanes.

Upon completion of their training, paratroopers from the 501st joined the 502nd Parachute Infantry as cadre. When this unit activated on July 1, 1941, its commander, Lieutenant Colonel William C. Lee—who had assisted the test platoon—called for volunteers. The response was so overwhelming, including noncommissioned officers willing to take a reduction in rank to join the battalion, that Lee and his cadre could be extremely selective in admitting only the most physically and mentally qualified.

The success of the test platoon and parachute battalions, combined with news about German and Soviet parachute operations in the early stages of World War II, encouraged the Americans to plan for additional airborne units. By the time of the Japanese attack on Pearl Harbor, the army had plans for several airborne divisions. To expedite parachute training, the U.S. Army Parachute School began operations at Fort Benning on May 15, 1942. Upon completion of basic training, volunteers reported to Fort Benning for airborne training and then transferred to their units.

It was also during this period that the army began experiments with other methods of delivering soldiers from the air to the ground. The army activated the 88th Glider Infantry Battalion on October 10, 1941. Transport aircraft pulled gliders airborne and then released them to sail silently to their targets. The plywood-and-canvas gliders carried a ten-man squad, or a light artillery piece or other small vehicle. Little training for the infantrymen passengers was necessary. Early glider veterans explained, "You took off, you flew, you landed, you were scared as hell in that damn flimsy bird."

Glider pilots required the bulk of the training, but they were not typical aviators. Many were the leaders of the squads they flew and, once on the ground, they left their small cockpits and fought as infantrymen. Members of the glider infantry battalions did not share in the few dollars of "hazardous pay" of their paratrooper brothers. However, the two groups got along well. The glider men thought anyone who jumped out of a perfectly good airplane must be crazy, while the paratroopers placed more confidence in their silk canopies than in the "cloth and board" gliders.

Throughout 1942 the parachute and glider schools increased their enrollments to fill the ranks of five authorized airborne divisions. While many of the army's infantry battalions and regiments traced their lineage back to the American Revolution, and their colors carried battle streamers from every previous war, most of the airborne units assumed numerical designations that were new. Units of the 82nd Airborne Division had the most history, but its regiments dated their existence back only to World War I.

The 101st Airborne Division, formed on August 16, 1942, at Camp Claiborne, Louisiana, was more typical of the new paratrooper units. At the activation ceremony, William C. Lee, now a major general and in command of the division, declared, "The 101st has no history, but it has a rendezvous with destiny."

The 101st and the other airborne divisions kept that rendezvous and wrote their own histories as they gained campaign streamers and battle honors in Europe and the Pacific. Throughout the war the airborne divisions spearheaded invasions, seized important objectives, assisted in breakthroughs, and cut off retreating enemy forces. They also reinforced units in danger of being cut off or surrounded.

The fighting abilities and spirit of the airborne shone when they reinforced infantry units at the Battle of the Bulge in December 1944. Upon arrival at the battle area near Bastogne, reporters asked several enlisted paratroopers if they would be able to stop the German offensive. They confidently responded, "We are the 82nd Airborne, they will go no further."

When the Germans surrounded Bastogne and demanded that the paratroopers surrender, they received an even briefer message. "Nuts," replied Brigadier General Anthony McAuliffe, the acting commander of the 101st Airborne. A few days later the paratroopers broke the German lines and began to push them back toward the Rhine River.

The Americans also discovered during World War II that parachutes could transport more than regiments and divisions to the battlefield. OSS and other agents parachuted behind enemy lines to gather intelligence, conduct sabotage, and organize resistance units.

The army deactivated many of its airborne units after World War II, but the concept of delivering large numbers of troops from the air by parachute remained an important part of its doctrine. The Korean War did not require large drops of paratroopers, but several parachute insertions by airborne regiments did occur during the conflict. Members of the Ranger companies who fought in Korea were also paratroopers.

All of the Special Forces and SEAL teams that served in Vietnam in the early years were airborne-qualified. American advisers also assisted the South Vietnamese in training their own airborne units. There were few instances in which battlefield requirements called for their skills in parachuting, but the South Vietnamese paratroopers, like their American brothers, earned the reputation as their country's best warriors.

The 173rd Airborne Brigade arrived in-country in May 1965 as the first American regular unit. A brigade of the 101st Airborne joined them two months later. The remainder of the 101st arrived in 1967, and a brigade of the 82nd Airborne Division deployed to Vietnam in the post-Tet buildup in 1968.

Although there was plenty of fighting for the paratroopers, there was little need for their parachuting skills. Troopers of the 173rd made the only massed parachute combat jump of the war on February 22, 1967, into Tay Ninh province, but the operation was more a validation of the concept than an influential combat action. SOG, Special Forces, and Force Recon conducted parachute insertions during the war, but never with more than a dozen or so men.

The size of Vietnam enabled the rapid movement of large units by helicopters. These "flying trucks" not only delivered troops to the ground but picked them up after the mission. Helicopters also proved invaluable in extracting units in danger of being overrun, evacuating wounded, and providing fire support.

By the end of the Vietnam War the helicopter had become so integral to warfare that the 101st no longer required its men to be jump-qualified, transitioning from an airborne to an airmobile division. In 1974 the division opened its Air Assault School to train its soldiers in the complexities of airmobile warfare.

Still, helicopters—which have limited range and are vulnerable to ground fire—have not totally replaced the need for an airborne strike force. At no time since World War II, including today, has the army not had at least one airborne division in its active ranks. The airborne has maintained its status as the most rapidly deployable ground combat unit. A battalion, and at times a brigade, of airborne troops remain packed and prepared to deploy anywhere in the world in less than twenty-four hours, the remainder of the division to follow within days.

Over the decades the 82nd Airborne Division has acted as the army's "ready force" to deploy worldwide. The 82nd joined the Rangers in Grenada and Panama and was the first on the ground in Saudi Arabia to hold the line during the allied buildup to retake Kuwait in Operation Desert Storm.

While the 82nd has remained the primary airborne unit, the army has maintained several other airborne battalions and brigades over the past decades. On January 25, 2002, the U.S. Southern European Task Force activated the 2nd Battalion (Airborne), 503rd Infantry, to join other airborne units at Vicenza, Italy. On June 12 the army combined the 503rd and other airborne units at Vicenza under the colors of the 173rd Airborne Brigade.

While the soldier who hangs under a parachute canopy on the way to the ground is not necessarily a blood warrior, graduation from airborne school is a qualification shared by all the American military elites. The army continues its airborne training at Fort Benning, where it still uses the 250-foot towers from the 1939 New York World's Fair to simulate jumps. Although the equipment and the aircraft have changed since the first units trained there in early World War II, today's jump students still take off from Lawson Army Airfield and made their first parachute jump over nearby Fryar Drop Zone.

The parachute school has had several names over the past sixty years, currently operating officially as the U.S. Army Basic Airborne Course. Cadre and students are organized into the 1st Battalion (Airborne), 507th Infantry Regiment. The cadre, also known as black hats because of their distinctive headgear, serve in the battalion's leadership positions, while the students fill the ranks. Its headquarters and headquarters company provide administrative support and command and control, while Company E contains parachute rigger support. The four line companies—A, B, C, and D—execute the school's program of instruction. Most of the cadre are soldiers, but naval, marine, and air force noncommissioned officers are also members of the companies.

Qualifications for attendance at the Basic Airborne Course are fairly simple. Student volunteers must be less than thirty-six years of age, graduates of appropriate basic military skills training, and physically fit. The most important part of the assessment physical test is the ability to complete a four-mile run within thirty-six minutes.

Students reporting to the school join a line company, where their cadre squad leaders and platoon sergeants remain with them during the entire training process—ground, tower, and jump weeks. Each class contains 320 students. Most of these come from the army, but other services, as well as a few foreign countries, are represented. Officers wear their rank during the training but receive no special treatment. With forty-five classes annually, the Basic Airborne School produces more than fourteen thousand paratroopers each year.

The army restricted attendance at airborne school to males during its first forty years. On December 14, 1973, two female soldiers completed a modified version of the school, made their five jumps, and received their wings. Since that time women have attended the regular course, meeting the same standards as the male students. At about this time the army began allowing West Point and ROTC cadets to attend the training to earn their jump wings during their summer "vacations."

The airborne school also reinforces the idea that parachuting is more than merely a means of transportation. Subordinates accompany their salutes with the greeting, "All the way, sir!" Salutes are returned with an enthusiastic, "Airborne!"

In addition to the fighting spirit of the airborne, the school recognizes that it instills more than just the traditions of those who have gone before. Its objective statement clearly relates that the purpose of the school is to qualify the student as a parachutist by performing five satisfactory jumps. It concludes, however, that the airborne training develops a sense of leadership, self-confidence, and aggressive spirit.

The airborne school cadre has understood since the first classes in the early 1940s that its special soldiers deserve special recognition. Graduates receive a silver badge of a winged parachute. Since the original test platoon, paratroopers have worn their jump boots with the trousers bloused into the tops with all uniforms—including their Class A's. Various special insignias also adorn the envelope or overseas cap. Although it did not become official until 1949, many paratroopers were already wearing the two-and-a-quarter-inch red-bordered blue disk surrounding a white parachute and glider. More recently, paratroopers assigned to the regular airborne divisions wear the maroon beret common to jump units around the world.

Even those airborne-qualified soldiers who are not blood warriors have proven themselves to be dedicated soldiers. They take their business seriously but have a sense of humor about the parachutes that mean life and death to them. Paratroopers often say about jumping, "All you have to worry about is if your chute opens or not. If it opens you have nothing to worry about. If it doesn't, there is nothing to worry about."

Riggers, who are also airborne-qualified, issue parachutes to paratroopers before each jump. For more than sixty years they have made the same remark as they hand over a newly packed chute: "If it doesn't work, bring it back."

CHAPTER 18

✻✻✻✻✻✻✻✻

Conclusions

*I*N the fourth century B.C. the Greek philosopher Plato proclaimed, "Only the dead have seen the end of war."

Twenty-three centuries later the U.S. Army Chief of Staff General George C. Marshall noted in a speech on February 3, 1939, "When the smoke cleared away, it was the man with the sword, or the crossbow, or the rifle who settled the final issue on the field."

In these opening years of the twenty-first century the words of both Plato and Marshall still ring true. Wars continue, and it is the infantryman who ultimately decides the outcome. That is not to say, however, that the means of fighting conflicts and achieving victory are not in a constant state of change.

The Vietnam War taught the U.S. military that it could not attain victory without the total commitment of its resources and the support of the American public. In Grenada in 1983, in Libya in 1986, and in Panama in 1989, the United States struck hard with overwhelming combat forces to accomplish its objectives in a short period of time with minimum casualties. It continued this strategy with coalition support in Iraq in 1991 and with UN forces in Bosnia in 1995.

Never in the annals of world history has there been a power as dominant as the United States. More influential than Alexander's Greece, Caesar's Rome, Napoleon's France, and Hitler's Germany, the United States of the twenty-first century stands as the only super-, or mega-, or hyperpower.

The Americans achieved their singular dominant role with

an amazing lack of friendly casualties during the Cold War, the "small wars" of the 1980s, and Desert Storm and Bosnia in the 1990s. Although the war against terrorism is not yet over, American casualties have remained few as the U.S. military has destroyed the Taliban and its allies.

In fact, during the four decades since the Vietnam War, terrorist attacks against U.S. embassies abroad and the assaults against the World Trade Center in New York City on September 11, 2001, killed more American civilians than all the military personnel lost in direct combat in the same time period.

Americans have come to expect their wars to be relatively bloodless for their sons and daughters in uniform. They have also grown confident that the professional armed forces can accomplish their missions and maintain the power status of the United States with an all-volunteer force. It is noteworthy that the great patriotic demonstrations and flag waving in the immediate aftermath of the September 11 attacks did not carry over to the military recruiting offices. Unlike the millions who stepped forward to join the military in World War II after the attack on Pearl Harbor, acceptable volunteers did not rush to recruiting offices after September 11. Americans still expect a few to defend the many.

Today's armed forces total only 1.4 million soldiers, airmen, sailors, and marines. On April 18, 2002, the four service chiefs asserted that the level of operations in Afghanistan and the heightened level of security in the U.S. has severely taxed the armed forces. Senior officers in the Pentagon contend that they need authorization for an additional fifty thousand men and women. Political leaders remain reluctant to increase manpower—and conscientiously avoid any reference to a possibility of resuming the draft.

Technology and tactics have aided the armed forces in accomplishing their missions and doing so with a minimum number of casualties. Until recently, neutralizing enemy targets required hundreds of airplanes dropping thousands of bombs. Today a single plane with a single "smart bomb" can accomplish the same mission. Missiles fired from aircraft or ships hundreds of miles from their targets can attack other objectives.

In still other instances, drones, or pilotless aircraft, can fly over enemy territory providing moving and still photos for intelligence units far behind the lines. There is even discussion that at some future date most or even all pilots may fly their missions from a computer console in the rear rather than from the cockpit.

Naval operations have also changed. With no threat to its dominance on the high seas, the U.S. Navy has focused on operations close to the shore to better support land operations. Marine Expeditionary Units can remain pre-positioned near trouble areas and be delivered and supported ashore within hours. In the war against the Taliban in Afghanistan, the army's special operations forces used navy carriers as offshore bases to launch their attacks inland. Some leaders are proposing that the army acquire large ships to support its operations in a manner similar to the marines.

The war against Saddam Hussein proved that American conventional armored and mechanized forces were unmatched. Those Iraqi troops who did not retreat or surrender died in place while inflicting nearly negligible casualties on the U.S. forces. Today there is not a single viable conventional threat on land, at sea, or in the air that can challenge American military and economic superiority.

That is not to say, however, that the Americans and their allies do not have formidable opponents. These enemies readily use terror as their primary tactic, through attacks against undefended civilian centers and women and children. Blood warriors will continue to be the primary weapon against these terrorists, but they will have to pay the price to preserve America's freedoms, defend its shores, maintain its interests, and extend its influence around the world.

The war against the Taliban and the al-Qaeda terrorists in Afghanistan offers keen insights into the capabilities and risks of the blood warriors. As of May 2002 the most intense battle of the war occurred during Operation Anaconda. On March 4 the Americans launched three infantry battalions and several special operations teams into the Shah-i-Kot Valley south of Kabul with the mission of neutralizing a concentration of Taliban and al-Qaeda forces.

Early in the attack a rocket-propelled grenade struck a helicopter carrying a special ops team. The explosion knocked one operator out of the aircraft onto the ground in the midst of the enemy. Other teams, following their code of never leaving a fellow soldier behind, converged on the area. In a daylong battle the blood warriors recovered the body of their comrade and killed many of the terrorists.

The price they paid to accomplish their mission was high. Eight Americans died in the fight—the largest number of combat deaths in a single battle since Mogadishu in 1993. The dead from Operation Anaconda represent nearly all the blood-warrior units—three Rangers, a Green Beret, a SEAL, a combat controller, a PJ, and an air force flight engineer.

The American political and military leadership has warned that the fight against terrorism will be a long one. Undoubtedly the blood warriors, as a part of the U.S. Special Operations Command, will continue to be in the heaviest action. The responsibility could be in no better hands.

In 2000 the senior officer in USSOCOM, General Peter J. Schoomaker, wrote, "We look forward to meeting the security challenges of this new century as we work to ensure that America's SOF remain the most carefully selected, most fully prepared, and the best-equipped and trained special operations fighting force in the world. Our country deserves no less."

An earlier leader of USSOCOM made even more succinct remarks about the role of his command and its blood warriors. In 1997 General Henry H. Shelton wrote, "The U.S. is increasingly challenged in unconventional ways, and the SOF have the skills and leadership to meet tomorrow's challenges. SOF are truly the force of the future."

APPENDIX A

✳✳✳✳✳✳✳✳

Standing Orders: Rogers's Rangers, 1759

1. Don't forget nothing.
2. Have your musket clean as a whistle, hatchet scoured, sixty rounds of powder and ball, and be ready to march at a minute's warning.
3. When you are on the march, act the way you would if you were sneaking up on a deer. See the enemy first.
4. Tell the truth about what you see and what you do. There is an army depending on us for correct information. You can lie all you please when you tell other folk about the Rangers, but don't ever lie to a Ranger or officer.
5. Don't ever take a chance you don't have to.
6. When we're on the march we march single file, far enough apart so one shot can't go through two men.
7. If we strike swamps, or soft ground, we spread out abreast, so it's hard to track us.
8. When we march, we keep moving till dark, so as to give the enemy the least possible chance at us.
9. When we camp, half the party stays awake while the other half sleeps.
10. If we take prisoners, we keep 'em separated till we have time to examine them, so they can't cook up a story between 'em.
11. Don't ever march home the same way. Take a different route so you won't be ambushed.
12. No matter whether we travel in big parties or little ones, each party has to keep a scout twenty yards on each flank and twenty yards in the rear, so the main body can't be surprised and wiped out.
13. Every night you'll be told where to meet if surrounded by a superior force.
14. Don't sit down to eat without posting sentries.

15. Don't sleep beyond dawn. Dawn's when the French and Indians attack.
16. Don't cross a river by a regular ford.
17. If somebody's trailing you, make a circle, come back onto your tracks, and ambush the folks that aim to ambush you.
18. Don't stand up when the enemy's coming against you. Kneel down, lie down, hide behind a tree.
19. Let the enemy come till he's almost close enough to touch. Then let him have it and jump out and finish him up with your hatchet.

APPENDIX B

****

Rogers's Rules of Discipline

1. All Rangers are to be subject to the rules and articles of war; to appear at roll-call every evening on their own parade ground, each equipped with a firelock, 60 rounds of powder and ball, and a hatchet, at which time an officer from each company is to inspect them to see that they are in order, so as to be ready to march at a minute's warning; and before they are dismissed the necessary guards are to be chosen, and scouts for the next day appointed.

2. Whenever you are ordered out to the enemy's forts or frontiers for discoveries, if your number is small, march in single file, keeping such a distance from each other as to prevent one shot from killing two men; sending one man or more forward and the like on each side, at the distance of twenty yards from the main body, if the ground you march over allows it, to give the signal to the officer of the approach of an enemy and of their number, etc.

3. If you march over marshes or soft ground, change your position and march abreast of each other to prevent the enemy from tracking you (as they would do if you marched in single file), until you get over such ground, and then resume your former order and march till it is quite dark before you encamp; which do, if possible, on a piece of ground that may afford your sentries the advantage of seeing or hearing the enemy at some considerable distance, keeping one half of your whole party alternately awake through the night.

4. Some time before you come to the place you would like to reconnoiter, make a stand and send one or two men in whom you can confide to look for the best ground for making your observations.

5. If you have the good fortune to take any prisoners, keep

them separate until they are examined, and return by a route other than the one you used going out so that you may discover any enemy party in your rear and have an opportunity, if their strength is superior to yours, to alter your course or disperse, as circumstances may require.

6. If you march in a large body of 300 or 400 with a plan to attack the enemy, divide your party into three columns, each headed by an officer. Let these columns march in single file, the columns to the right and left keeping twenty yards or more from the center column, if the terrain allows. Let proper guards be kept in the front and rear and suitable flanking parties at a distance, as directed before, with orders to halt on all high ground to view the surrounding ground to prevent ambush and to notify of the approach or retreat of the enemy, so that proper dispositions may be made for attacking, defending, etc. And if the enemy approaches in your front on level ground, form a front of your three columns or main body with the advanced guard, keeping out your flanking parties as if you were marching under the command of trusty officers, to prevent the enemy from pressing hard on either of your wings or surrounding you which is the usual method of savages if their number will allow it, and be careful likewise to support and strengthen your rear guard.

7. If you receive fire from enemy forces, fall or squat down until it is over, and then rise and fire at them. If their main body is equal to yours, extend yourselves occasionally; but if they are superior, be careful to support and strengthen your flanking parties to make them equal with the enemy's, so that if possible you may repulse them to their main body. In doing so, push upon them with the greatest resolve, with equal force in each flank and in the center, observing to keep at a due distance from each other, and advance from tree to tree, with one half of the party ten or twelve yards in front of the other. If the enemy pushes upon you, let your front rank fire and fall down, and then let your rear rank advance through them and do the same, by which time those who were in the front will be ready to fire again, and repeat the same alternately, as occasion requires. By this means you will keep up such a constant fire that the enemy will not be able to break your order easily or gain your ground.

8. If you force the enemy to retreat, be careful in pursuing them to keep out your flanking parties and prevent them from gaining high ground, in which case they may be able to rally and repulse you in their turn.

9. If you must retreat, let the front of your whole party fire and fall back until the rear has done the same, heading for the best ground you can. By this means you will force the enemy to pursue you, if they pursue you at all, in the face of constant fire.

10. If the enemy is so superior that you are in danger of being surrounded, let the whole body disperse and every one take a different road to the place of rendezvous appointed for that evening. Every morning the rendezvous point must be altered and fixed for the evening in order to bring the whole part, or as many of them as possible, together after any separation that may occur in the day. But if you should actually be surrounded, form yourselves into a square or, in the woods, a circle is best; and if possible make a stand until darkness favors your escape.

11. If your rear is attacked, the main body and flanks must face about the right or left, as required, and form themselves to oppose the enemy as directed earlier. The same method must be observed if attacked in either of your flanks, by which means you will always make a rear guard of one of your flank guards.

12. If you determine to rally after a retreat in order to make a fresh stand against the enemy, by all means try to do it on the highest ground you come upon, which will give you the advantage and enable you to repulse superior numbers.

13. In general, when pushed upon by the enemy, reserve your fire until they approach very near, which will then cause them the greater surprise and consternation and give you the opportunity to rush upon them with your hatchets and cutlasses to greater advantage.

14. When you encamp at night fix your sentries so they will not be relieved from the main body until morning, profound secrecy and silence being often of the most importance in these cases. Each sentry, therefore, should consist of six men, two of whom must be constantly alert, and when relieved by their fellows, it should be without noise. In case those on duty see or hear anything that alarms them, they

are not to speak. One of them is to retreat silently and advise the commanding officer so that proper dispositions can be made. All occasional sentries should be fixed in a like manner.

15. At first light, wake your whole detachment. This is the time when the savages choose to fall upon their enemies, and you should be ready to receive them.

16. If the enemy is discovered by your detachments in the morning, and if their numbers are superior to yours and a victory is doubtful, you should not attack them until the evening. Then they will not know your numbers and if you are repulsed your retreat will be aided by the darkness of the night.

17. Before you leave your encampment, send out small parties to scout around it to see if there are any signs of enemy force that may have been near you during the night.

18. When you stop for rest, choose some spring or rivulet if you can, and dispose your party so as not to be surprised, posting proper guards and sentries at a due distance, and let a small party watch the path you used coming in, in case the enemy is pursuing.

19. If you have to cross rivers on your return, avoid the usual fords as much as possible, in case the enemy has discovered them and is there expecting you.

20. If you have to pass by lakes, keep at some distance from the edge of the water, so that, in case of an ambush or attack from the enemy, your retreat will not be cut off.

21. If the enemy forces pursue your rear, circle around until you come to your own tracks and form an ambush there to receive them and give them the first fire.

22. When you return from a patrol and come near our forts, avoid the usual roads and avenues to it; the enemy may have preceded you and laid an ambush to receive you when you are almost exhausted with fatigue.

23. When you pursue any party that has been near our forts or encampments, do not follow directly in their tracks, lest you be discovered by their rear guards who, at such a time, would be most alert. But endeavor, by a different route, to intercept and meet them in some narrow pass, or lie in ambush to receive them when and where they least expect it.

24. If you are to embark in canoes, or otherwise by water, choose

the evening for the time of your embarkation, as you will then have the whole night before you to pass by any enemy parties on hills or other places that command a view of the lake or river.

25. In paddling or rowing, order that the boat or canoe next to the last one wait for it, and that each wait for the one behind it to prevent separation and so that you will be ready to help each other in any emergency.

26. Appoint one man in each boat to look out for fires on the adjacent shores, from the number and size of which you may form some idea of the number that kindled them and whether you can attack them or not.

27. If you find the enemy encamped near the banks of a river or lake that you think they will try to cross for their security when attacked, leave a detachment of your party on the opposite shore to receive them. With the remainder, you can surprise them, having them between you and the water.

28. If you cannot satisfy yourself as to the enemy's number and strength from their fires and the like, conceal your boats at some distance and ascertain their number by a patrol when they embark or march in the morning, marking the course they steer, when you may pursue, ambush, and attack them, or let them pass, as prudence directs you. In general, however, so that you may not be discovered at a great distance by the enemy on lakes and rivers, it is safest to hide with your boats and party concealed all day, without noise or show, and to pursue your intended route by night. Whether you go by land or water, give out patrol and countersigns in order to recognize one another in the dark, and likewise appoint a station for every man to go to in case of any accident that may separate you.

APPENDIX C

✳✳✳✳✳✳✳✳

U.S. Army Ranger Creed

Recognizing that I volunteered as a Ranger, fully knowing the hazards of my chosen profession, I will always endeavor to uphold the prestige, honor, and high esprit de corps of my Ranger Regiment.

Acknowledging the fact that a Ranger is a more elite soldier who arrives at the cutting edge of battle by land, sea, or air, I accept the fact that as a Ranger my country expects me to move further, faster, and fight harder than any other soldier.

Never shall I fail my comrades. I will always keep myself mentally alert, physically strong, and morally straight and I will shoulder more than my share of the task whatever it may be, one hundred percent and then some.

Gallantly will I show the world that I am a specially selected and well-trained soldier. My courtesy to superior officers, neatness of dress, and care of equipment shall set the example for others to follow.

Energetically will I meet the enemies of my country. I shall defeat them on the field of battle for I am better trained and will fight with all my might. Surrender is not a Ranger word. I will never leave a fallen comrade to fall into the hands of the enemy and under no circumstances will I ever embarrass my country.

Readily will I display the intestinal fortitude required to fight on to the Ranger objective and complete the mission, though I be the lone survivor.

APPENDIX D

✳✳✳✳✳✳✳✳

U.S. Army Ranger Course

From SH 21-75 "Ranger Course Pamphlet,"
October 1995

The Benning Phase (21 days)

The Benning Phase of Ranger training is designed to assess and then to develop the military skills, physical and mental endurance, stamina, and confidence a soldier must have to successfully accomplish combat missions. It is also designed to teach the Ranger student to properly sustain himself, his subordinates, and maintain his equipment under difficult field conditions during the subsequent phases of Ranger training. If a student is not in TOP PHYSICAL CONDITION when he reports to the Ranger Course, he will have extreme difficulty keeping up with the fast pace of Ranger training, especially during the initial phase.

The Benning Phase is executed in two parts. The first part is the Ranger Assessment Phase (RAP) conducted at Camp Rogers in the Harmony Church area of Fort Benning. This phase consists of an Army Physical Fitness Test (APFT) and Combat Water Survival Test (CWST), five-mile run, three-mile run with an obstacle course, a 12-mile foot march, night and day land navigation tests, medical considerations class, and 10-event Ranger Stakes. Advanced physical training assures physical and mental endurance and the stamina required for enhancing basic Ranger characteristics, commitment, confidence, and toughness. Additionally, the student completes the Water Confidence Test at Hurley Hill (Victory Pond) and seven and one-half hours of combatives vicinity Camp Rogers.

The second part of the Benning Phase is conducted at nearby Camp William O. Darby. The emphasis at Camp Darby is on the instruction in and the execution of squad combat operations. The Ranger student receives instruction on airborne/air assault operations, environmental and fieldcraft training, executes the Darby Queen obstacle course, and learns the fundamentals of patrolling, the warning order/operations order format, and communications. The fundamentals of combat operations include battle drills (React to Contact, Break Contact, React to Ambush, Platoon Raid, Demolitions Training, Airborne Operations, Air Assault Operations, Crawl, Walk, Run FTX), principles and techniques that enable the squad to successfully conduct reconnaissance and raid missions.

The Ranger must then demonstrate his expertise through a series of cadre and student led tactical operations. As a result, the Ranger student gains tactical and technical proficiency, confidence in himself, and prepares to move to the next phase of the course—the Mountain Phase. Following the Benning Phase, students are normally provided a short break to launder uniforms, get haircuts, and purchase sundry items or TA50 they may have lost, destroyed, or exhausted prior to their departure to Camp Frank D. Merrill, Dahlonega, Georgia.

The Mountain Phase (21 days)

During the Mountain Phase, students receive instructions on military mountaineering tasks as well as techniques for employing a platoon for continuous combat operations in a mountainous environment. They further develop their ability to command and control a platoon size element through planning, preparing, and executing a variety of combat missions. The Ranger student continues to learn how to sustain himself and his subordinates in the adverse conditions of the mountains. The rugged terrain, severe weather, hunger, mental and physical fatigue, and the emotional stress that the student encounters afford him the opportunity to gauge his own capabilities and limitations as well as that of his "Ranger Buddies."

In addition to combat operations, the Ranger student receives five days on military mountaineering. During the first three days of mountaineering (Lower) he learns about knots, belays, anchor points, rope management, and the basic fundamentals of climbing and rappelling. His mountaineering training culminates with a two day exercise (Upper) at Yonah Mountain applying the skills learned during Lower mountaineering. Each student must make all prescribed climbs at Yonah Mountain to continue in the course. During the FTX, Ranger students perform a mission that requires the use of their mountaineering skills. Combat missions are directed against a conventional equipped force in a Mid-Intensity Conflict scenario. These missions are conducted both day and night over an eight-day field training exercise (FTX) and include moving cross country over mountains, conducting vehicle ambushes, raiding communications/mortar sites, and conducting a river crossing or scaling a steep sloped mountain.

The Ranger Student reaches his objective in several ways: cross-country movement; airborne insertion into small, rugged drop zones; air assaults into even smaller landing zones on the sides of mountains; or an 8–10 mile foot march over the Tennessee Valley Divide (TVD). The stamina and commitment of the Ranger student is stressed to the maximum. At any time, he may be selected to lead tired, hungry, physically expended students to accomplish yet another combat mission.

At the conclusion of the Mountain Phase, the students move by bus or parachute assault into the Third and final (Florida) Phase of Ranger training, conducted at Camp Rudder, near Eglin Air Force Base, Florida.

The Florida Phase

The Third or capstone Phase of Ranger School is conducted at Camp James E. Rudder (Auxiliary Field #6), Eglin AFB, Florida. Emphasis during this phase is to continue the development of the Ranger student's combat arms functional skills. He must be capable of operating effectively under conditions of extreme mental and physical stress. This is accomplished through practical exercises in extended platoon level operations in a jungle/swamp environment. Training further develops the students' ability to plan for and lead small units on independent and coordinated airborne, air assault, small boat, and dismounted combat operations in a Mid-Intensity combat environment against a well trained, sophisticated enemy.

The Florida Phase continues the progressive, realistic Opposing Force (OPFOR) scenario. As the scenario develops, the students receive "in-country" technique training that assists them in accomplishing the tactical missions later in the phase. Technique training includes: small boat operations, expedient stream crossing techniques, and skills needed to survive and operate in a jungle/swamp environment.

The Ranger students are updated on the scenario that eventually commits the unit to combat during techniques training. The 12-day FTX is a fast-paced, highly stressful, challenging exercise in which the students are further trained, but are also evaluated on their ability to apply small unit tactics/techniques. They apply the tactics/techniques of raids, ambushes, and movement to contact to accomplish their missions.

Upon completion of the Florida Phase of training, students move by parachute assault or bus to Fort Benning, Georgia. Ranger students graduate two days later if they have passed all requirements.

Summary

High standards are required and maintained despite the stressful environment in Ranger training. The Ranger Course produces a mentally hardened soldier, who possesses an enhanced capability to perform combat arms related associated functional skills and is more confident in his ability to withstand the stresses of combat to overcome all obstacles to accomplish his mission under extremely adverse conditions.

The Ranger proves during the Ranger course that he can overcome seemingly insurmountable mental and physical challenges. He has demonstrated, while under simulated combat conditions, that he has acquired the professional skills and techniques necessary to plan, organize, coordinate, and conduct small unit operations. He has demonstrated that he has mastered basic skills needed to plan and execute dismounted small-unit day and night operations, low altitude mountaineering, and infiltration as well as exfiltration techniques via land, air, and sea. As a result of proving that he can successfully accomplish these tasks during the Ranger Course, he is authorized to wear the Ranger Tab. The graduate of the Ranger Course is the epitome of the U.S. Infantryman.

APPENDIX E

✳✳✳✳✳✳✳✳

U.S. Army Special Forces A-Team

Position	Rank
Detachment Commander	Captain
Executive Officer	Warrant Officer
Operations Sergeant	Master Sergeant
Operations and Intelligence NCO	Sergeant First Class
Weapons NCO	Sergeant First Class
Assistant Weapons NCO	Staff Sergeant
Engineer NCO	Sergeant First Class
Assistant Engineer NCO	Staff Sergeant
Medical NCO	Sergeant First Class
Assistant Medical NCO	Staff Sergeant
Communications NCO	Sergeant First Class
Assistant Communications NCO	Staff Sergeant

The Special Forces Operational Detachment-A, or A-Team, is the fundamental building block for all Special Forces units. There are six A-Teams in a Special Forces Company. All team members are Special Force qualified and cross-trained in different skills as well as being multi-lingual. In each company one of the six teams is trained in combat diving and another is qualified in military free-fall parachuting.

In general, A-Teams are armed with individual and perimeter defense weapons, as well as night-vision devices, and electric and non-electric demolitions. Their communications equipment includes high-powered systems such as tactical satellite communications, burst transmission devices, high frequency radios, and global positioning systems. Medical kits include, but are not limited to, field surgical kits, dental supplies, water testing kits, and veterinary equipment. Equipment for underwater infiltration includes SCUBA (Self-Contained Underwater Breathing Apparatus) with open circuit twin-80 tanks and closed-circuit Dragger (rebreather). Zodiac boats and Klepper kayaks support waterborne infiltration. Teams qualified for free-fall infiltration are equipped with ram-air parachutes complete with oxygen systems.

A-Team capabilities include:

- Plan and conduct SF operations separately or as part of a larger force;
- infiltrate and exfiltrate specified operational areas by air, land, or sea;
- conduct operations in remote areas and hostile environment for extended periods of time with a minimum of external direction and support;
- develop, organize, equip, train and advise or direct indigenous forces up to battalion size in special operations;
- train, advise, and assist other U.S. and Allied forces and agencies;
- plan and conduct unilateral SF operations;
- perform other special operations as directed by higher authority.

APPENDIX F

✳✳✳✳✳✳✳✳

U.S. Army Special Forces Missions

From Official Department of the Army Documents

Unconventional Warfare (UW):

A broad spectrum of military and paramilitary operations conducted in enemy-held, enemy-controlled or politically sensitive territory. UW includes, but is not limited to, the interrelated fields of guerrilla warfare, evasion and escape, subversion, sabotage, and other operations of a low visibility, covert, or clandestine nature. Conduct a broad spectrum of military and paramilitary operations.

- Long-duration, indirect activities including guerrilla warfare and other offensive, low visibility, or clandestine operations.
- Mostly conducted by indigenous forces organized, trained, equipped, supported, and directed in varying degrees by special operations forces.

Direct Action (DA):

Either overt or covert action against an enemy force. Seize, damage, or destroy a target; capture or recover personnel or material in support of strategic/operational objectives for conventional forces.

- Short-duration, small-scale offensive actions.
- May require raids, ambushes, direct assault tactics; emplace mines and other munitions; conduct standoff attacks by firing from the air, ground or maritime platforms; designate

or illuminate targets for precision-guided munitions; support for cover and deception operations; or conduct independent sabotage normally inside enemy-held territory.

Special Reconnaissance (SR):

Special Forces teams are infiltrated behind enemy lines to provide the theater commander with intelligence on the enemy or to gather information on the terrain, local populace, etc. of an area. Verify, through observation or other collection methods, information concerning enemy capabilities, intentions, and activities in support of strategic/operational objectives or conventional forces.

- Reconnaissance and surveillance actions conducted at strategic or operational levels to complement national and theater-level collection efforts.
- Collect meteorological, hydrographic, geographic, and demographic data; provide target acquisition, area assessment, and post-strike reconnaissance data.

Foreign Internal Defense (FID):

FID operations are designed to help friendly developing nations by working with host country military and police forces to improve their technical skills, understanding of human rights issues, and to help with humanitarian and civic action projects. FID missions assist another government in any action program taken to free and protect its society from subversion, lawlessness, and insurgency.

- U.S. government interagency activity to foster internal development of economic, social, political, and military segments of a nation's structure.
- Train, advise, and assist host-nation military and paramilitary forces.

Counter-Terrorism (CT):

Offensive measures taken to prevent, deter, and respond to terrorism. Preempt or resolve terrorist incidents. Interagency activity using highly specialized capabilities.

Psychological Operations (PSYOPs):

Induce or reinforce foreign attitudes and behavior to objectives of the United States. Influence emotions, motives, and behavior of foreign governments, organizations, groups, and individuals.

Civil Affairs (CA):

Establish, maintain, influence, or exploit relations among military forces, civil authorities, and civilian populations to facilitate military operations.

- May be conducted as stand-alone operations or in support of a larger force.
- May include military forces assuming functions normally the responsibility of the local government.

Coalition Warfare/Support (CW/S):

Ensures the ability of a wide variety of foreign troops to work together effectively, in a wide variety of military exercises or operations. Draws upon the SOF soldier's maturity, military skills, language skills, and cultural awareness.

Humanitarian and Civic Action (HCA):

SOF soldiers' diversified skills, language capabilities, and cultural training make them a natural choice for supporting humanitarian and civic action operations.

Other Individual Missions:

Besides the individual skills of operations and intelligence, communications, medical aid, engineering and weapons, each Special Forces soldier is taught to train, advise, and assist host-nation military and paramilitary forces. Special Forces soldiers are highly skilled operators, trainers, and teachers. Area-oriented, these soldiers are specially trained in their area's native language and culture.

Other Special Operations Missions:

In addition to the above specialized missions, the various Special Operations Commands must:

- Prepare assigned forces to carry out special operations missions as required and, if directed by the president or secretary of defense, plan for and conduct special operations.
- Develop doctrine, tactics, techniques, and procedures for special operations forces.
- Conduct specialized courses of instruction for all special operations forces.
- Train assigned forces and ensure inter-operability of equipment and forces.
- Monitor the preparedness of special operations forces assigned to other unified commands.
- Develop and acquire unique special operations equipment, material, supplies, and services.
- Consolidate and submit program and budget proposals.
- Monitor promotions, assignments, retention, training, and professional development of all special operations forces personnel.

APPENDIX G

✳✳✳✳✳✳✳✳

U.S. Army Special Forces Creed

I am an American Special Forces Soldier. A professional!

I will do all that my nation requires of me.

I am a volunteer, knowing well the hazards of my profession.

I serve with the memory of those who have gone before me: Rogers's Rangers, Francis Marion, Mosby's Rangers, the first Special Service Forces, the Ranger Battalions of World War II, and the Airborne Ranger Companies of Korea.

I pledge to uphold the honor and integrity of all I am—in all I do.

I am a professional soldier. I will teach and fight wherever my nation requires. I will strive always to excel in every art of war.

I know that I will be called upon to perform tasks in isolation, far from familiar faces and voices, with the help and guidance of my God.

I will keep my mind and body clean, alert and strong, for this is my debt to those who depend upon me.

I will not fail those with whom I serve. I will not bring shame upon myself or the Forces.

I will maintain myself, my arms, and my equipment in an immaculate state as befits a Special Forces soldier.

I will never surrender, though I be the last man. If I am taken, I pray that I may have the strength to spit upon my enemy.

My mission is to succeed in any mission—and live to succeed again.

I am a member of my nation's chosen soldiers. God grant that I may not be found wanting, that I will not fail this sacred trust.

APPENDIX H

✳✳✳✳✳✳✳

Officer Assignment Opportunities in Delta Force

From a U.S. Army Personnel Command On-Line Announcement in 1999

The U.S. Army's 1st Special Forces Operational Detachment—Delta (1st SFOD-D) plans and conducts a broad range of special operations across the operational continuum. Delta is organized for the conduct of missions requiring rapid response with surgical applications of a wide variety of unique skills, while maintaining the lowest possible profile of U.S. involvement.

Assignment to 1st SFOD-D involves an extensive prescreening process, successful completion of a three to four week mentally and physically demanding Assessment and Selection Course, and a six month Operator Training Course. Upon successful completion of these courses officers are assigned to an operational position within the unit.

As an officer in the 1st SFOD-D, you will have added opportunities to command at the captain, major, and lieutenant colonel levels. You may also serve as an Operations Officer. After service with 1st SFOD-D, there are a wide variety of staff positions available to you at Department of Defense (DOD), Joint Chiefs of Staff (JCS), Department of the Army (DA), U.S. Army Special Operations Command (USASOC), U.S. Special Operations Command (USSOCOM), and other joint headquarters because of your training and experience. In addition, there are interagency positions available to you as well.

The prerequisites for an officer are:

- Male
- Volunteer
- U.S. citizen
- Pass a modified Class II flight physical
- Airborne qualified or volunteer for airborne training

- Pass a background security investigation and have at least a Secret Clearance
- Pass the Army Physical Fitness Test (55 pushups in two minutes, 62 situps in two minutes, and a two-mile run in 15:06 or less)
- Minimum of two years active service remaining upon selection to the unit
- Captain or Major (Branch immaterial)
- Advance Course Graduate
- College Graduate (BA or BS)
- Minimum of 12 months successful command (as a captain)

1st SFOD-D conducts worldwide recruiting twice a year to process potential candidates for the Assessment and Selection Course. Processing for the March course is from October through January. Processing for the September course takes place April through July.

Assignments with 1st SFOD-D provide realistic training and experiences that are both personally and professionally rewarding.

APPENDIX I

✳✳✳✳✳✳✳

U.S. Navy Basic Underwater Demolition/SEAL School (BUD/S)

From School Documents

Indoctrination

BUD/S indoctrination is five weeks in length. This is a mandatory course designed to give the student an understanding of the techniques and performance required of him. The first obstacle a student faces is the BUD/S Physical Screen Test. He must pass the test in order to class up and begin training. At the end of the indoctrination course, he will be given a more advanced version of the BUD/S Physical Screen Test that must be passed in order to enter the First Phase of BUD/S.

First Phase—Basic Conditioning

First Phase is eight weeks in length. Continued physical conditioning in the areas of running, swimming, and calisthenics grow increasingly difficult as the weeks progress. Students participate in weekly four-mile runs in boots and timed obstacle courses. They swim ocean distances up to two miles in fins and learn small boat seamanship.

The first two weeks of First Phase prepare you for the third week, known as "Hell Week." Students participate in five and one-half days of continuous training, with a maximum of four hours sleep for the entire week. This week is designed as the ultimate test of one's physical and mental motivation while in First Phase. During Hell Week, you will learn the value of the mainstay of SEAL teams: TEAMWORK! The remaining five weeks are devoted to teaching methods of conducting hydrographic surveys, preparing hydrographic charts, and instruction in basic maritime operations.

Second Phase—Diving

By completing First Phase, you prove to the instructor staff that you are motivated to participate in more in-depth training. The diving phase is seven weeks in length. Physical training continues during this period, and the times are lowered for the four-mile run, two-mile swim, and obstacle course.

Second Phase concentrates on combat SCUBA (Self-Contained Underwater Breathing Apparatus). Students are taught two types of SCUBA: open circuit (compressed air) and closed circuit (100% oxygen). You participate in a progressive dive schedule emphasizing the basic combat swimmer skills necessary to qualify as a combat diver. These skills will enable you to operate tactically and to complete your combat objective. These are the skills that separate SEALs from all other special operations forces.

Third Phase—Land Warfare

The demolitions, reconnaissance, weapons, and tactics phase is ten weeks long. Physical training grows more strenuous as the run distances increase and minimum passing times are lowered for the runs, swims, and obstacle course. Third Phase concentrates on teaching land navigation, small-unit tactics, rappelling, military land and underwater explosives, and weapons training. The final four weeks of Third Phase are spent on San Clemente Island, where students apply in a practical environment the techniques acquired throughout training.

Post-BUD/S Schools

BUD/S graduates receive three weeks of basic parachute training at the Army Airborne School, Fort Benning, Georgia, prior to reporting to their first Naval Special Warfare assignment.

Navy corpsmen who complete BUD/S and Basic Airborne

Training also attend two weeks of Special Operations Technician training at the Naval Special Warfare Center, Coronado. They also participate in an intense course of instruction in diving medicine and medical skills called 18-D (Special Operations Medical Sergeant Course). This is a 30-week course where the students receive training in treating burns, gunshot wounds, and trauma.

After assignment to a team and successful completion of a six-month probationary period, qualified personnel are awarded a Naval Special Warfare Classification (NEC) Code and Naval Special Warfare Insignia. New combat swimmers serve the remainder of their first enlistment (2.5 to 3 years) in either a SDV or SEAL Team.

A broad range of advanced training opportunities are available. Advanced courses include Sniper School, Dive Supervisor, language training, SEAL tactical communication, and many others. Shore duty opportunities are available in research and development, instructor duty, and overseas assignments.

Fitness Standards

The intense physical and mental conditioning required to become a SEAL begins with Basic Underwater Demolitions/SEAL (BUD/S) training. During this six-month program, recruits are pushed to their physical and mental limits.

BUD/S students participate in challenging training and daily encounter opportunities to develop and test their stamina and leadership. BUD/S training is extremely thorough—both physically and mentally—but through adequate preparation and a positive attitude you can meet its challenges with confidence.

Physical Fitness Standards

First Phase

50 meter underwater swim	Pass/fail
Underwater knot tying	Pass/fail
Drown-proofing test	Pass/fail
Basic lifesaving test	Pass/fail
1200 meter pool swim with fins	45 minutes

1 mile bay swim with fins	50 minutes
1 mile ocean swim with fins	50 minutes
1.5 mile swim with fins	70 minutes
2 mile ocean swim with fins	95 minutes
Obstacle course	15 minutes
4 mile timed run	32 minutes

Post–Hell Week

2000 meter condition pool swim without fins	Completion
1.5 mile night bay swim with fins	Completion
2 mile ocean swim with fins	85 minutes
4 mile timed run in boots	32 minutes
Obstacle course	13 minutes

Second Phase

2 mile ocean swim with fins	80 minutes
4 mile timed run in boots	31 minutes
Obstacle course	10.5 minutes
3.5 mile ocean swim with fins	Completion
5.5 mile ocean swim with fins	Completion

Third Phase

Obstacle Course	10 minutes
4 mile timed run in boots	30 minutes
14 mile run	Completion
2 mile ocean swim with fins	75 minutes

Required academic standards on all written tests

| Officers | 80% or above |
| Enlisted | 70% or above |

APPENDIX J

✳✳✳✳✳✳✳✳

U.S. Air Force Combat Control Team Training

From USAF Documents

Combat Control Orientation
2 Weeks
Lackland AFB, TX

The two-week orientation focuses on preparing airmen to meet the challenges of future training. In addition to administrative processing the airmen begin physical training while also attending classes in CCT history, training techniques, and fundamentals.

Combat Control Operator Course
15.5 Weeks
Keesler AFB, MS

The Combat Control Course teaches aircraft recognition and performance, air navigation aids, weather determination and effects, airport traffic control, flight assistance service, communication procedures, conventional approach control, radar procedures, and air traffic rules. This is the same course all other air traffic controllers attend and is the heart of the Combat Controller's job.

In addition to satisfactorily meeting academic requirements, students must pass a physical fitness test that includes swimming 1000 meters in less than 26 minutes and completing a three-mile run in less than 22.5 minutes.

U.S. Army Airborne School
3 Weeks
Fort Benning, GA

The army's airborne school teaches basic parachuting skills required to infiltrate an objective by static line airdrop. It lasts three weeks and includes ground operations week, tower week, and jump week composed of five actual parachute jumps. Personnel who complete the training are awarded the basic parachute rating and are authorized to wear the parachute badge.

USAF Basic Survival School
2.5 Weeks
Fairchild AFB, WA

This course teaches basic survival techniques for remote areas using minimal equipment. It includes instruction on principles and procedures for survival regardless of conditions, environment, or distance from friendly lines.

Combat Control School
13 Weeks
Pope AFB, NC

The combat control school provides final CCT qualifications. Training includes physical fitness, small unit tactics, land navigation, communications, fire support coordination, weapons orientation, and demolitions. Upon completion of the course each airman is assigned the designation of 3 Skill Level and awarded the scarlet beret and CCT flash.

Advanced Skills Training (AST)
Up to 12 Months
Hurlburt Field, FL

Upon completion of the Pipeline those who have successfully met the requirements to reach 3 Skill Level report to Hurlburt

Field, Florida, for advanced training. During this training the Combat Controllers join Pararescue (PJs) in the Special Tactics Initial Familiarization Course. The course uses both the classroom and field exercises to advance their knowledge in airfield seizure operations, combat search and rescue, fire support coordination with fixed and rotary wing aircraft, and other operations related topics.

During this period the Combat Controllers attend the U.S. Army Combat Divers School at Key West, Florida, to learn the use of open and closed circuit SCUBA equipment. They also develop their parachuting skills at the U.S. Army Military Free Fall Parachutist School at Fort Bragg, North Carolina, and Yuma Proving Grounds, Arizona, while the U.S. Navy Underwater Egress Training at Pensacola Naval Air Station, Florida, teaches them how to safely escape from an aircraft that has ditched into the water.

Upon the completion of Advanced Skills Training the Combat Controllers report to their Special Tactics Squadrons for operations—and continued training and retraining.

APPENDIX K

****

U.S. Special Operations Command Missions

Special Operations Command Posture Statement Published in 2000 by the Office of the Assistant Secretary of Defense

Principal Missions

SOF are organized, trained, and equipped specifically to accomplish their assigned roles, as described below, in nine mission areas:

1. Counter-proliferation (CP): Combat proliferation of nuclear, biological, and chemical across the full range of U.S. efforts, including the application of military power to protect U.S. forces and interests; intelligence collection and analysis, and support the diplomacy, arms control, and export controls. Accomplishment of these activities may require coordination with other U.S. government agencies.
2. Combating Terrorism (CT): Preclude, preempt, and resolve terrorism actions throughout the entire threat spectrum, including anti-terrorism (defense measures taken to reduce vulnerability to terrorist acts) and counter-terrorism (offensive measure taken to prevent, deter, and respond to terrorism), and resolve terrorist incidents when directed by the National Command Authorities or the appropriate unified commander or requested by the Services or other government agencies.
3. Foreign Internal Defense (FID): Organize, train, advise, and assist host nation military and paramilitary forces to enable those forces to free and protect their society from subversion, lawlessness, and insurgency.

4. Special Reconnaissance (SR): Conduct reconnaissance and surveillance actions to obtain or verify information concerning the capabilities, intentions, and activities of an actual or potential enemy or to secure data concerning characteristics of a particular area.

5. Direct Action (DA): Conduct short-duration strikes and other small-scale offensive actions to seize, destroy, capture, recover, or inflict damage on designated personnel or material.

6. Psychological Operations (PSYOP): Induce or reinforce foreign attitudes and behaviors favorable to the originator's objectives by conducting planned operations to convey selected information to foreign audiences to influence their emotions, motives, objective reasoning, and ultimately, the behavior of foreign governments, organizations, groups, and individuals.

7. Civil Affairs (CA): Facilitate military operations and consolidate operational activities by assisting commanders in establishing, maintaining, influencing, or exploiting relations between military forces and civil authorities, both governmental and non-governmental, and the civilian population in friendly, neutral, or hostile areas of operation.

8. Unconventional Warfare (UW): Organize, train, equip, advise, and assist indigenous and surrogate forces in military and paramilitary operations normally of long duration.

9. Information Operations (IO): Actions taken to achieve information superiority by affecting adversary information and information systems while defending one's own information and information systems.

Collateral Activities

Based on their unique capabilities, Special Operations Forces are frequently tasked to participate in the following activities:

1. Coalition Support (CS): Integrate coalition units into multinational military operations by training coalition partners on tactics and techniques and providing communications.

2. Combat Search and Rescue (CSAR): Penetrate air defense systems and conduct joint air, ground, or sea operations deep within hostile or denied territory, at night or in adverse weather, to recover distressed personnel during wartime or

contingency operations. SOF are equipped and manned to perform CSAR in support of SOF missions only. SOF performs CSAR in support of conventional forces on a case-by-case basis not to interfere with the readiness of or operations of core SOF mission.

3. Counter-drug (CD) activities: Train host-nation CD forces and domestic law enforcement agencies on critical skills required to conduct individual and small-unit operations in order to detect, monitor, and interdict the cultivation, production, and trafficking of illicit drugs targeted for use in the United States.

4. Humanitarian De-mining (HD) activities: Reduce or eliminate the threat to noncombatants and friendly forces posed by mines and other explosive devices by training host-nation personnel in their recognition, identification, marking, and safe destruction; provide instruction in program management, medical, and mine-awareness activities.

5. Humanitarian Assistance (HA): Provide assistance of limited scope and duration to supplement or complement the efforts of host-nation civil authorities or agencies to relieve or reduce the results of natural or manmade disasters or other endemic conditions such as human pain, disease, hunger, or privation that might present a serious threat to life or that can result in great damage to, or loss of, property.

6. Security Assistance (SA): Provide training assistance in support of legislated programs which provide U.S. defense articles, military training, and other defense-related services by grant, loan, credit, or cash sales in furtherance of national policies or objectives.

7. Special Activities: Subject to limitations imposed by Executive Order and in conjunction with a presidential finding and congressional oversight, plan and conduct actions abroad in support of national foreign policy objectives so that the role of the U.S. government is not apparent or acknowledged publicly.

******

U.S. Army Special Operations Command Organization Chart

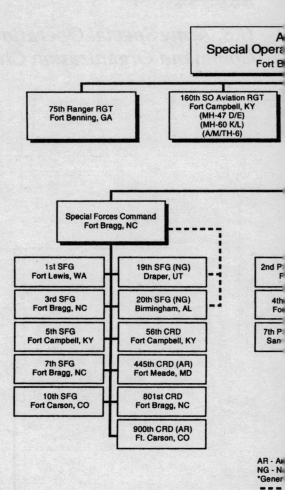

A
Special Opera
Fort B

75th Ranger RGT
Fort Benning, GA

160th SO Aviation RGT
Fort Campbell, KY
(MH-47 D/E)
(MH-60 K/L)
(A/M/TH-6)

Special Forces Command
Fort Bragg, NC

1st SFG Fort Lewis, WA	19th SFG (NG) Draper, UT	2nd P
3rd SFG Fort Bragg, NC	20th SFG (NG) Birmingham, AL	4th
5th SFG Fort Campbell, KY	56th CRD Fort Campbell, KY	7th P
7th SFG Fort Bragg, NC	445th CRD (AR) Fort Meade, MD	
10th SFG Fort Carson, CO	801st CRD Fort Bragg, NC	
	900th CRD (AR) Ft. Carson, CO	

AR - A
NG - N
*Gener
- - -

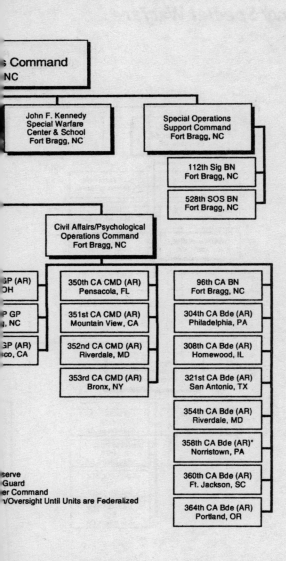

```
                    s Command
                    NC
```

John F. Kennedy Special Warfare Center & School Fort Bragg, NC	Special Operations Support Command Fort Bragg, NC

112th Sig BN
Fort Bragg, NC

528th SOS BN
Fort Bragg, NC

Civil Affairs/Psychological
Operations Command
Fort Bragg, NC

GP (AR) OH	350th CA CMD (AR) Pensacola, FL	96th CA BN Fort Bragg, NC
P GP g, NC	351st CA CMD (AR) Mountain View, CA	304th CA Bde (AR) Philadelphia, PA
GP (AR) sco, CA	352nd CA CMD (AR) Riverdale, MD	308th CA Bde (AR) Homewood, IL
	353rd CA CMD (AR) Bronx, NY	321st CA Bde (AR) San Antonio, TX
		354th CA Bde (AR) Riverdale, MD
		358th CA Bde (AR)* Norristown, PA
		360th CA Bde (AR) Ft. Jackson, SC
		364th CA Bde (AR) Portland, OR

serve
Guard
er Command
n/Oversight Until Units are Federalized

APPENDIX M
U.S. Navy Special Warfare

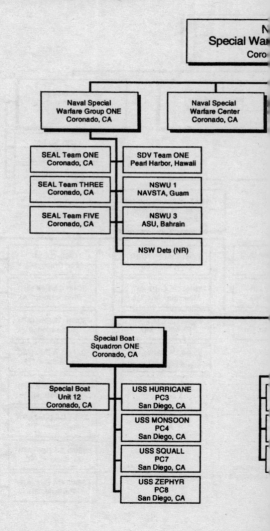

Special Warfare
Coro...

Naval Special
Warfare Group ONE
Coronado, CA

Naval Special
Warfare Center
Coronado, CA

SEAL Team ONE
Coronado, CA

SDV Team ONE
Pearl Harbor, Hawaii

SEAL Team THREE
Coronado, CA

NSWU 1
NAVSTA, Guam

SEAL Team FIVE
Coronado, CA

NSWU 3
ASU, Bahrain

NSW Dets (NR)

Special Boat
Squadron ONE
Coronado, CA

Special Boat
Unit 12
Coronado, CA

USS HURRICANE
PC3
San Diego, CA

USS MONSOON
PC4
San Diego, CA

USS SQUALL
PC7
San Diego, CA

USS ZEPHYR
PC8
San Diego, CA

Command Organization Chart

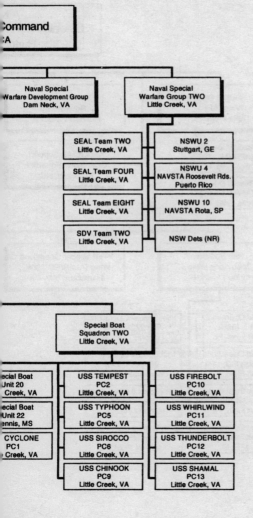

Command
:A

Naval Special Warfare Development Group Dam Neck, VA	Naval Special Warfare Group TWO Little Creek, VA

SEAL Team TWO Little Creek, VA	NSWU 2 Stuttgart, GE
SEAL Team FOUR Little Creek, VA	NSWU 4 NAVSTA Roosevelt Rds. Puerto Rico
SEAL Team EIGHT Little Creek, VA	NSWU 10 NAVSTA Rota, SP
SDV Team TWO Little Creek, VA	NSW Dets (NR)

Special Boat
Squadron TWO
Little Creek, VA

ecial Boat Unit 20 Creek, VA	USS TEMPEST PC2 Little Creek, VA	USS FIREBOLT PC10 Little Creek, VA
ecial Boat Unit 22 ennis, MS	USS TYPHOON PC5 Little Creek, VA	USS WHIRLWIND PC11 Little Creek, VA
CYCLONE PC1 Creek, VA	USS SIROCCO PC6 Little Creek, VA	USS THUNDERBOLT PC12 Little Creek, VA
	USS CHINOOK PC9 Little Creek, VA	USS SHAMAL PC13 Little Creek, VA

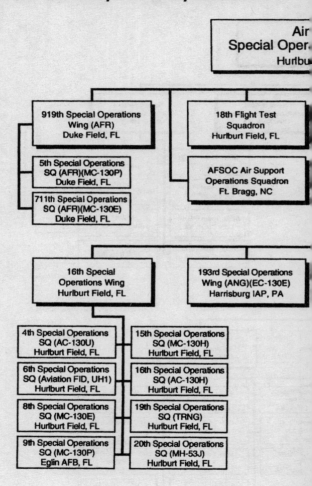

Command Organization Chart

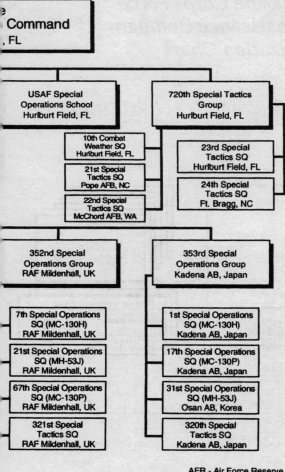

	Command
	, FL

USAF Special Operations School
Hurlburt Field, FL

720th Special Tactics Group
Hurlburt Field, FL

10th Combat Weather SQ
Hurlburt Field, FL

21st Special Tactics SQ
Pope AFB, NC

22nd Special Tactics SQ
McChord AFB, WA

23rd Special Tactics SQ
Hurlburt Field, FL

24th Special Tactics SQ
Ft. Bragg, NC

352nd Special Operations Group
RAF Mildenhall, UK

353rd Special Operations Group
Kadena AB, Japan

7th Special Operations SQ (MC-130H)
RAF Mildenhall, UK

21st Special Operations SQ (MH-53J)
RAF Mildenhall, UK

67th Special Operations SQ (MC-130P)
RAF Mildenhall, UK

321st Special Tactics SQ
RAF Mildenhall, UK

1st Special Operations SQ (MC-130H)
Kadena AB, Japan

17th Special Operations SQ (MC-130P)
Kadena AB, Japan

31st Special Operations SQ (MH-53J)
Osan AB, Korea

320th Special Tactics SQ
Kadena AB, Japan

AFR - Air Force Reserve
ANG - Air National Guard

APPENDIX O

✱✱✱✱✱✱✱✱

U.S. Marine Corps Force Reconnaissance Company Organization Chart

1ST FORCE RECON ORGANIZATION

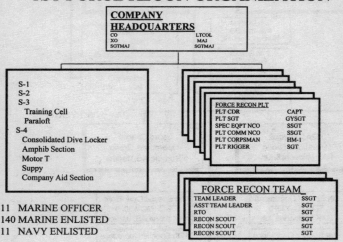

COMPANY HEADQUARTERS

CO	LTCOL
XO	MAJ
SGTMAJ	SGTMAJ

S-1
S-2
S-3
   Training Cell
   Paraloft
S-4
   Consolidated Dive Locker
   Amphib Section
   Motor T
   Suppy
   Company Aid Section

FORCE RECON PLT

PLT CDR	CAPT
PLT SGT	GYSGT
SPEC EQPT NCO	SSGT
PLT COMM NCO	SSGT
PLT CORPSMAN	HM-1
PLT RIGGER	SGT

FORCE RECON TEAM

TEAM LEADER	SSGT
ASST TEAM LEADER	SGT
RTO	SGT
RECON SCOUT	SGT
RECON SCOUT	SGT
RECON SCOUT	SGT

11 MARINE OFFICER
140 MARINE ENLISTED
11 NAVY ENLISTED

APPENDIX P

✳✳✳✳✳✳✳✳

U.S. Army Sniper School Training Schedule

The following schedule is from the sniper class of 24 February–29 March 2001. Other class schedules may vary slightly. Lesson numbers and administrative remarks have been deleted.

Day 0, Sunday

0800–Until Completion	Records screening, weigh-in, PT test

Day 1, Monday

0500–0530	Draw weapons/Load vehicles
0530–0700	PT retest
0700–0800	Breakfast
0800–0830	Welcome briefing
0830–1130	Intro to the M-24 Sniper Weapon System
1130–1215	Lunch
1215–1530	Field sketches/Range Card & Log Book
1530–1630	Practical Exercise
1630–1830	Ghillie suit construction
1830–1900	Dinner
1900–2200	Ghillie suit construction/ Weapons maintenance
2200–2215	Movement to 4700A (quarters)
2215–2230	Turn in weapons

Day 2, Tuesday

0500–0530	Draw weapons/Load vehicles
0530–0600	Movement to Sniper School
0600–0700	Physical Training
0700–0800	Breakfast
0800–1100	Fundamentals of marksmanship
1100–1500	Range Estimation
1500–1800	Ballistics/Data Book
1800–1830	Dinner
1830–2200	Ghillie suit construction
2200–2230	Movement to 4700A
2230–2245	Turn in weapons

Day 3, Wednesday

0500–0530	Draw weapons/Load vehicles
0530–0600	Movement to Sniper School
0600–0700	PT—Three-mile run
0700–0800	Breakfast
0800–1600	Field fire M24 (Zero at 100/300/500 meters)
1600–1730	Range Estimation
1730–1800	Dinner
1800–2000	Command & Control use and employment
2000–2200	Ghillie suit construction
2200–2230	Movement to 4700A
2230–2245	Turn in weapons

Day 4, Thursday

0500–0530	Draw weapons/Load vehicles
0530–0600	Movement to Sniper School
0600–0700	PT—Three-mile road march
0700–0800	Range Estimation
0800–0830	Draw ammo and MRE (Meal Ready to Eat) for Lunch
0830–1800	Field fire M24 (500–900 meters)
1800–1930	Moving targets

1930–2000	Dinner
2000–2200	Weapons/Ghillie maintenance
2200–2230	Movement to 4700A

Day 5, Friday

0500–0530	Draw weapons/Load vehicles
0530–0600	Breakfast
0600–0700	Movement to Sniper School
0700–1600	Field fire M24 (400–600 meters)
1600–1700	Range Estimation
1700–1800	Ghillie suit construction
1800–1830	Dinner
1830–2200	Weapons/Ghillie suit maintenance
2200–2230	Movement to 4700A

Day 6, Saturday

0600–0630	Draw weapons/Load vehicles
0630–0700	Breakfast
0700–0730	Movement to Sniper School
0730–0900	Range Estimation
0900–1300	Field fire M24 (400–600 meters)
1300–1330	Movement to 4700A

Day 7, Sunday

No Training Scheduled

Day 8, Monday

0530–0600	Draw weapons/Load vehicles
0600–0630	Breakfast
0630–0700	Movement to Sniper School
0700–1530	Field fire M24 (Moving targets, 400–600 meters)
1530–1630	Range Estimation
1630–1700	Dinner
1700–2200	AN/PVS10 Sniper Night Scope (300, 400, 500 meters)

| 2200–2330 | Weapons/Ghillie suit maintenance |
| 2330–2400 | Movement to 4700A |

Day 9, Tuesday

0530–0600	Movement to Sniper School
0600–0700	PT—three-mile road march
0700–0800	Breakfast
0800–0900	Range estimation
0900–1630	Field fire M24
1630–1730	Dinner
1730–2200	AN/PVS10 Sniper Night Scope (400, 500, 600 meters)
2200–2230	Movement to 4700A
2230–2400	Weapons/Ghillie suit maintenance

Day 10, Wednesday

0530–0600	Breakfast
0600–0630	Movement to Range 4882
0630–0800	Range estimation, cover and concealment
0800–1530	Field fire M24
1530–1730	Range Estimation
1730–1800	Dinner
1800–2200	AN/PVS10 Sniper Night Scope (400, 500, 600 meters)
2200–2215	Movement to 4700A
2215–2400	Weapons/Ghillie suit maintenance

Day 11, Thursday

0530–0600	Breakfast
0600–0630	Movement to Sniper School
0630–0700	Individual mentoring
0700–0900	Countersniper operations
0900–1100	Range Estimation

1100–1700	Field fire M24—moving targets (400–700 meters)
1700–1800	Dinner
1800–2200	AN/PVS10 Sniper Night Scope (300–600 meters)
2200–2230	Movement to 4700A
2230–2400	Weapons/Ghillie suit maintenance

Day 12, Friday

0530–0600	Breakfast
0600–0630	Movement to Sniper School
0630–0900	Camouflage and concealment
0900–1300	Stalking techniques
1300–1730	Target detection
1730–1830	Dinner
1830–2030	Select, construct, occupy sniper position
2030–2100	Written Exam
2100–2200	Weapons/Ghillie suit maintenance
2200–2230	Movement to 4700A

Days 13 and 14, Saturday and Sunday
No Training Scheduled

Day 15, Monday

0500–0600	Breakfast
0600–0630	Movement to Sniper School
0630–1000	Stalking techniques
1000–1330	Target detection
1330–1730	Unknown distance firing (300–900 meters)
1730–1800	Dinner
1800–2100	Weapons/Ghillie maintenance
2100–2130	Movement to 4700A

Day 16, Tuesday

0500–0600	PT—two-mile run
0600–0630	Breakfast
0630–0700	Movement to Sniper School
0700–1200	Stalking techniques
1200–1300	Target detection
1300–1800	Unknown distance firing (300–900 meters)
1800–1830	Dinner
1830–2030	Unknown distance firing (300–900 meters)
2030–2200	Weapons/Ghillie suit maintenance
2200–2230	Movement to 4700A

Day 17, Wednesday

0500–0600	Breakfast
0600–0700	Individual mentoring
0700–1200	Stalking techniques
1200–1330	Target detection
1330–1730	Unknown distance firing (300–900 meters)
1730–1800	Review written Exam
1800–1830	Dinner
1830–2100	Stalking retraining/Weapons maintenance
2100–2130	Movement to 4700A

Day 18, Thursday

0530–0600	Breakfast
0600–0630	Movement to Sniper School
0630–0700	Individual mentoring
0700–1130	Stalking techniques
1130–1330	Target detection
1330–1730	Unknown distance firing (300–900 meters)
1730–1800	Dinner

1800–2100	Countersniping techniques
2100–2130	Weapons/Ghillie suit maintenance
2130–2200	Movement to 4700A

Day 19, Friday

0530–0600	Breakfast
0600–0630	Movement to Sniper School
0630–0700	Individual mentoring
0700–1130	Stalking techniques
1130–1300	Target detection
1300–1700	Unknown distance firing (300–900 meters)
1700–1900	Elevation and windage holds
1900–1930	Dinner
1930–2100	MOUT/Urban sniping
2100–2200	Weapons/Ghillie suit maintenance
2200–2230	Movement to 4700A

Day 20, Saturday

0700–0730	Breakfast
0730–0800	Movement to Sniper School
0800–1200	Urban operations
1200–1300	Target detection
1300–1330	Weapons/Ghillie suit maintenance
1330–1400	Movement to 4700A

Day 21, Sunday

No training scheduled

Day 22, Monday

0530–0600	Breakfast
0600–0630	Movement to Sniper School
0630–0800	Stalking techniques
0800–1100	Urban sniping

1100–1300	Target detection
1300–1700	Urban sniping
1700–1800	Stalking techniques
1800–1830	Dinner
1830–2100	Night stalking techniques
2100–0500	Practical exercise—hide construction/target detection

Day 23, Tuesday

0800–0830	Breakfast
0830–0900	Movement to Sniper School
0900–1100	Stalking techniques
1100–1330	Target detection
1330–1800	Urban sniping
1800–1830	Dinner
1830–1930	Weapons/Ghillie suit maintenance

Day 24, Wednesday

0530–0600	Breakfast
0600–0630	Movement to Sniper School
0630–1200	Stalking techniques
1200–1330	Target detection
1330–1730	.50 caliber orientation
1730–1830	Dinner
1830–2100	AN/PVS10 Sniper Night Scope
2100–2200	Weapons/Ghillie suit maintenance
2200–2230	Movement to 4700A

Day 25, Thursday

0530–0600	Breakfast
0600–0700	Movement to Sniper School
0700–1100	Stalking techniques
1100–1300	Target detection
1300–1700	.50 caliber alts and holds
1700–1800	Dinner

1800–1900	Weapons/Ghillie suit maintenance
1900–1930	Movement to 4700A

Day 26, Friday

0700–0800	Breakfast
0800–0830	Movement to Sniper School
0830–1200	.50 caliber fire exercise
1200–1600	Reconnaissance fundamentals
1600–1900	Field Exercise Operations Order/Preparation
1900–2000	Weapons/Ghillie suit maintenance
2000–2030	Movement to 4700A

Days 27 and 28, Saturday and Sunday
Additional training as needed

Day 29, Monday

0430–0500	Breakfast
0500–0530	Movement to Sniper School
0530–0630	Preparation for air insertion
0630–1000	Air mission, Field Training Exercise (FTX) insertion
1000–2400	FTX

Day 30, Tuesday

0001–2400	FTX

Day 31, Wednesday

0001–0730	FTX
0730–0930	Air mission/FTX recovery
0930–1300	Final M24 record fire
1300–1500	Mission debriefing
1500–1900	Weapons/Ghillie suit maintenance

| 1900–1915 | Movement to 4700A |
| 1915–1930 | Turn in weapons |

Day 32, Thursday

0730–0830	Breakfast
0830–0900	Movement to Sniper School
0900–1000	Sniper sustainment program
1000–1800	Out processing
1800–1815	Movement to 4700A

Day 33, Friday

0800–0900	Breakfast
0900–1100	Out processing
1100–1145	Graduation rehearsal
1145–1230	Graduation/dismissal

APPENDIX Q

✻✻✻✻✻✻✻✻

U.S. Army Basic Airborne Course

Course description provided by the School

The purposes of the Basic Airborne Course (BAC) are to:

1. Qualify the BAC student in the use of the parachute as a means of combat employment. The qualification is accomplished by:
   a. Developing the student's confidence through repetitious training to overcome the student's natural fear of jumping from an aircraft while in flight.
   b. Maintaining the level of physical fitness required of military parachutists through daily physical training.
   c. Qualifying the student as a parachutist by performing five satisfactory parachute jumps from an aircraft in flight.

2. Develop a sense of leadership, self-confidence, and an aggressive spirit through mental and physical conditioning.

BAC course content and structure:

Ground Training Week (Week 1)

During Ground Training Week, you begin an intensive program of instruction to build individual airborne skills, prepare you to make a parachute jump, and land safely. You will train on the mock door, the 34-foot tower, and the lateral drift apparatus (LDA). To go forward to Tower Training Week, you must individually qualify on the 34-foot tower, the LDA, and pass all PT requirements.

Tower Training Week (Week 2)

The individual skills learned during Ground Week are refined during Tower Week and a team effort or "mass exit" concept added to the training. The apparatuses used this week are the 34-foot towers, the swing landing trainer (SLT), the mock door for mass exit training, the suspended harness, the wind machine, and the 250-foot tower. You must qualify on the mass exit procedures, the SLT, and pass all PT requirements to advance to Jump Training Week.

Jump Training Week

Week Three is devoted to your five qualifying jumps. Before you make your first jump you will receive a review of malfunctions and aircraft orientation and be organized and manifested for the jump. Unless restricted by the lack of jump aircraft or weather (in which case training will continue into the next week until the five jumps are accomplished) graduation is conducted on Friday of Week Three at the Airborne Walk. Guests are welcome to observe jumps at Fryar Field, watch graduation, and participate in awarding wings.

ANNOTATED BIBLIOGRAPHY

General Elites

Adams, James. *Secret Armies*. New York: Atlantic Monthly Press, 1988. General insights into American, Soviet, and European special forces.

Adkin, Mark. *Urgent Fury*. Lexington, MA: Lexington Books, 1989. Includes actions by Rangers, SEALs, and Delta Force during the operation to liberate the island of Grenada.

Arostegui, Martin C. *Twilight Warriors*. New York: St. Martin's Press, 1996. A general study of special forces worldwide.

Bohrer, David. *America's Special Forces*. Osceola, WI: MBI Publishing Company, 1998. A coffee-table pictorial book about the weapons, training, and missions of the elites.

Donnelly, Thomas. *Operation Just Cause*. New York: Lexington Books, 1991. Includes information on special operations units in the invasion of Panama.

Emerson, Steven. *Secret Warriors: Inside the Covert Military Operations of the Reagan Era*. New York: Putnam, 1988. A journalist's account of special operations during the administration of President Ronald Reagan.

Marquis, Susan L. *Unconventional Warfare*. Washington, D.C.: Brookings Institution Press, 1997. The history of the rebuilding of U.S. special operations forces after Vietnam according to an academic.

McRaven, William H. *Spec Ops: Case Studies in Special Operations Warfare*. Novato, CA: Presidio Press, 1995. A series of stories on modern special operations around the world.

Neillands, Robin. *In the Combat Zone*. Washington Square, New York: New York University Press, 1998. A former British officer's account of special operations, primarily U.S. and British, since 1945.

O'Donnell, Patrick K. *Beyond Valor*. New York: The Free Press, 2000. An oral history collection of the experiences of World War II Rangers and airborne veterans.

Paddock, Alfred H. *U.S. Special Warfare: Its Origins*. Lawrence, KS: University Press of Kansas, 2002. A study of special warfare units from World War II to the present.

Waller, Douglas C. *Commandos*. New York: Simon & Schuster, 1994. A journalist's view of "America's secret soldiers" in Operation Desert Storm.

Zedric, Lance Q., and Michael F. Dilley. *Elite Warriors*. Ventura, CA: Pathfinder Publishing, 1996. Detailed history of American fighting elites.

Airborne

Ambrose, Stephen E. *Band of Brothers*. New York: Touchstone Books, 2001. The story of E Company, 506th Parachute Regiment of the 101st Airborne Division from Normandy to the end of World War II.

Blair, Clay, Jr. *Ridgeway's Paratroopers*. New York: Doubleday, 1985. General history of the American airborne in World War II.

Bradley, Francis X., and H. Glen Wood. *Paratrooper*. Harrisburg, PA: Stackpole Books, 1967. Illustrated history of the airborne and of paratrooper training of the period.

Breuer, William B. *Geronimo!* New York: St. Martin's Press, 1991. A history of American paratroopers in World War II.

Burgett, Donald R. *Currahee!: A Screaming Eagle at Normandy*. Novato, CA: Presidio Press, 1999. Personal narrative of a paratrooper in the 101st during the invasion of Europe.

Flanagan, Edward M. *Angels at Dawn*. Novato, CA: Presidio Press, 1999. The rescue of Japanese-held prisoners at Los Banos in the Philippines by the 11th Airborne Division in 1945.

Gabel, Kurt. *The Making of a Paratrooper*. Lawrence, KS: University Press of Kansas, 1990. Overview of airborne training and combat during World War II.

Halberstadt, Hans. *Airborne*. Novato, CA: Presidio Press, 1988. A history of American paratroopers.

Hickey, Michael. *Out of the Sky.* New York: Scribners, 1979. A general history of airborne units worldwide.

Hoyt, Edwin Palmer. *Airborne.* New York: Stein and Day, 1979. A general history of U.S. airborne forces.

Ryan, Cornelius. *A Bridge Too Far.* New York: Touchstone Books, 1995 (reprint). Detailed history of the failed Allied airborne Operation Market Garden in World War II.

Thompson, Leroy. *United States Airborne Forces: 1940–1986.* New York: Blandford Press, 1986. A general history of American paratroopers.

Delta Force

Adams, James. *Secret Armies: The Full Story of the SAS, Delta Force, and Spetsnaz.* New York: Atlantic Monthly Press, 1988. Discusses some past missions but has few other details on Delta.

Beckwith, Charlie A., and Donald Knox. *Delta Force.* New York: Harcourt Brace Jovanovich, 1983. The account of the founding of Delta by its first commander. (The book was re-released in paperback by Avon Books in 2000 with a brief epilogue by C. A. Mobley.)

Bowden, Mark. *Black Hawk Down.* New York: Atlantic Monthly Press, 1999. Includes Delta participation in the 1993 Battle of Mogadishu.

———. *Killing Pablo: The Hunt for the World's Greatest Outlaw.* New York: Atlantic Monthly Press, 2001. Includes Delta participation in the death of Colombian drug lord Pablo Escobar.

Griswold, Terry, and D. M. Giangreco. *Delta.* Osceola, WI: MBI Publishing Company, 1992. A history, mostly pictorial, of Delta's weapons, equipment, and more.

Haney, Eric L. *Inside Delta Force.* New York: Delacorte, 2002. The story of Delta's early years by a retired sergeant major who was one of the unit's founders.

Livingstone, Neil C. *The Cult of Counterterrorism.* Lexington, MA: Lexington Books, 1989. Includes some early Delta history.

Force Recon

Hamblen, Donald M., and Bruce H. Norton. *One Tough Marine.* New York: Ivy Books, 1993. Story of a marine's career spent mostly in Force Recon, including tours in Vietnam.

Jacques, Maurice A., and Bruce H. Norton. *Sergeant Major: U.S. Marines.* New York: Ivy Books, 1995. Covers Jacques's career as a marine including three tours in Vietnam, mostly with First Force Recon.

Lanning, Michael Lee, and Ray W. Stubbe. *Inside Force Recon: Recon Marines in Vietnam.* New York: Ivy Books, 1989. General history of Force Recon and detailed account of their service in the Vietnam War.

Lee, Alex. *Force Recon Command: A Special Marine Unit in Vietnam.* Annapolis: Naval Institute Press, 1995. Operations by the Third Force Recon Company in 1969 and 1970 in Vietnam by its commanding officer.

Norton, Bruce H. *Force Recon Diary: 1969.* New York: Ivy Books, 1991. Personal narrative of a navy corpsman's tour with First Force Recon Company in Vietnam.

————. *Force Recon Diary: 1970.* New York: Ivy Books, 1992. Covers Norton's continued tour with First Force Recon.

————. *Stingray.* New York: Ballantine, 2000. An overview of Force Recon in the Vietnam War.

Meyers, Bruce F. *Fortune Favors the Brave.* Annapolis: Naval Institute Press, 2000. The story of First Force Recon by its first company commander.

Peters, Bill. *First Force Recon Company.* New York: Ivy Books, 1999. A personal narrative of an officer's tour with First Force in Vietnam in 1969.

Vetter, Lawrence C., Jr. *Never Without Heroes.* New York: Ivy Books, 1996. General history of Third Reconnaissance Battalion in Vietnam from 1965 to 1970 by an officer who served as a platoon leader in the unit.

Young, Paul R. *First Recon—Second to None.* New York: Ivy Books, 1992. Personal narrative of a lieutenant with the First Recon Battalion in 1967.

Rangers

Black, Robert W. *Rangers in Korea*. New York: Ivy Books, 1989. Detailed account of Ranger units and operations in the Korean War.

———. *Rangers in World War II*. New York: Ivy Books, 2001. Detailed account of Ranger units and operations in the Second World War.

Burford, John. *LRRP Team Leader*. New York: Ivy Books, 1994. Personal narrative of a veteran of the LRRPs with the 101st Airborne Division in 1968.

Camper, Frank. *L.R.R.P. The Professional*. New York: Dell, 1988. Personal narrative of a LRRP in the 4th Infantry Division in 1967.

Chambers, Larry. *Death in the A Shau Valley*. New York: Ivy Books, 1998. Personal narrative of a Ranger with the 101st Airborne Division in 1970.

———. *Recondo*. New York: Ivy Books, 1992. Personal narrative of a LRRP with the 101st Airborne Division in 1969 including training at Recondo School.

Darby, William O., and William H. Baumer. *Darby's Rangers: We Led the Way*. San Rafael, CA: Presidio Press, 1980. The story of the World War II Rangers based on the autobiography written by Darby before his death near the end of the war.

Ericson, Don, and John L. Rotundo. *Charlie Rangers*. New York: Ivy Books, 1989. An early personal narrative of C Company Rangers in Vietnam in 1969 and 1970.

Foley, Dennis. *Special Men*. New York: Ivy Books, 1994. Personal narrative of an officer's tour with the provisional LRRPs of the 101st Airborne Division in Vietnam.

Ford, Gary D. *4/4: A LRP's Narrative*. New York: Ivy Books, 1993. Personal story of an enlisted soldier with F Company, 51st LRPs, in Vietnam in 1967.

Goshen, Bill. *War Paint*. New York: Ballantine, 2001. Personal narrative of a LRRP with the 1st Infantry Division in Vietnam from 1968 to 1970.

Hall, Don C., and Annette R. Hall. *I Served*. Bellevue, WA: A. D. Hall, 1994. Personal narrative of a LRRP with II Field Force in Vietnam in 1967 and 1968.

Hogan, David W. *Raiders or Elite Infantry?* Westport, CT: Greenwood

Press, 1992. A study of the changing role of Rangers from World War II through Grenada.

Jorgenson, Kregg P. J. *Acceptable Loss.* New York: Ivy Books, 1991. Personal narrative of a tour with the LRRP/Rangers of the 1st Cavalry Division in Vietnam in 1969 and 1970.

———. *Ghosts of the Highlands.* New York: Ivy Books, 1999. An overview of operations by the LRRPs of the 1st Cavalry Division in Vietnam in 1966 and 1967.

———. *LRRP Company Command.* New York: Ballantine, 2000. An overview of the 1st Cavalry LRRPs in Vietnam during 1968 and 1969.

———. *MIA Rescue.* New York: Ivy Books, 1996. Details a LRRP team's cross-border mission into Cambodia in 1970.

Lanning, Michael Lee. *Inside the LRRPs: Rangers in Vietnam.* New York: Ivy Books, 1988. General Ranger background and detailed history of LRRPs/Rangers in the Vietnam War.

Leppleman, John. *Blood on the Risers.* New York: Ivy Books, 1991. Personal narrative of nearly three years in Vietnam including a tour with the Rangers of the 173rd Airborne Brigade.

Linderer, Gary A. *Eyes of the Eagle.* New York: Ivy Books, 1991. Personal narrative of LRRPs in Vietnam with the 101st Airborne Division in 1968.

———. *Eyes Behind the Lines.* New York: Ivy Books, 1991. Continuation of personal narrative by a LRRP in the 101st.

———. *Phantom Warriors.* New York: Ballantine, 2000. A collection of LRRP/Ranger war stories from the Vietnam War.

———. *Phantom Warriors, Book 2.* New York: Ballantine, 2001. More war stories of LRRP/Rangers in Vietnam.

———. *Six Silent Men, Book 3.* New York: Ivy Books, 1999. The third in a series of books about the LRRP/Rangers of the 101st Airborne Division in the Vietnam War.

Lock, John D. *To Fight with Intrepidity.* New York: Pocket Books, 1998. A detailed history of American Rangers from 1622 to the present.

Martinez, Reynel. *Six Silent Men, Book 2.* New York: Ivy Books, 1997. The second in a series of three books on LRRP/Rangers of the 101st Airborne Division in Vietnam.

Miller, Kenn. *Six Silent Men, Book 1.* New York: Ivy Books, 1997. The first in a series of three books on LRRP/Rangers of the 101st Airborne Division in Vietnam.

Ogburn, Charlton, Jr. *The Marauders.* New York: Harper & Brothers,

1959. Detailed history of Merrill's Marauders in World War II by one of its veterans.

Sides, Hampton. *Ghost Soldiers*. New York: Doubleday, 2001. The rescue of prisoners held by the Japanese at Cabanatuan in the Philippines by Rangers in World War II.

Stanton, Shelby L. *Rangers at War*. New York: Orion Books, 1992. A history of LRRPs in Vietnam based on after-action reports from the National Archives.

Walker, James W. *Fortune Favors the Bold*. New York: Ivy Books, 1998. Personal narrative by a British citizen who volunteered for a tour in Vietnam with the LRRPs of the 101st Airborne Division.

SEALs

Best, Herbert. *The Webfoot Warriors*. New York: John Day Company, 1962. A detailed history of the Navy's underwater demolition teams.

Bosiljevac, T. L. *SEALs: UDT/SEAL Operations in Vietnam*. New York: Ivy Books, 1989. An in-depth account of SEAL operations in the Vietnam War.

Chalker, Dennis. *One Perfect Op*. New York: William Morrow, 2002. An enlisted SEAL's personal narrative of training, the invasion of Grenada, and operations with Red Cell.

Constance, Harry, and Randall Fuerst. *Good to Go*. New York: Avon, 1998. Personal narrative of a SEAL officer's tours with Team Two in Vietnam during the late 1960s.

Couch, Dick. *The Warrior Elite: The Forging of SEAL Class 228*. New York: Crown, 2001. A former SEAL comments on today's training.

Cummings, Dennis. *The Men Behind the Trident*. New York: Bantam, 1998. A history of SEAL Team One in Vietnam.

Dockery, Kevin. *Navy SEALs: A History of the Early Years*. New York: Berkley Books, 2001. A collection of oral histories of early members of the UDT and SEALs.

Dockery, Kevin, and Bill Fawcett. *The Teams*. New York: William Morrow, 1998. An oral history of the SEALs.

Enoch, Barry, and Greg Walker. *Teammates!* New York: Pocket, 1998. Personal narrative of a veteran of SEAL Team One in Vietnam.

Fawcett, Bill. *Hunters and Shooters: An Oral History of the U.S. Navy SEALs in Vietnam.* New York: Avon, 1996. A collection of fifteen war stories.

Halberstadt, Hans. *U.S. Navy SEALs in Action.* Osceola, WI: Motorbooks International, 1995. A pictorial account of SEAL training.

Hoyt, Edwin P. *SEALs at War.* New York: Dell, 1993. The history of UDTs and SEALs from World War II through Desert Storm.

Kelly, Orr. *Brave Men, Dark Waters.* New York: Pocket Books, 1993. A history of UDTS and SEALs from their origins through Desert Storm.

———. *Never Fight Fair!* New York: Pocket Books, 1996. A collection of SEAL war stories from World War II through the Persian Gulf.

Marcinko, Richard, and John Weisman. *Rogue Warrior.* New York: Pocket, 1992. Personal narrative of Marcinko's naval career, including time with UDTs, SEALs, and his formation of SEAL Team Six.

Miller, Rad. *Whattaya Mean I Can't Kill 'Em.* New York: Ivy Books, 1998. Personal narrative of a SEAL's tour in Vietnam in 1969.

O'Dell, James D. *The Water Is Never Cold.* Washington, D.C.: Brasseys, 2000. Overview of the origins of U.S. naval combat demolitions units, UDTs, and SEALs.

Roat, John Carl. *Class-29.* New York: Ballantine, 2000. Personal narrative of SEAL training in the early 1960s and today.

Smith, Gary R., and Alan Maki. *Death in the Delta.* New York: Ivy Books, 1996. Personal narrative of a veteran of five tours with SEALs in Vietnam.

———. *Death in the Jungle.* New York: Ivy Books, 1995. Personal narrative of Smith's tours with SEALs in Vietnam.

———. *Master Chief.* New York: Ivy Books, 1996. Personal narrative of Smith's last SEAL tour in Vietnam.

Walsh, Michael J. *SEAL!* New York: Pocket, 1996. Personal narrative of a veteran of twenty-six years with the SEALs.

Waterman, Steven L. *Just a Sailor.* New York: Ballantine, 2000. Personal narrative of a UDT diver's tour in Vietnam.

Watson, James, and Kevin Dockery. *Point Man.* New York: William Morrow, 1993. Personal narrative of a career sailor with UDT and later with SEAL Team Two in Vietnam.

Young, Darryl. *The Element of Surprise.* New York: Ivy Books, 1990. Personal narrative of a navy SEAL in Vietnam in 1970.

——. *Seals, UDT, Frogmen: Men Under Pressure.* New York: Ivy Books, 1994. Sixty-one stories of SEALs in training and war from their beginnings to the present.

Snipers

Culbertson, John J. *A Sniper in the Arizona.* New York: Ivy Books, 1999. Personal narrative of a 5th Marine Regiment sniper in Vietnam in 1967.

Gilbert, Adrian. *Sniper.* New York: St. Martin's Press, 1995. A history of snipers around the world; includes chapters on U.S. marksmen in Vietnam.

——. *Stalk and Kill.* New York: St. Martin's Press, 1997. More on the history of sniping around the world.

Henderson, Charles. *Marine Sniper: 93 Confirmed Kills.* New York: Berkley Books, 1988. The story of Carlos Hathcock, one of the marines' most successful snipers in Vietnam.

——. *Silent Warrior.* New York: Berkley Books, 2001. More on the career of Carlos Hathcock.

Kugler, Ed. *Dead Center.* New York: Ivy Books, 1999. Personal narrative of a 4th Marine Regiment sniper from 1966 to 1968.

Lanning, Michael Lee. *Inside the Crosshairs: Snipers in Vietnam.* New York: Ivy Books, 1998. A comprehensive look at sniper history and their use by both sides during the Vietnam War.

Plaster, John L. *The Ultimate Sniper.* Boulder, CO: Paladin Press, 1993. Contains training guidance for military and police marksmen.

Sasser, Charles W., and Craig Roberts. *One Shot—One Kill.* New York: Pocket Books, 1989. Oral histories of American combat snipers in World War II, Korea, Vietnam, and Beirut.

Senich, Peter R. *Limited War Sniping.* Boulder, CO: Paladin Press, 1982. Includes information on sniping in Korea and Vietnam.

——. *The Complete Book of U.S. Sniping.* Boulder, CO: Paladin Press, 1988. Information on U.S. military snipers from the Civil War through Vietnam; includes extensive illustrations of weapons.

——. *The Long Range War: Sniping in Vietnam.* Boulder, CO: Paladin Press, 1994. History, including many pictures, of army and marine snipers in Vietnam.

————. *The One-Round War: USMC Scout Snipers in Vietnam.* Boulder, CO: Paladin Press, 1996. History, including many pictures, of marine snipers in Vietnam.

————. *U.S. Marine Corps Scout Snipers: World War II and Korea.* Boulder, CO: Paladin Press, 1993. Extensive photographs and some documents on marine snipers in the Second World War and Korean conflict.

Ward, Joseph T. *Dear Mom: A Sniper's Vietnam.* New York: Ivy Books, 1991. Personal narrative of a sniper with the First Marine Division in Vietnam during 1969 and 1970.

Special Forces

Clancy, Tom. *Special Forces.* New York: Berkley, 2001. The famed novelist's survey of Special Forces.

Craig, William T. *Lifer.* New York: Ivy Books, 1994. Personal narrative of a career soldier who served as an infantryman in the Korean War and with Special Forces in Southeast Asia.

————. *Team Sergeant.* New York: Ivy Books, 1998. Continued personal narrative with details of his experiences with Special Forces during the Tet Offensive.

Donahue, James C. *Blackjack 33.* New York: Ivy Books, 1999. Personal narrative of a Special Forces medic's tour in Vietnam in 1967.

————. *Blackjack 34.* New York: Ivy Books, 2000. More on the author's experiences during his tour with Special Forces in Vietnam.

————. *Mobile Guerrilla Force.* Annapolis: Naval Institute Press, 1996. The first in the series about the author's tour with Special Forces in Vietnam.

Dooley, George E. *Battle for the Central Highlands.* New York: Ballantine, 2000. Personal narrative of a Green Beret's tour in the Central Highlands of Vietnam.

Miller, Franklin D. *Reflections of a Warrior.* Novato, CA: Presidio Press, 1991. The narrative of a Medal of Honor recipient about his six tours in Southeast Asia.

Morris, Jim. *War Story.* New York: St. Martin's Press, 2000. Covers the early years of Special Forces in Vietnam by a three-tour veteran.

Plaster, John L. *SOG: The Secret Wars of America's Commandos in*

Vietnam. A three-tour SOG veteran tells the story of the Studies and Observations Group.

Schemmer, Benjamin F. *The Raid.* New York: Ballantine, 2002. A detailed look at the failed raid by Special Forces of the Son Tay prison near Hanoi.

Simons, A. J. *The Company They Keep: Life Inside the U.S. Army Special Forces.* New York: The Free Press, 1997. A look at Special Forces training and family life in the late 1990s by a female Ph.D. anthropologist.

Simpson, Charles M. *Inside the Green Berets.* Novato, CA: Presidio Press, 1983. A history of the first thirty years of the Special Forces by a veteran officer.

Stanton, Shelby L. *Green Berets at War.* Novato, CA: Presidio Press, 1985. An overview of Special Forces in Southeast Asia from 1956 to 1975.

Wade, Leigh. *Assault on Dak Pek.* New York: Ivy Books, 1998. A veteran's account of the fight for a Special Forces camp in 1970 in Vietnam.

————. *Protected Will Never Know.* New York: Ivy Books, 1998. Personal narrative of a tour with Special Forces and SOG in Vietnam in 1965.

————. *Tan Phu.* New York: Ivy Books, 1997. Personal narrative of a Special Forces radioman defending a camp in the Mekong Delta in 1963.

Yedinak, Steven M. *Hard to Forget.* New York: Ivy Books, 1998. Personal narrative of a Special Forces officer's tour with a Mobile Guerrilla Force of Cambodians in the Vietnam War during 1966.

USAF Special Tactics

Brehm, Jack and Pete Nelson. *That Others May Live.* Three Rivers, MI: Three Rivers Press, 2001. Details of the PJ efforts during "the perfect storm" in the North Atlantic in 1991.

Drury, Bob. *The Rescue Season.* New York: Simon & Schuster, 2001. The story of the rescue of three mountain climbers by PJs in Alaska.

Chinnery, Philip D. *Any Time, Any Place.* Annapolis: Naval Institute Press, 1994. A history of Air Force special operations from 1944 to 1994.

Hirsh, Michael. *Pararescue: The Skill and Courage of the Elite 106th Rescue Wing.* New York: Avon, 2001. The rescue by PJs of the crew of a sinking ship in the mid-Atlantic.

Junger, Sebastian. *The Perfect Storm.* New York: W. W. Norton, 1997. Includes mention of PJ operations during a storm in the North Atlantic in 1991.

Pushies, Fred J. *U.S. Air Force Special Ops.* Osceola, WI: MBI Publishing, 2000. A pictoral history of air force special operations.

U.S. Special Operations Command (USSOCOM)

Clancy, Tom, and Carl Stiner. *Shadow Warriors.* New York: Putnam, 2002. The story of special operations as mostly told through the experiences of General Carl Stiner, who commanded USSOCOM from 1990 to 1993.

Department of Defense. *United States Special Operations Command History.* MacDill AFB, FL: Headquarters, USSOCOM, 1998. The official history of SOCOM.

———. *United States Special Operations Command 10th Anniversary History.* MacDill AFB, FL: Headquarters, USSOCOM, 1997. An earlier official history of SOCOM.

Locher, James R., III. *Defense Organization: The Need for Change.* Washington, DC: U.S. Government Printing Office, 1985. An important study that helped lead to the authorization of SOCOM.

Office of the Assistant Secretary of Defense. *United States Special Operations Forces Posture Statement.* Washington, DC: Pentagon, 2000. The official current status of SOCOM.

Walker, Greg. *At the Eye of the Hurricane.* New York: Ivy Books, 1994. An overview of special operations forces from Vietnam to Desert Storm.

Index

Don't miss this memorable book
by Michael Lee Lanning

INSIDE THE CROSSHAIRS
Snipers in Vietnam

Here noted military historian Michael Lee Lanning
shows how U.S. snipers in Vietnam—combining
modern technology in weapons, ammunition, and
telescopes—used the experience and traditions of
centuries of expert shooters to perfect their craft.
To provide insight into the use of American snipers
in Vietnam, Lanning interviewed men with combat
trigger time, as well as their instructors, the
founders of the Marine and U.S. Army sniper programs, and the generals to whom they reported.
Backed by hard information and firsthand
accounts, the author demonstrates how the skills
these one-shot killers honed in the jungles of
Vietnam provided an indelible legacy that helped
save American lives in Grenada, the Gulf War, and
Somalia and continues to this day with
American troops in Bosnia.